ST. ROSE OF LIMA

Cross and Crown Series of Spirituality

LITERARY EDITOR

Reverend Jordan Aumann, O.P., S.T.D.

NUMBER 36

Sister Mary Alphonsus, O.SS.R.

ST. ROSE
OF
LIMA

Patroness of the Americas

TAN BOOKS AND PUBLISHERS, INC.
Rockford, Illinois 61105

IMPRIMATUR:
✠ John J. Carberry
Archbishop of St. Louis
June 7, 1968

Originally published by B. Herder Book Co., St. Louis, Missouri, and London, England.

Copyright © 1968 by B. Herder Book Co.

Copyright © 1982 by TAN Books and Publishers, Inc.

Library of Congress Catalog No.: 81-86444

ISBN: 0-89555-172-1

Printed and bound in the United States of America

TAN BOOKS AND PUBLISHERS, INC.
P.O. Box 424
Rockford, Illinois 61105
1982

IN MEMORY OF

MY

PARENTS,

ESPECIALLY MY MOTHER,

WHO HELPED ME

WITH

THIS BOOK.

PREFACE

THIS BOOK tells the story of a humble young lady of second class nobility of seventeenth-century Lima. She was so poor that at times she had to work miracles to feed her family. She hated parties, although she was the center of every one she went to. She turned down the suitors that flocked to her door. Her exits from home were to the neighboring church of the Dominicans or at times to the homes of friends. She was deft with her fingers, skilled in the garden, a gifted musician and poet. She played her guitar, nursed the sick, passed out free mixtures of herbs to the poor. When she died, the whole city mourned her.

The room where they first laid her out shone with glory. Her body stayed flexible, her skin soft, her cheeks were flushed. Her eyes would not close, nor her mouth, which curved up in a smile. A clamor of people outside, a dense stream of mourners passing by the bier, an influx of persons from beyond Lima's limits were but the beginning. Soon, such a tumult arose within the house where she lay that the viceroy sent his private guard to keep order.

Her body was moved to the church of St. Dominic. There, the wonders began. From morning till night, for two days and a half, the crowd milled around it. Time after time, relic-seekers cut her habit to shreds. In vain was it replaced. When the coffin was wheeled into the chapel of Our Lady of the Rosary, the statue of Mary and the Infant Jesus moved. All saw it. The Queen of heaven smiled; both she and her Son bowed to the body. "A saint! She's a saint!" murmured the throng.

When the archbishop was singing her Requiem Mass, his

voice and the choir were drowned out. The Dominican friars had to give up and say the psalms in private. At night her body was moved into the convent and placed in the novices' chapel. There the community and many eminent men of the laity prayed until morning.

At noon on the third day, the throng was importunate. She could not be buried for fear of a riot, so the friars and bishops tried a ruse. They left ostentatiously at noon as though for their meal and siesta. The people left, too. The instant they were gone, the clergy returned, took the body and buried it under an unmarked slab in the cloister.

But it was not left there. Barely three years later it was solemnly transferred and enshrined at the altar. Relics were cut from her bones and given to the faithful. Pope Urban VIII gave the permission to begin the formal Process for beatification and canonization. Her relics had to be taken from the church. Violent were the protests, loud the laments. The people loved her frantically and they would not be deprived of her relics or her public cult.

The formal Process began. It was soon concluded. The pope who canonized her named her Patroness of the Americas. Her name? A fragrant one: St. Rose of Lima.

Rose was made for God and lived for him. She loved him intensely. When she turned that love towards people, the flame flared whitehot. She opened her heart and adobe infirmary to all the poor: white, black and brown. This she did in a place and at a time when such love was unthinkable. She shocked her conventional fellow-citizens; she urged them to love like Christ. She poured out her strength working for them, praying for them, mortifying her flesh to gain grace for them. If anything counts with God, it is love; if anything counts in this world, it is love. This was Rose's secret.

But her love for the poor and all races was no mere philanthropy. There was nothing impersonal, nothing fugitive about it. Sometimes charitable gifts are a mask for cowardice, while the giver shrinks from giving himself. Rose's love was no mask. The first proof came in her choice of personal friends. When it came to choosing them, she knew no distinction. The noble, rich and eminent Spanish Peruvians loved her, and she loved them. An Indian maid was her lifelong confidante. The Dominican friars and the Jesuits made friends with Rose and she took their friendship simply; but, of her own accord, she sought out a Negro lay-brother, Martin de Porres, as an intimate friend. To him she spoke artlessly of her soul and life. The second proof came in the variety of those for whom she worked miracles after her death.

Such was St. Rose. Her life is a spotless mirror in which we see ourselves, whatever our color, our station, our land and our age, whatever our chosen vocation. Like St. Thérèse of Lisieux, Rose took our Lord by the heart. In taking him, she took his church. Her life is our boast, our crown, our defense, and a challenge to love completely.

GEOGRAPHICAL NOTE

PERU is a stylishly thin South American republic poised tip-toe on the Chilean desert with the blue Pacific behind her, burly Brazil before her and Ecuador, Colombia and a tuft of Brazilian jungle above her. She has three great geographical zones: the coastal, Andean and river-forest. The Andean zone is called the *sierra*, which in Spanish means "saw" and so, de-rivatively, "a mountain range." The river-forest zone is called the *montaña* or mountain. The coastal zone forms 10 % of Peruvian territory, the *sierra* 25% and the *montaña* 65%.

The coastal zone is arid and treeless, except where streams from the Andes bisect it as they flow to the sea. Port towns and cities huddle in these watered oases, leaving the rest of the zone to the lizards and birds, a few miners and such others as chose to dwell there in pastoral peace on planta-tions. Sandhills, plains strewn with moving sand dunes, dry basins fit only for borax mining, salt plains and deserts of drifting volcanic ash complete the scene. The Andes, which run southeast to northwest from Chile to Ecuador, prevent rain from falling between themselves and the sea. Cacti flour-ish in variety but other vegetation can grow only with artifi-cial irrigation. Sugar and cotton have been so produced; the mild, even temperature makes field work bearable and even pleasant.

Moving inland from the coastal zone, one soon reaches the Andes. This mountain range is approximately 1,500 miles long and from 100 to 300 miles wide. It creates knotty transporta-tion problems for the Peruvian government and people. As might be assumed, the *sierra* is cold. Rain and snow beat upon rocks and ravines where a smattering of Indians eke out a destitute existence on shallow land-islands. The *sierra* is the great snowy graveyard of Peru, where many thousands of Indians and Spaniards froze to death in the course of army marches during the Conquest and the Civil Wars. But the foothills are terraced and fertile, yielding well to the diligent. Valleys are fertile, too, when watered by mountain streams, and the climate at such levels is mild and agreeable. The vast, flat uplands yield pasturage for great herds. Above these run rugged rocky ranges, rich in minerals, dotted with lakes. The ice-peaked cordilleras tower over all.

The southern part of the *sierra* is veiled beneath the fish-teeming waters of a great inland sea, Lake Titicaca. It was near the blue bosom of this lake, bordered by swamps saffron with water-weed and dense with flocks of scarlet flamingoes, that three of the most fascinating cultures known to us sprang up, matured and died: the cultures of the Tia people, the Aymara and the Incas of Cuzco.

To the west, on the coastal zone, the pre-Incan culture of Chan-Chan sparkled in jewel-encrusted glory. Some three hundred miles to the south of this entrancing city stood Pachacamác, the great center of Nascan worship. Its ruins still stand and are but a short distance from Lima.

The third geographical zone of Peru is reached as one descends the eastern flank of the Andes. After the weird formations of the rocky zone, one abruptly meets the line of vegetation. From this line onward the Andean streams pour eastward to the Amazon. The climate is temperate and not unhealthy, the soil rich, the foliage semi-tropical. This region is distinct from the Brazilian jungle known to missionaries as "the green hell." It has remained until recent times largely uncultivated and unsettled. Its Indians are not homogeneous but divided into approximately twelve tribal strata. They are largely uncivilized and live in idyllic barbarism. The slightest civilized Campas tribe cultivates large plantations of maize, potatoes, bananas and other vegetables and fruits. Missionary work among these forest savages has been handicapped in the past, but it is to be hoped that eventually these tribes will be assimilated into the Christian populace of Peru.

ACKNOWLEDGMENTS

THE AUTHOR expresses heartfelt thanks to the following persons who were especially helpful in the writing of this book: Michael Cardinal Browne, O.P., former Master General of the Dominican Order; Reverend Norbert Georges, O.P.; Reverend Francis N. Wendell, O.P.; Reverend Ruben Vargas Ugarte, S.J.; Reverend Peter Sheehan, C.S.B.; Dom Mary James Fox, O.C.S.O.; Reverend Charles Auth, O.P.; Very Reverend F.M. Drouin, O.P.; Reverend William Hinnebusch, O.P.; Reverend Thomas Charland, O.P.; Mr. Robert I. Clifton; Mr. Joseph Waterer; Miss Hilda Conlan; Mr. John Neal Waddell; the librarians of the University of Toronto and the Barrie Public Library.

CONTENTS

CHAPTER ONE

A Tale of Two Peoples

Peoples are like persons, with good qualities and defects. They have aspirations to do good, but sometimes they fail. Like persons, too, peoples have two parents, the native and the conquering races. Much that is rich in the life of a land flows from each blood-stream. This is exemplified in Peru, where there was frequent mingling of blood between conquerors and conquered. Most of it was illicit, but much good has come of it.

The first two saints born on Peruvian soil typify this mingling. St. Martin de Porres was half Negro and half Spanish. St. Rose of Lima was Spanish, but it is almost certain that her maternal great-grandmother was Incan. The Incas were white. The union of an Incan woman and a Spaniard produced fine-featured white children, with light brown or auburn hair. St. Rose's hair was fair and the sun danced in her eyes. St. Martin was dark and negroid. These two saints were friends. Their friendship has an urgent message for us, whatever the color of our skin, as it had for Peru.

When Pizarro and his men reached Cajamarca in 1532, Peru was already old. Her culture spanned three thousand years. Who the first Peruvians were is uncertain, but they had a Flood Myth. Noah and his wife are not mentioned, but only six persons, three men and three women, presumably his sons and their wives. But archaeologists have found no trace of the flood in Peru, so the Flood Myth seems to have been imported.

1

The people of Peru slowly developed farming, husbandry, architecture, spinning, weaving, metallurgy and other arts of civilization. They do not seem to have had the wheel unless, as a few archeologists have thought, two immense stone discs found near Lake Titicaca just beyond the border between Peru and Bolivia were wheels.

The city of Chan-Chan, the Chimu port which flourished in the time of Christ, enjoyed a high degree of culture. The city was shielded from foes by a fortress and strong walls. Its artisans were skilled; their pottery reached the level of sculpture in portrait vases manufactured from molds; their textiles were exquisite, ranging from fragile loom-made lace to richly worked brocades, unequalled by any other known civilization, including our own; wood carving was superb and lavish, even on common objects; mosaic work and mother-of-pearl inlay were perfect. Gold, silver and platinum were mined and smelted. A process of plating was used which rivalled electroplating. The secret of this technique has not been rediscovered. Metals were hammered, welded and soldered by the Chimu. They were cast, embossed, engraved, etched and pressed.

High in the Andes lies Tiahuana, near Lake Titicaca. Its ruins tell many tales. Here architectural feats have been accomplished that have to be imagined. Our modern engineering and masonry experts stand staring, awestruck. Some stones of two hundred tons have been used here; stones weighing fifty to a hundred tons are common. Each stone is of different size and shape, yet all have been so perfectly measured and cut that no cement is needed to hold them in place.

Who were the Tiahuanans and when did they live? Where did they go and why? These are questions long disputed by archeologists. One truth emerges: these ruins are not uniform. They show distinct stages of civilization. But where did the Tia people go? Where are their descendents? Was the city wiped out by some calamity such as a flood or earth-quake? Amid all suggested possible answers, one stands out: Tiahuana was unfortified. Her people were peace-loving, intent on worship, the arts and crafts. Nearby were fierce tribes crazed by blood and plunder. Life at Tia was no longer safe; a city people were forced back to nomadry.

They went, it would seem, to Zapolo, where they studied revenge. Of all their foes, the Aymara of Cuzco were the worst and nearest. Their desire to build an empire brought them on raids of Tiahuana, but the Tia warriors swooped upon them over fifty miles of mountains and won the fray. They settled there as lords in a feudal system, forcing on their captives a much superior culture. The Aymara peasants worked the fields of Cuzco while white Incas with brown or auburn hair and aquiline noses ruled the city and the Aymar Empire. They pushed its boundaries north, east, south and west, until it embraced a third of South America.

The Tia people had the image of a bearded man in their temple. They also had the cross, which appeared repeatedly in decorative designs. The Cuzco Incas also had the cross and paid it worship, but they had forgotten its meaning. Their legends told of the passage of a bearded white man through their land, a preacher who had given them good laws and worked many wonders. He had planted the cross on the hill above Cuzco. Even his dress was mysterious and strange; the Tia and Cuzco peoples wore knee-length tunics but he wore a long white robe. Whoever this preacher was, his doctrines had not wholly died in this land of his labors.

Spiritually, though not materially, the Incan culture excelled that of Chan-Chan. In the coastal city sodomy was so common that it found a place in the temple rites; in the Incan Empire it was a crime even to speak the word. Although divorce was legal, adultery brought death. Stealing was a crime loathed and despised. Lies were the object of horror and the truth was told without human respect. The Incas cared for the old and sick, the deformed, handicapped and widowed. Under the Incan feudal system, all worked hard and lived frugally.

Pachacamác, the Indian "Holy City," flourished long before the Incan dynasty and was brought into the empire shortly after it began. It was protected by the fortress Limatambo, where centuries later St. Martin de Porres planted olive trees.

The Nascas of Pachacamác worshipped the "Creator Spirit." Like other Peruvian peoples, they used graven images to express God's attributes, especially two. These found apt expression in the so-called images of the "condor god," which symbolized the belief that God, although spirit, was somehow like man. He dwelt in inaccessible heights like the condor, a bird which soars so high as to be lost to the sight. The condor is also a bird of prey, so the strength and power of God and the weakness of creatures before him are shown in this image. The sacrificial aspect of Nascan worship is also expressed in it. As the condor swoops on his prey and devours it, so God accepts sacrifices and consumes them. Man must sacrifice to show his utter dependence on God for every moment of life, as well as in expiation of sin.

It was part of the Incan policy to establish the cults of Cuzco in newly conquered regions, but this did not mean the exclusion of native worship. Indeed, the cults of subject peoples were brought to Cuzco and added to those in vogue. And what was the adulteration which lowered the cult of the Creator Spirit in Pachacamác? It was the cult of sex which had been encouraged in the Cuzco area when unnatural vice was stamped out, never to reappear. The procreative faculty was seen as a phase of the Creator's power acting in the world through creatures and in time it assumed a divine entity.

The bearded man-god, Vira-Cocha, was also worshipped there. According to Peruvian Indian belief he was the divine son of the Creator Spirit. A trio of legends preserved throughout Peru tell of his preaching of the cross and his performance of many miracles. It seems that Vira-Cocha was a composite figure, a confusion of Christ with some apostle who came preaching his name. Was he St. Thomas, as some Indians and Spaniards have claimed?

At first, as the legends say, the ancestors of the Indians around Cuzco worshipped the Creator Spirit alone. Then came the worship of idols and sun-worship. The sun, said one Supreme Inca, served the Creator as Lord of the sky. It should be worshipped too. Then moon-worship came, based on the same conclusions and flanked by the worship of angels and propitiation of devils. Still, God the Creator was held to be supreme.

The Aymara "found" spiritual entities in all creatures. These they called "grandfather spirits." Due to this doctrine all things became *huaca* or holy, and as such might be worshipped. Devils often spoke from idols and other inanimate objects as well as animals and birds. Although the Incas made sun-worship the official religion of their class, the *huacas* always held first place as the chief cult of the peasants. Most favored among these were stone love-charms; deep faith was placed in them.

The Incas had *huacas* too, among them the cross, and their faith held many Catholic teachings: the resurrection of the body, heaven, hell, purgatory, a sense of sin, confession and penance imposed by a priest. Fasts were rigorous; they might last a month, six months or longer, depending on one's piety or need. Not only were infractions of the moral code confessional matter, but natural misfortunes were also included. They were thought to be sent by God as punishment for sin and were therefore signs of guilt, if not actual sins.

Unlike many pagans, the Incas prized chastity. By the Temple of the Sun was a convent, the "Dwelling-of-those-set-apart." Here, girls chosen from the whole empire for their beauty were secluded from the world. Supervised by a house-mother, they prayed and did manual work. Their prayers were for the needs of the empire and special intentions recommended to them; their work was spinning and weaving. When the girls matured, some took vows of virginity and remained in the "Dwelling." They were called "Wives of the Sun." Others were wedded to distinguished men or joined the household of the Supreme Inca.

Sometimes human sacrifice was offered to the sun, and as these virgins were physically flawless and had led lives of purity and prayer, they were the most precious of possible victims. It was believed that their holocaust brought them full remission of the punishment due to sins and heaven at once. Among the Incas heaven had come to be called "the sun." One who died after a good life "went to the sun." This was considered a place of brightness, light and bliss where, in the presence of the sun-god and the Creator Spirit, virtue was rewarded.

Incan marriage laws were like those established or permitted by God for the Jews in Old Testament times. Concubinage and divorce were permitted but death was the punishment for adultery. However, not all Incan moral standards measured up to those of the Jews. For example, divining was a widespread practice in Peru. The future tantalized the Incas and Indians. Of the thirteen classes of priests whom they gladly supported, ten were diviners.

The Incas and Aymara were homeloving peoples; there was no traveling for pleasure. It is true that there were some temporary exiles from the hearth; soldiers, shepherds of the llama herds, construction gangs employed on the roads and couriers lived in isolation. But they knew that their terms of duty were defined; eventually they would be placed in other work congenial to nature.

Couriers were trained to carry great loads on their backs; a two-hundred-pound pack was nothing to groan over. They ran with perishable foods from the coast to Cuzco in twenty-mile relays. Llama trains carried produce and raw material that were not perishable. Each llama took a hundred pounds and a train of a hundred llamas was common. When Francisco Pizarro threaded his men and horses over these roads and bridges, the Incan Empire had 12,000,000 citizens. It covered 380,000 square miles. Although the tribes within it spoke many tongues, all had a common language: Quechua. This was imposed on all Incan subjects for the sake of ease in administration.

So much for St. Rose's probable Incan background; now let us see the Spanish. As an inevitable result of their history, the Spaniards were fighters. From her mythological age until 1492 A.D., Spain was either being invaded or striving to throw off some occupying power. First came the Celts; they were followed by the Phoenicians, and then the Romans. During the Roman rule Sts. Paul and James came, preaching Christ. At their summons and that of seven apostolic men who preached in their wake, the Spaniards flocked to the Church. The Roman Empire crumbled and the Tartars poured in on Spain. They were hurled back. Then came the Visigoths. By 466 A.D. they held the peninsula, but their empire declined; and as it did, Hispano-Roman power grew and the Church flourished. But the Moslems conquered much of the land, mutilating, enslaving and martyring countless Christians. Soon the Arab kingdom split into more than twenty small units. Three times African Moors swept in to help them, but fruitlessly. After the Battle of El Salado they held only Granada, which they lost in 1492 to King Ferdinand the Catholic. The reconquest was complete.

In that same year, Christopher Columbus reached the Bahamas. At the urging of a Dominican and a Franciscan friar, Spain financed his voyage. A new world was about to be born and she was to sire it. The Church would baptize it; men would call it America.

At the close of the fifteenth century the Church was sorely tried. Politically she tossed with the times, making fresh pacts and foes with every sweep of the wind. Since all Europe was Catholic, her foes were Catholic. Spiritually her power was weakened by the Avignon exile, the Great Schism and its lesser satellites, the failures of the clergy and simony. Nepotism and the papal army's campaigns had also played their part in alienating peoples from her.

While Catholic kings fought one another, the Turks advanced across Europe; the popes pleaded almost in vain for the cause of the Crusade. In matters of ecclesiastical policy and discipline they also met with little cooperation. Whenever they took some course of action that offended either the princes of the Church or state, these threatened schism. Sometimes, too, they demanded a Council or called one without the pope's consent.

As soon as King Ferdinand of Spain had thrown off the Moslems, he began to have differences of opinion with the pope. He refused to pay the sum customarily given by newly crowned kings to the popes who confirmed them in office. Soon after this, he and Queen Isabella opposed the pope's nominations for two Spanish prelacies. The Queen won her case, and the pope even granted her the privilege of naming prelates. But King Ferdinand was less happy in his cause; the pope stood firm. The king flew into a rage and schismatized, creating for himself an anti-pope with his own college of cardinals. The schism in no way reflected the attitude of the Spanish people and the king wisely brought it to a close.

Many nations were fast becoming hotbeds of heresy, but Spain kept the faith. However, she suffered from the indiscretions of those who ruled her, as well as the defection of some of her children. Her inward torments were therefore not less than those of other European nations, though their causes were different. The faults committed by Spanish kings and lesser authorities were due to zeal for the Church and fear of her enemies.

Although the popes opposed it, Spanish Jews were pressed to become Christians. Rather than leave their country or suffer on account of their adherence to the Law of Moses, many were received into the Church without changing their inner convictions. In public they worshipped as Catholics, in private as Hebrews. When this fact was disclosed, pressure changed to persecution and the Jewish bitterness increased. All Jews were ordered to be baptized or to leave Spain. Some fled to Portugal rather than feign Christianity; others took refuge in the Papal States, even Rome itself. Fearing a similar fate, many Moors in Spain also posed as Christians.

The chief weapon used by the Church to maintain purity of doctrine was the Inquisition, a Church court which judged upon matters of faith. It questioned witnesses, heard the accused and passed sentence on them. Those condemned went to civil prisons prior to their execution. Rome promulgated rules to safeguard suspects. Pre-trial inquiries were to be secret, prisons were to be liveable, milder torture was to be applied than that used in prosecuting civil cases. It could be applied only once and with discretion. Bishops were to keep a check on the inquisitors and the latter were to inform them of the cases in process.

The few who held absolute power in Spain circumvented these safeguards in spite of repeated papal protests. Secrecy was sometimes cast aside; the bishops were not informed; prisons were pest-houses in which suspects sometimes died of

torture. The rack was used one day and again the next, not as
fresh torture but a prolongation of the first. When under torture, a suspect would plead guilty, whereupon he would be released from the rack. By the time a priest arrived to hear his
confession, he would be pleading innocent as when first
charged.

Other abuses drew reproofs from Rome. Persons were tried
and acquitted only to find themselves accused again. False
charges were made against the rich, whether Jew or Gentile,
because the goods of those convicted were confiscated by the
crown. Many innocent Jews were acquitted by the Inquisition
only to find themselves stripped of their fortunes.

In spite of these abuses, the Inquisition did much to preserve the purity of Catholic doctrine. However, the exile of
the popes in Avignon, the ensuing French influence on the
Church, the schisms and the long delay in reforming the
clergy combined to produce the great heresies. These no Inquisition could stem.

When it became clear that Columbus had reached unknown lands, Portugal claimed them on the grounds that he
was a Portuguese. Spain fought the claim, as the queen had
helped finance him. The pope was asked to judge between
the two claims, and he ruled that since Portugal had the right
of conquest over the west coast of Africa, Spain should have
it in the Indies. However, this was granted her on one condition: that she preach the Gospel to the natives. To the pope,
it seemed like a providential opportunity to spread Christ's
church; to the Spaniards, it seemed to ensure God's blessing
on their empire-building. Yet, it proved to be a mistake.
From the dawn of the Conquest, Spaniards fought with one
hand and baptized with the other. In the eyes of many native South Americans, therefore, the cross became a sword-
hilt.

CHAPTER TWO

The Founders of a Family

ST. ROSE'S paternal grandparents sailed to Puerto Rico around the year 1531 in a galleon of three decks, a combination sailboat and rowboat which looked like a huge insect as it plied the waters. In fair weather, the galleon was water-tight enough but comfortless; during storms it tossed and plunged like a shell. Ocean travel in the sixteenth century was no relaxation; only destitution in Spain and the lure of the fabulous wealth of the Indies brought most voyagers to risk the crossing.

It is said that St. Rose's father was born in 1531. If so, he must have been no more than an infant in arms when his parents made the voyage. Perhaps he was still unborn, for when the couple registered with the civil authorities in Puerto Rico he was young enough to be tabulated as having been born there. However, he is claimed by Toledo, too, so we can only guess at his birthplace.

The monotony of the voyage was gruelling, time of storm excepted; then, terror reigned. Fresh foods ran out long before the galleon reached Puerto Rico; water was strictly rationed, stale and tepid. The voyagers whiled the time away, chatting of current news. Doubtless, the ladies dwelt on the latest scandal: Henry VIII of England was banishing his homely wife to marry the lovely Anne Boleyn, despite the pope's refusal to grant him an annulment. Among the gentlemen the talk was perhaps of the Crusade.

Gaspar's earliest memories would have thrilled any boy.

Every day brought his father home from work with tales of discovery and adventure. When Gaspar was a lad of six, he first heard of the conquest of Peru. A vast empire had been found where gold was used for kitchen utensils, where there was no coinage or wheeled conveyance, where no horse had been seen until the Spaniards came.

Gaspar heard his elders marvelling at the Battle of Cajamarca which had won Peru for the King of Spain. From twenty to forty thousand Indians had been slain in fifteen minutes without a single wound to a Spaniard, except one inflicted on Pizarro when he shielded the Supreme Inca.

But soon there were tales of dispute and bloodshed among the conquerors. First, Pizarro quarrelled with Almagro and exiled him to Chile. The next report was more grave: Francisco Pizarro's brother had executed Almagro. Would Almagro's son try to avenge his father's death? Everyone seemed to fear this except Francisco Pizarro until it was too late, and he lay dying in pools of his own blood on the pavement of his palace apartment.

The Almagro revolt soon paled before a greater evil. The viceroy, Blasco Núñez, had made himself odious to the holders of large land grants worked by Indian labor. He had applied the Spanish laws against enslavement of the Indians, and the outraged colonists threatened revolt. A man less rigorous and more prudent would have marked time to learn whether or not the king wished to risk losing Peru for the sake of the land reforms. Not so this viceroy, who lacked both judgment and self-control.

The crisis came when an insolent knight named Suárez de Carbajal was called to the palace to answer for his plots against the viceroy. The interview took place at night and in secret, for Blasco Núñez wished to hush up the matter. The two men soon fell into an argument and the viceroy ran Carbajal through. Terrified, he hid the body; when it was found, the clamor against him grew louder, this time with justice.

Meanwhile Gonzalo Pizarro and an army of rebels were about to attack the viceregal forces. Ostensibly to save them, the viceroy proposed that the people of Lima evacuate the city by sea while he proceeded to meet Pizarro. Actually he feared that Lima would betray him. The court opposed the plan and deposed him unconstitutionally. He was ordered to await a ship to take him to Spain. However, in the zero hour the judge gave him his freedom, and he marched towards Quito, swelling his forces as he went.

In the meantime, Gonzalo Pizarro captured Lima and had himself made provisional governor. He then marched on Blasco Núñez. The viceroy was stunned in battle and fell from his horse, and as he lay unconscious on the ground, the brother of the assassinated Carbajal had him decapitated by a negro slave. Pizarro attended the funeral as chief mourner. He showed mercy to the viceroy's men and won them over; his return march to Lima was a triumph.

As master of Peru he lived like a prince, but without lessening his loyalty to Spain. Confident that his action would be praised and that he would be confirmed in office, he sent messengers to Spain with explanations of his actions. When this news reached Puerto Rico, Gaspar Flores made a quiet decision.

"I am going to Panama if you will permit me," he told his father. It was at Panama that the next major clash could be expected.

Gaspar was not more than fifteen years old when he went to Panama. An inexperienced stripling, he nevertheless managed to fend for himself among the seasoned soldiers of the port. His life consisted in a series of military drills and studies interspersed with short leaves.

Gaspar's thirst for combat was soon to be satisfied. Pizarro's heavily manned navy lay anchored in the gulf; Panama was governed by a man of his party. Meanwhile, the newly appointed president, Father Pedro de la Gasca, landed at Santa Marta in present-day Colombia. He heard of the battle between Pizarro and Blasco Núñez and the latter's death. The president had no army, but as representative of the king of Spain, he could offer pardon to Gonzalo and his partisans. He now turned this power to good account. First he won over Meixa, who held the port of Nombre de Dios; then he turned to the governor of Panama.

At first the governor parried, sending to Gonzalo for instructions, but when Gonzalo's messengers to the king, having stopped at Panama, went over to Gasca, he followed them. Years later, Gaspar Flores still loved to describe the ceding of the fleet. Like all official Spanish acts, it was carried out with consummate pomp. A brilliantly liveried herald read Father Gasca's proclamation of amnesty. The governor of Panama and his captains gave their documented resignations to Gasca. Then, while the throng listened in tense silence, the former adherents of Pizarro took the oath of allegiance to the king. While the whole squadron stood reverently at attention, the standard of Castile was raised aloft.

Gaspar's emotions were profoundly stirred and his young mind was deeply impressed. But exuberance soon swept over him as he saw combat service within his grasp. Volunteers were being sought for the war against Pizarro. Gaspar was surely one of the first to offer himself. But another winter of waiting followed, for Gasca's *armada* could not sail until April, 1547.

Gasca's four-vessel *armada* set out on a serene sea but trouble soon came. The galleons entered conflicting currents and progress was slow. Then came bad weather. The sea was convulsed; mountainous waves towered above the decks while beneath yawned watery chasms into which the prows plunged headlong. Sheets of rain plummeted down; nothing could be seen in the darkness. Then came repeated flashes of lightning. Seasoned sailors begged to turn back. Gaspar and his companions turned pale with nausea, clutched the walls and muttered prayers or imprecations.

Between storms they reached Gorgona, crawled to Manta, and from there sailed for Tumbez. Once more on deck, Gaspar peered landward. It was an hour of excited chatter. Tumbez was an historical city, for it was here that Francisco Pizarro had sighted the first Incan raft or *balsa*.

When he left again for Tumbez he had three galleons, twenty-seven *caballeros* and almost two hundred soldiers. The Indians welcomed him, thinking the Spaniards gods on account of their white skin and beards. Their god Vira-Cocha had a beard; the Incas were smooth-faced.

Back in Lima, Gonzalo Pizarro was furious and worried. Now that the land-holders no longer feared the loss of their *repartimientos* and Indian slaves, they were cooling towards him. He intercepted secret messages sent to his enemies; his heart hardened. He would revolt openly against the king, but one of his best men, Centeno, turned on him and captured Cuzco. Gonzalo fled from Lima to Arequipa for more soldiers, but hardly had he left Lima when its people opened the gates to Aldana. He took possession of the city for Father Gasca, amid frantic acclamations.

On June 13, the Gasca *armada* reached Tumbez. Here the priest-president split his forces. While he went to the rich and fertile valley of Xauxa, Hinojosa marched to Cajamarca for reinforcements. As a matter of course, Gaspar went with his detachment. The route followed the famous Incan highway, cursed by the cavalry and extolled by the infantry. Gaspar climbed up and down the numberless steps that girdled the mountains; he gazed giddily on the gorges below as he picked his way across the tenuous swinging bridges.

Wide-eyed he gazed on Cajamarca, the thousand-acre Incan fortress city. It was set like a coral bead on a bed of emerald green velvet at the foot of a terraced mountain. Built in circular form, it was impregnable; yet there was no city wall. All the outer walls of the buildings were windowless and the masonry finished so that no foothold could be found. To enter the city, one had to pass through a narrow gate which was the only break in the granite wall.

We may suppose that it was in Cajamarca that Gaspar saw his first Aymara and Incas. It was at Cajamarca, too, that Gaspar learned more about the battle that had been fought there the year after his birth. We may reconstruct the scene as follows:

Atahualpa, the Supreme Inca, was at war with his brother, Huascar. When he was told of Francisco's coming, he sent word offering him the freedom of the city, which was empty at the time. He hoped that Francisco would help him conclude the civil war. Atahualpa promised to come unarmed, though some claim that his bodyguards had daggers hidden in their tunics; but why did they not use them?

When Atahualpa and his escort joined the Spaniards, Pizarro and the archbishop (he was a simple friar then) spoke through their interpreter. The archbishop tried to convert the Inca on the spot, but it was too sudden. Atahualpa listened for a while, then held the archbishop's book to his ear, thinking that it would speak like the *huacas*. When it did not, he threw it down on the pavement. The archbishop shouted something and Pizarro gave the battle-cry.

The Spaniards charged, slashing as they pleased. Some Incas fled over the wall but not one struck a blow in retaliation. Many crowded around Atahualpa to shield him. As one row was cut down, another took its place. In a few minutes, some eight thousand Incas were killed.

When Hinojosa had assembled his Cajamarca army, he rejoined Gasca at Xauxa. While Father Gasca's camp awaited news from Cuzco, Centeno sent word that he held the mountain passes through which Gonzalo would try to flee the country. Gaspar shared the general rejoicing, but his jubilation was brief. Bad news trod on the heels of the good. Gonzalo Pizarro had fought Centeno at Huarina and won a gory victory. Cuzco was his.

At Xauxa all were near despair; Gaspar must have shared his comrades' consternation. But Father Gasca's courage steadied the men so that not one deserted. He spoke to them of the support God gives to those whose cause is just and who place their trust in him. Then he made his first countermove. He ordered one detachment to Lima under Alvarado to enlist the royalists who had fled to the capital from the rout of Huarina. For the same purpose he sent a second detachment to Guamanga, a mere sixty leagues from Cuzco. Was Gaspar in either of these groups or did he stay with Gasca? We do not know.

When his army was reunited, Gasca crossed the *sierra*, a rigorous march under the best conditions. With the troops went priests of various ranks, three bishops and more than eight hundred fresh recruits under Valdivia, the conqueror of Chile. Despite the handicaps of the terrain and illness among the troops, Gasca's forces were strengthened spiritually and numerically. They needed every ounce of that added strength.

For three months they had waited at Andaguaylas; then one spring day Gasca gave the order to march on Cuzco. Their progress was slowed by the fact that many bridges had been burnt and had to be rebuilt for transit. The mountains increased the men's misery. Often the cavalry had to dismount and lead their horses past perilous chasms and over the thread-like swinging bridges. Reeling at the sight of the abysses beneath them, sometimes losing their packs in invisible depths, they made two leagues a day at most.

It was decided that the battle should be fought in the valley of Xaquixaguana. Gasco's army had to wait on the alert most of the night. When the attack came at last, it was a relief, and it also brought pleasant surprises. Cepeda, Vega, and perhaps twelve fusiliers deserted Gonzalo. Then a column of soldiers and a squadron of cavalry sent after the fugitives followed their example, joining Gasca's forces. Now the remainder of Pizarro's men lost their heads. Some wheeled their mounts about and spurred them off in flight. Others ran, arms raised, towards Gasca's camp.

"Let us die like Romans!" cried one of Gonzalo's remnant. But Pizarro cared more for his soul than his honor as a soldier.

"Better die like Christians!" he exclaimed, and went to give himself up, knowing that he would not be spared.

Gonzalo Pizarro died with serene dignity, even to the extent of giving edification. He did not lose his composure. Several priests stood around him suggesting acts of faith, hope, charity and other prayers. He answered devoutly and died as he had wished, like a Christian. As Gaspar watched from his vantage point on the fringe of the throng, he must have murmured to himself, as did so many others: "What a pity that he did not live more like one!"

Not all the rebels died as did Gonzalo. Carbajal remained hardened and flippant to the end, despite the pleadings of the priests sent to prepare him for death. Cepeda was sent home to Castile, tried and condemned; but he died in prison before the time fixed for his execution.

Father Gasca's entry into Lima was triumphant. Amid the delirious joy of the people, he rode on a mule, while on his right, in deference to the absent king, a magnificent horse moved in measured paces, bearing on its saddle the royal seal.

For the next three months Gaspar encamped with his comrades in the valley of Jauja, while Father Gasca untangled a maze of conflicting claims for special rewards. Having reached his conclusions, he wisely asked the archbishop of Lima to make them public. Archbishop Loaisa assembled the favor-seekers in his cathedral and read the president's itemized decree from the pulpit. He and Father Gasca were soon showered with abuse. No one, even the most favored, seemed to feel that justice had been done.

Did Gaspar share the widespread discontent? We hear of no complaints made by him and he was not sent on any of the conveniently distant expeditions which rid Lima of the most disgruntled. However, he left Hinojosa's service, for when the latter was assassinated at La Plata two years later, Gaspar was not with him.

Perhaps the young soldier attached himself at this time to Gasca's service, acting as escort for some of the officials sent to investigate the landed estates. An armed escort was needed, for the parties were in constant danger of raids by hostile Indians or Spaniards.

In the worst *encomiendas*, the owners had shed all pretense of instructing the Indians. They lived voluptuously in their spacious homes while they extracted from their Indian laborers every grain of wheat and ounce of energy that they could produce. They kept harems composed of defenseless Indian women and girls. Often such a house had as its mistress a baptized Incan concubine who dressed like a Spanish lady and had learned Castilian. Peruvian country gentlemen of that generation seldom sought the intervention of the Church in their domestic unions except to petition for the legitimacy of their sons so that they could inherit their fathers' estates or take holy orders. It seems probable that St. Rose's maternal grandmother was born of such a union.

In many *encomiendas* there were no resident priests. A compromise was reached in such cases by having a missionary come periodically, but most of them could not preach in Quechua or instruct Indian catechumens.

Father Gasca wished to ferret out the facts in each case, so he sent visitors who spoke Quechua. They interviewed the Indians and noted their complaints and requests. To abolish the slavery, the president resolved to treat personal service henceforth as a tax. He also put an end to the enforced mass migrations of Indians from one part of the country to another.

As Gaspar approached the age of twenty, Father Gasca's mission ended. He prepared to return to Spain, stopping at Panama on his way and taking some troops with him. Probably he asked men who had come from Panama, but Gaspar did not go. He chose Peru as his homeland. A strong standing army was needed by the governor, and although great battles were not fought, skirmishes saved the soldier's life from boredom.

When Gaspar was twenty-four, one of his dreams came true: a chance to be useful to the king. He had set out for Cuzco in company with two comrades, Juan Ramírez Zegarra, son of Hinojosa's predecessor as governor of Panama, and Pedro Luís de Cabrera. They had travelled as far as the Valley of Pincos when they learned that Francisco Hernández Girón was in revolt. The trio rushed back to Lima to warn the governor, but Girón's rebellion died and so did the governor. No reward came.

Again in interim power, the *audiencia* began to oppress the people. Gaspar, now in Cuzco, knew nothing of the growing discontent. With his distinguished friend, Pedro Luís de Cabrera, he made the rounds of the drawing-rooms where his recent exploit made him, like Pedro, the hero of the moment.

While stationed temporarily in a small hamlet near Cuzco, Gaspar discovered a second rebellion. It was divulged accidently by travellers putting up for the night at the inn. As soon as he could, he left the line with his mount and hastened along the dusty road to Cuzco. But again his service to the crown was passed over. One of lesser worth than Gaspar would have turned bitter, perhaps seeking an outlet for his zeal on the side of rebellion. Not so the father of St. Rose.

The year 1553 found Gaspar on the road between Lima and Potosí, a dangerous journey even thirty years later on account of Indian raiders. In this instance, however, the danger was less from Indians than from the rebel Francisco Hernández Girón, who was again at war. Gaspar took part in the battle which followed, but he was in no state to take part in the excesses that followed the victory. Attacked by illness, he had to leave camp and go to a friend's house for the care which he needed.

Scarcely was Gaspar regaining his strength when he was called back to camp. He went, hardly knowing what to expect, but he did not have to wait long in suspense. The order was given that very day to move to the Valley of Villacari. It must have been difficult for Gaspar; perhaps on this account he was given a mule.

Gaspar next took part in the march to Jauja and the subsequent battle of Pucara. This time he was assigned to the fusiliers, who were mounted. This was the most interesting unit in the army, for the weapon itself was still a novelty.

We do not know precisely what model of gun was given him, but the "arquebus," sometimes called a "hacbut" or "hagbut," was the father of the musket and grandfather of the rifle, having a bell-shaped muzzle. It was discharged by applying a lighted match to a touch-hole, but by Gaspar's time the matchlock had been added.

After the battle of Pucara, in which Hernández Girón was defeated, Gaspar went to his viceroy and asked for a new assignment. The result of this interview was Gaspar's transfer to Jaén de los Bracamoros (the Inca Pacamuru). He crossed the rugged country with Antonio de Oznayo's men, and during the march, made in frightful weather, Indian arrows flew thick and fast at times. The most dangerous moment came, however, when the detachment met Captain Juan de Salinas with a strongly armed force. Claiming the area by right of conquest, he refused to let them pass. He and his men were about to do battle with the viceroy's band when Gaspar's friend, Juan Ramírez Zegarra, arrived. By his imperious air and curt command he brought the threat of rebellion to nothing. To his great joy, Gaspar was ordered with some others to escort the hero to a place of safety far from Indian arrows.

After his return to the capital, Gaspar may have served under the Conde de Nieva, although his name is not in the muster rolls. This viceroy is known for his negligence and it is not unlikely that the clerks who worked for him took advantage of his slackness, not keeping their records up to date. In any case we are certain that Gaspar was in or near Lima. He had applied for a place in the viceregal guard and could not risk leaving the city for fear of losing his chance in the event of a vacancy. He had not long to wait; in 1564 the viceroy was recalled and during the interim rule of Lope García de Castro, Gaspar entered the guard. He was therefore waiting stiffly at attention, musket in hand, when Castro's successor stepped from the gangplank of the galleon in 1568.

So, at thirty-eight Gaspar was a semi-retired soldier and ready for rest after twenty years of combat. As a member of the viceroy's private guard, his duty was to present himself before the court and public immaculately groomed, distinguished in bearing, faultless in drill and discipline. He could do this with ease. His alert glance, even features and pointed beard made him a striking figure.

Gaspar's single life in Lima was happy. The city itself was attractive, its people gay. There even a Spaniard felt at home. Unlike Cuzco, where Incan buildings met the eye as often as those of Spanish type, Lima had a unified look. It had been built according to the detailed plan of Francisco Pizarro. It was in many ways a typical colonial city but its founder had stamped it with his own characteristic thoughts. He had chosen the site carefully, although the Indians shook their heads at his choice. For good reasons, they had not built there. Lima became a city of flowers but this at the cost of fogs, fevers and rheumatism. A thick pall of moisture clogs the air for six months of the year.

Two leagues from the sea, the city lies in a broad palm of lowland. The Rímac River rises to the east, shallow in summer but in winter swelling and flowing seaward. When the city was being laid out, a place was first chosen for the great *plaza* or square which was in sight of the principal buildings and on which the checkerboard streets converged. Ample room was provided for large civic gatherings, including bull fights and cavalry demonstrations. Space for a market was also provided. Lima was from the first a city of gardens. Every home had an irrigation trench running through its grounds, which were often extensive and terraced.

Gaspar, like his contemporaries, was proud of Lima. He saw nothing overdone in the incredible decoration of its buildings. He saw nothing overdone, either, in the manners and dress of his friends. In his eyes the diminutive puffed trouser legs and brilliant ballet hose worn by his male acquaintances detracted in no way from their virility. Their pointed beards, painted or gilded shoes and flamboyant hats seemed quite conservative. Used to formality, Gaspar thought nothing of rolling off a formidable line of titles when addressing a person of rank.

Ten or eleven years before Gaspar was appointed to the viceregal guard, a baby girl was born in Lima to a worthy couple of the same rank as himself: Francisco de Oliva and

Isabel de Herrera. The girl's childhood was dominated by the forceful personality of her mother. This lady, pious though she was later in life, had outstanding defects which may have resulted from the humiliations of her background. We may well believe that she kept both her husband and daughter firmly in check. As Francisco's occupation is unknown, it must have been a humble one, forced on him by poverty and the lack of special training or aptitude.

Doubtless it was on Isabel's insistence that their child was given one of those whimsical redundant names so tempting to parents whose surname has a meaning. Francisco's surname was Oliva. In a twist of fantasy their daughter became "María de la Oliva de Oliva." Her Christian name, according to Spanish custom, gave her our Lady as her patroness under a particular title. The title chosen was Our Lady of the Olive. Intimate friends and members of her family called her simply "Oliva."

The redundancy of her name has caused confusion in the minds of some biographers of St. Rose. I have followed the major fundamental source available: her Canonical Process. Oliva's name occurs often in the testimonies and the variations in its form are revealing. A little more than half the time she is referred to as María de Oliva, but almost as frequently she is called María de la Oliva. Those persons who knew her well enough to drop the predicate would have used this form.

One remark found in the Process proves beyond doubt that "Oliva" was not only her surname but also part of her Christian name. The remark in question occurs in a testimony given by a close friend of the family, Gonzalo de la Maza. This distinguished gentleman once called her simply "Oliva." He would never have omitted part of her Christian name unless he had been close to the family. On the other hand, it is unthinkable that he would have called her simply by her maiden name, without any Christian name before it.

If any further evidence be needed to prove this disputed point we have the words of St. Rose herself in a song of her own composition, in which she calls her mother not *"mi María"* but *"mi Oliva."*

So much for the true form of this good lady's name. How and to what extent she modelled her actions on those of the benign Queen of Peace is another matter. On reading the simple facts one cannot escape the thought that, had our Lord been given the choice of names, he would have teasingly called her "Daughter of Thunder." The apostles whom he nicknamed *"Boanerges"* were not more deserving of it.

CHAPTER THREE

The Family

❦❦❦

ONE OF Oliva's earliest memories was of that of a controversial event: the introduction of the Inquisition into Peru. She already knew what a death was meted out to those who fell from Catholicism, for there had been two burnings held in Lima prior to this. But now the Holy Office began its official inquiries and trials. Those potentially condemned included, by law, not only heretics but also usurers, bigamists, blasphemers, relapsed Jews and Moslems, sodomists and sorcerers. Indians, African slaves, freedmen and Jesuits were as yet exempt from investigation.

The child was about eleven years old when the first *auto de fé* (demonstration of faith) took place in Lima. The Inquisition had included three friars on its agenda. One had died in prison of torture but not before making his confession. He was shown to the public in effigy, dressed as a "reconvert." The other two were burned. A nun had been convicted of witchcraft not long before. Since she and at least one of the condemned friars had been reputed as saints, their crimes, trial and fate were the scandal of the moment. Oliva listened to her parents' discussion of the case and from that moment cultivated a great distrust of extraordinary manifestations of piety. Later, this would cause her and her daughter, Rose, a great deal of anguish. At the same time, an invincible horror of the Inquisition sprang up in her soul, and this was to cause the most painful crisis of her life.

There should be no need of underlining the effect of the first *auto de fé* on the sensitive little girl. She could hardly have witnessed it herself, but what she heard was enough to sear her soul for life. A green cross was erected in the plaza. All night long the inquisitors and many religious had kept vigil before it. All night, too, Dominican friars had tried to convert the impenitent. At noon the trumpets sounded to call the families of the condemned to the center of execution. Before the multitude they were forced to swear in an audible voice to yield up the guilty for trial without fear or favor. Again the trumpets sounded; the mace bearers of the University of San Marcos and the mayor of Lima entered the plaza, mounted on horseback. They were followed by the gentlemen, among whom Oliva's father marched. After them came the viceroy or his representative, escorted by his private guard.

Was Gaspar there? It would have been his duty to be there. He took part also in all subsequent *autos*, as long as he was physically able.

Moorish drums sounded eerily; then came the cavalry in full dress. At the end of the procession came the men and women who had been tried. Those whose innocence had been proved rode on white horses and carried palms of victory. Those who were guilty but repentant carried burning torches, for their faith and charity were alight; but a yellow cross on the front and back of each one's tunic signified the temporary betrayal of Christ. Finally, mounted on donkeys, came the impenitent who were to be burned. They were dressed in unrelieved black and carried extinguished torches to show that their supernatural faith and charity were dead. On their heads the condemned were made to wear tall conical caps decorated with pictures of devils and llamas. The latter was an addition to Spanish custom, peculiar to Peru.

Together with the terror which Oliva felt when she heard

her father's description of this procession and of the fiery
death meted out to the condemned before the adult populace, there sprang up in her a violent repugnance for doctrinal
error or any excess of devotion which might lead to such. She
was Catholic to the marrow; purity of doctrine was dearer to
her than life. She shared this tenacious, even violent faith
with her contemporaries of Spanish culture, including many
who did not practice that faith. There was no such incon-
sistency in Oliva's case. Her parents trained her well and she
never swerved from the path of strict religious duty.

At about the same time as the first Peruvian *auto* took
place, Lima was the scene of a heated debate during a council
of all the bishops of the New World. The prime study of
the council was the spiritual plight of the Indians. The learning of Quechua, essential to the Indian apostolate, was neglected by the priests charged with it. The effect on the Indians was fearful. At best, the religious instruction that they received was nominal; their confessions were not understood
and sermons were in Spanish. Many Indians resorted to the
use of interpreters rather than die without the sacrament of
penance.

All possible pressure was brought on the bishops to prevent
the reforms. Embroiled in the issue were four orders: Franciscans, Dominicans, Augustinians and Mercedarians. All administered parishes in Lima, while other parishes were diocesan. Hence the faithful were strongly partisan on one side
or the other, depending on who administered the parish in
which they lived. There is strong evidence that Oliva's family
lived in the parish of the major diocesan church over which
the archbishop of Lima presided. Consequently Oliva showed
little interest in the *doctrineros*.

When Oliva was about ten years old, trouble broke out
with the Incas on a major scale. As a matter of policy, the

Spaniards had used puppet Supreme Incas to pacify the natives, but the puppets were not always docile or long-lived. Titi-Cusi the second last of these, had become Christian and kept the peace; but when he died the Indians blamed an Augustinian friar, and not without reason. His potent prescription for pleurisy sent the soul of the Inca through the pearly gates with the speed of an astronaut. The next Supreme Inca, his younger half-brother, Amaru, ordered the friar to be killed. This might have passed as an incident but Amaru went further. He had the viceroy's envoy slain. This was the signal for a large-scale revolt.

Amaru removed the women and children to the mountain-peak fortress city of Vilcapampa. Then he went down to fight the Spaniards in the valley. He was captured and his army crushed by the viceroy's forces. Far downstream from the battle proper, fifty soldiers turned on Vilcapampa. Having no arms other than those which God had given them, for four days and nights the women and children hurled rocks at the Spaniards who were trying to climb the narrow stone road. At last, ready to drop from exhaustion, the women surrendered, but first they set fire to their city. The captive Amaru was brought up the mountain and led through the smoking streets in humiliation before the anguished women. After this victory parade, the heroes proceeded to the temple, where the idol of the god Punchau was enshrined. They wrenched the precious image from its niche and seized an incredible loot in jewels and household articles of gold. Then, in a gesture of contempt, they fed the fire which was razing the city. A month later, on the ashes, they built an Indian reduction called San Francisco de la Vitoria.

The sensation caused throughout Peru by this double battle was tremendous. Oliva listened avidly to the tales related by her father and questioned him eagerly about the news. She perhaps did not suspect that she herself might be partly Incan. Only later, when she realized that the date of her mother's birth almost excluded the possibility of a Spanish maternal grandmother, could the thought have come to her.

The viceroy was pleased that an example had been made at Vilcapampa and now resolved on Amaru's execution, but his resolution was not shared by many members of his court and private guard. Amaru had become a Christian, with his wife and daughter, and most of the Spaniards in Cuzco felt that if he were allowed to live he could convert his people and reconcile them to their state as vassals. He himself asked for this opportunity. But the viceroy said no. Amaru had shed his envoy's blood and revolted against Spain. He must die, Christian or not. Gaspar stood by at attention during the scene that followed the publication of the sentence.

Seven illustrious men were announced, entered the audience room and dropped to their knees before the viceroy. The onlookers gasped. Who were these men? The Archbishop of Mexico, an Augustinian, a Mercedarian, the prior of the Dominicans, a Franciscan, a Jesuit and a diocesan priest comprised the group. Their pleas for the life of Amaru would have moved any heart less hardened than the viceroy's, but he froze like an Andean peak; and lest someone intervene to save Amaru, he sent word in haste to have the ceremony of execution cut short.

Amaru was beheaded in the plaza of Cuzco, his capital and the capital of his fathers. Before he died he made a speech. He abjured his former paganism in public as he had already done in private, begging his subjects to do the same and keep peace with the Spaniards. He died praising the Trinity.

The Church claimed his body and the viceroy dared not withhold it, but he would not give up the head. He had it impaled on a pike and left under guard in the plaza. The Indians who packed the square kept vigil around it, and as they wailed, all the church bells in Cuzco tolled. A man was dead; with him had died an empire and a civilization.

Most of the Spaniards in Cuzco were furious. That night many Spaniards, Gaspar probably among them, went back to the plaza to pray before the head. It was plainly visible. In life Amaru had been handsome; in death he was glorious. Heavenly beauty shone from his face and around it. All present spoke of the wonder with awe. From his room the viceroy Toledo stared morosely into the night. He had done his duty despite all opposition; he had crushed the Incan power forever. Why then was he not happy?

The next six years passed quickly and busily for Oliva. While Gaspar remained with Toledo in Cuzco, she worked hard at her books, needlework and practical nursing. She may have studied music, too, for it formed part of a well-educated young lady's training and later she would have her daughter, Rose, learn the guitar. While Gaspar was staying with the viceroy in La Plata and Potosí and fighting the Chiriguanos fruitlessly, his future wife was maturing in mind and body.

By the time Gaspar was returning from the south via Arequipa, early in 1576, her dreams for the future were taking shape. She was already forming specifications for her future husband. He must be noble, dignified, a man of character and virtue. He must be brave, daring, experienced in the ways of the world, dependable, honest, loyal, intelligent, with contacts among distinguished families. She would like him to be a soldier also.

Was wealth listed among Oliva's demands of her husband-to-be? Undoubtedly at first; but she was too practical not to realize as she grew older that many of the noblest families in Lima were impoverished. Her own was of limited means, despite her father's sacrifices, her mother's ingenuity and her own talent at sewing and dress designing. She could not aspire at once to a place in the highest rank of society. The most that she could do was to marry a man who might some day rise to the coveted circle.

We do not know where or how she met the handsome middle-aged Gaspar Flores, but he cannot have taken any romantic interest in her before 1576. Probably Gaspar was invited to her home and she met him there. Although poor, he held an honored post; he knew the viceroy and the whole court.

When he first met Oliva, Gaspar was in high spirits. He had much to tell that would be of interest to the young girl and her parents. If at this time he was still a self-defensive bachelor, he soon found himself marvelling at her precocious poise, elegance and cultivation of mind.

What did the enamored couple speak of in their carefully chaperoned meetings, besides Gaspar's adventures? The reign of St. Pius V, which began in Oliva's childhood, was a verdant springtime full of growth, pruning and promise. The papal court, the sacred college, the Roman clergy, the Swiss guards and the whole city of Rome became a kind of monastery, as the wits remarked. But this was only a prelude to the saint's fundamental work, the work dearest to his heart: the implementing of all the decrees of the Council of Trent. By the time of his death in May, 1572, he had done all that was most urgent in this respect.

In 1576, when Gaspar came courting, St. Pius was still far from canonized by many Spaniards at home and in the colonies. They had found him too firm a father. Had he restricted his work to ecclesiastical matters, he might have escaped with a few acid jokes and anecdotes, but he turned his attention to something highly cherished in Spain. He forbade bullfights in Spanish territory, European and colonial. Most of the Spanish bishops resisted the pope's will by not publishing the prohibition formally, but the papal nuncio outwitted them by making it known everywhere through the Lenten preachers.

Needless to say, there were violent repercussions in Peru, as everywhere in the Spanish empire, and there was great joy when a new pope revoked the prohibition promulgated by Pius V. This was the prime topic of conversation when Gaspar first came courting Oliva.

For another fault as well, St. Pius V had found it necessary to upbraid Spain. In the diocese of Calahorra class friction grew so sharp that churches were the scene of disturbances and damage. The people were divided into two classes: the *hildagos*, who were exempt from taxes, and the *pecheros* (commoners), who were not. The *hildagos* claimed the first places in church at Mass, in receiving the sacraments and in religious processions. The civil government decreed that churches should be divided lengthwise and the *hildagos* seated on one side, the *pecheros* on the other. The pope abolished the law and decreed the excommunication of anyone who claimed a special place in church. His action stirred up much bitterness against him, not only in the diocese in question, but wherever such abuses existed. In Peru various confraternities were at war with one another over precedence. St. Pius V had outraged Spaniards by still another rebuke, this time to priests. The Council of Trent decreed that clerics in minor orders should receive the sacraments of penance and Communion at least once a month, those in major orders were to receive these sacraments twice a month and priests were to celebrate Mass at least once a week. Pope Pius had also forced an outraged King Philip II to permit the giving of Communion to condemned convicts. It had been denied them in Spain and the Spanish dominions by custom, through a rigorous respect to our Lord. Human nature being what it is, we have no difficulty in believing that many found these changes offensive and hoped for a reverse decision from the new pope, Gregory XIII. He had already withdrawn the excommunication attached to bullfights; would he grant further concessions to the Spanish national sensibilities?

It was probably about the time of Oliva's sixteenth birthday that Gaspar asked for her in marriage and his proposal was accepted. Now came months of high activity for Oliva; she revelled in it. All her days were spent in spinning, weaving and needlework, or in choosing house furnishings. What she bought had to be simple and cheap; yet her sense of design kept the whole harmonious.

Now Oliva's interest in world affairs abruptly ceased. Even her delight in the gossip of Lima suffered some eclipse. Instead of chatting with her friends over the latest scandal, she sketched plans and examined possible sites for her future home. She and Gaspar had decided to build. Together they strolled through the city, pausing to comment on each vacant lot. Finally their search took them along Calle Santo Domingo, a pleasant street which took its name, like most colonial city streets, from a building located on it. This was the Church of St. Dominic, administered by the Dominican friars of the adjacent Convent of the Holy Rosary.

"What a large garden that is behind Espíritu Santo!" cried Oliva eagerly, as the couple walked a short distance beyond Santo Domingo. "Does the hospital own it all?"

"I believe so," Gaspar answered reflectively. "All the land was donated by the founder. See those roses, Oliva?" he asked as they stopped and peered into the garden. "They all came from the first rose seed planted in Peru. That was before your birth."

"Oh Gaspar!" Oliva exclaimed in delight, "let us try to build here."

The Espíritu Santo sold the property and Oliva had her wish. Soon Indian builders were at work on the house. Gaspar could not afford oven-baked brick, so it was of adobe.

Was it by accident that they built their home on part of

the plot of land where the first rose seed was planted in Peru? No one who believes in a provident God can say yes; for, only thirty-four years later, St. Rose of Lima grew and bloomed on that same plot: the first rose of charity canonized in South America.

The wedding of Oliva and Gaspar went off on schedule with the greatest pomp possible. Oliva was lavishly gowned and bejeweled despite her poverty. Undoubtedly all the members of the viceregal guard were present at the ceremony and the celebration that followed. Perhaps the viceroy himself came to the wedding.

Gaspar's post in the viceregal guard was a high stepping stone. From its ranks the viceroys drew royal officials who enjoyed their confidence—generals, admirals and governors of provinces. Oliva could hope that Gaspar might some day be a highly paid governor or an admiral. Then they would be accepted by the first class nobility.

In the very year of their marriage Lima was threatened by pirates. Since the conquest, incredible wealth had flowed from Peru across the sea to Spain and the stream was still continuing. It was to go on until more than half the gold in Europe glittered in Spanish coffers. The galleons putting out from Callao, the seaport of Lima, were therefore frequent targets of buccaneers blessed by predatory European kings and queens. The attacking ships in this case were English.

Sailing under Francis Drake, these naval gangsters sailed through the Strait of Magellan and followed the coast of Chile, where they seized 25,000 golden pesos. Made more audacious by this triumph, they pounced on Callao when the Peruvian fleet was absent. Coming close enough to land, they cut twelve galleons from their moorings and proceeded to rifle them. It took time to accomplish this, and the two leagues between Callao and Lima were soon covered by a galloping courier. In a matter of minutes the city was in a panic.

While men rushed to arms, women and children fled to the churches. But the pirates did not attack the capital.

Drake's attack was the first of its kind experienced by Callao. In Lima fear gave way to anger when the pirates sailed away with their loot. A deputation of noble ladies confronted the viceroy, offering to defend the nation's treasures "since the men are unable to do so."

Oliva's plight was extreme on the day of Drake's attack, for she was already pregnant. Gaspar, whether or not he was at home when the news came, must have rushed at once to Callao. Oliva's parents lived in a distant quarter of the city, so she could not easily join her mother. They were too poor to own a carriage and there was no question of crossing the city on foot amid the clamor. With her Indian servant girl, Oliva therefore fled with the other women of the quarter to one of the neighboring churches. There she prayed fervently to God and the Virgin of Atocha to protect her, her dear ones and her unborn child.

Great was her grief and that of Gaspar when despite their prayers they lost that child, then a second and a third, perhaps in consecutive years. But after this triple loss and trial of their faith, the Giver of life began to reward them beyond their dreams. In 1581 a daughter was born and baptized Bernardina. She thrived, and for the first time Oliva and Gaspar felt that they enjoyed real happiness. However it was not long before Oliva's father became seriously ill and died. His loss was painful to Isabel and Oliva, as well as Gaspar, and it brought a heavy cross to Gaspar's household in the person of the newly widowed Isabel.

Scarcely was she established in her daughter's house when she began to resume her imperious rule over her daughter. In Oliva's childhood it had been more tolerable and justifiable; it was so no longer. Oliva, determined to retain her rightful place, resisted violently. Gaspar, who had found his home a place of refreshment and joy, now found it a battlefield. It was perhaps at that time that he and Oliva had another son, Gaspar.

Between 1582 and 1584 Oliva gave birth to two more children. The first was a daughter whose name is unknown. We shall call her "Mercedes." She was soon joined by a baby brother, and there is some doubt as to whether he was Matthias or Andrew. By the close of 1585 Gaspar and Oliva had six living children. They must have added at least one room to their house. Rising prices made Gaspar's wage more inadequate by the month. Oliva resolved to help him; she began a day school for children, holding her classes in the house. Oliva was a competent teacher. Already used to the training of children, she knew how to combine training in the natural and supernatural life. Oliva's pupils advanced in Christian virtue while they studied books and needlework. Later, when it seemed advisable to close the school, Oliva found herself ready to begin what was a work worthy of her supreme attention: the character formation and education of a saint.

The earnings which Oliva added to the family income were welcome, but the school seems to have injured her health. The presence of the pupils in the house day after day increased the friction between Oliva and her mother. Of Oliva's children, only Bernardina and Mercedes were old enough to attend the classes; the others were left in Isabel's care. Like most grandmothers, she treated them with an indulgence which made them unruly. This led to bitter disputes between the two women.

Meanwhile Gaspar had other worries. The viceroy, Toledo, was a man of high morals and a fearless sense of duty, but from the very beginning he had been disliked. His execution of Amaru and the crushing burden of his legislative system set both Indians and Spaniards against him. The king had shown his displeasure by cutting the personnel of his private guard as well as their salaries. The viceroy had often been denounced to King Philip II since then.

Despite the increasing hostility, Toledo persisted in making fresh enemies. He crushed all who crossed him; his path was strewn with broken men. Some deserved punishment, spoliation or exile, but this fact made them no less formidable as foes. At Panama, even before he reached Peru, he had ordered back to Spain all immoral men. Concubinage was common between Spaniards and baptized negresses, whom they ruined but would not marry. Toledo forced all such to marry. This news reached Peru before the viceroy, and Peruvian spines were even then stiffened against him. His later policies fed their first antagonism.

Toledo's quarrel with the priests and hierarchy of Peru began on his arrival. His rigid fervor quickly noted every abuse. He sent a stinging memorial to the king, who studied Toledo's reports intently. The genuinely worthy archbishops and priests lost no occasion of stating their side of the case, but their appeals were offset by the unworthy priests who, when censured by their diocesan superiors, ran to the *audiencia*. This played directly into the viceroy's hands; he informed the king that the ecclesiastical courts were encroaching on the rights of the *audiencia*.

In justice to Toledo, it must be admitted that the clergy of Peru at that time had its faults. The failure of the *doctrineros* (most of them religious) to learn Quechua and the collusion of their superiors against the efforts of diocesan prelates to force them to have been mentioned. Desperately poor, many diocesan priests accepted part-time work to meet the high cost of living. This injured the respect and piety of the people. Moreover, many priests who engaged in such work spent their earnings on silken cassocks not only of the more sombre hues but even of spectacular colors. They wore painted shoes and their capes and hats were lavishly adorned. Many had sailed for Peru without permission; some were fugitives seeking escape from punishment for past offenses. A number of them wandered from place to place without discipline or care of souls.

Toledo's move was ruthless. He had brought from Spain officials to set up the Inquisition. Now he proposed to the king that it be turned against the Peruvian clergy.

Vehement though the viceroy was against evils in the clergy, he did not wish their reform to come from the Church. Therefore, when in 1573 Archbishop Loaisa wished to call a council of bishops, the viceroy blocked it. The archbishop died in 1575, and the next archbishop got no further. When he was promoted to Badajaz and the see of Lima was again vacant, King Philip II did one of the most commendable things recorded in his life: he named Toribio Mogrovejo as archbishop of Lima. He was not a priest when the king named him archbishop, but a quiet, studious bachelor buried happily in his books and classrooms in Granada. He had spent most of his life in the universities of Valladolid, Salamanca and Coimbra, but now a papal dispensation hastened his way to the priesthood and soon he was ready to embark for Lima. He was forty-three years old.

While St. Toribio was changing from a scholar to an apostle, the viceroy Toledo was in the throes of his final battle, this time against the Jesuits. At first he had a high opinion of them, despite his scorn for all other Peruvian clergy and prelates, but they refused to serve in his war against the Dominicans by taking charge of the University of San Marcos which the Dominicans had founded and long administered. This did not prevent the viceroy from seizing the University and setting it up as a civil institution under the patronage of King Philip II in 1574. If he restored it to the Order of Friars Preachers in 1580, he was doing them no favor, for he had succeeded in throwing its finances into wild disorder.

Enraged at the Jesuits for refusing to act as his pawns, Toledo began to plot the closing of their seminary. At the same time, he thought to use the Jesuits to strike a blow at the diocesan clergy. The archbishop had been struggling to found a diocesan seminary so the viceroy asked the Jesuits to assume its administration. But the learned Jesuit Provincial, Acosta, was more astute than the viceroy. When he refused the care of the diocesan seminary, Toledo forbade the Jesuits to teach in the University of San Marcos, where they held several chairs, or even in their own college. He also prohibited others from teaching in their classrooms.

Many memorials reached the king from eminent persons pleading for justice. In the meantime, the viceroy forbade the founding of a Jesuit house in Arequipa on flimsy pretexts. His motives were so obvious that the Jesuit Provincial opened the house. Toledo ordered it to be closed, and he himself closed the College at Potosí which had been founded without his consent by the *audiencia* of Charcas. All Peru was in ferment.

What were Gaspar's views during this storm? We cannot know, but we do know that if he at any time shared the viceroy's anti-Jesuit fury, he later lost it, for he permitted his mother-in-law and daughter, Rose, to go to the Jesuits for spiritual direction. While most of Peru raged against the viceroy, Gaspar had to present a bland face. He found it necessary to guard his tongue even with his friends, and his anxiety lest Oliva, Isabel or one of his older children pass some imprudent remark which might be reported to the viceroy must have been intense. Moreover, Gaspar's support of Toledo, necessary though it was and superficial though it may have been, bore with it the danger of dismissal by the king whenever the storm should break in Spain.

In 1581, while Gaspar was absorbed in these apprehensions, Francisco de Toledo was recalled. Amid fervent rejoicing, his successor, Martín Enríquez de Almansa, arrived in Callao on May 4, 1581. A week later, Archbishop Toribio arrived. Many receptions were held in honor of the archbishop, his sister, Grimanesa, and her husband, Francisco Quiñones. As a matter of course, Gaspar and Oliva were invited to many of them and eventually Oliva and Grimanesa became cordial friends.

The arrival of the new viceroy and archbishop provided the people some diversion from the tension caused by Toledo. One of Martín's first acts was to permit the opening of the Jesuit College which his petulant predecessor had closed.

On October 29 of the same year, the Inquisition held its second *auto de fé* in the city. As always, it was a strenuous day for Gaspar, who had to be present at the long ceremony. The attendance of the viceroy was of supreme importance at that particular *auto* because the archbishop could not attend, being out of the city. Twenty persons were sentenced, among whom a Flemish Lutheran attracted most attention. For three years he had alternated between retracting errors and confessing his faith. Finally, the inquisitors gave him over to the secular arm for sentence.

In the meantime, the viceroy was having trouble with the people of Huancavelica. In an uncomplimentary report to the king, he called them "the most unquiet people of the Indies." Looking about for a man of firm character who might be able to restore calm to the district, he chose Captain Juan Maldonado de Buendía, who had been a witness at the wedding of Gaspar and Oliva. The couple congratulated their friend with sincere joy mingled with pride, and they spent much money to give him a suitably elegant farewell party. But they would not have been human had they not felt a pang of disappointment that, once again, Gaspar had been ignored. The disappointment was even sharper because at the same time Martín named another member of his private guard to a lucrative post in the provincial administration.

At the end of January, 1582, a violent earthquake flattened the city of Arequipa and its suburbs. When this news reached Lima, the Flores family, like all the citizens of Lima, were horrified and fearful. Out of their poverty, like their friends and neighbors, they sent aid to the stricken city.

On March 12, 1583, the viceroy died. He had been a man of virtue, loyal in his service to God and the crown. The mourning of the citizens was genuine. They buried him with due pomp in the Church of St. Francis, and although Isabel was herself unwell, she arose from her bed to attend the funeral.

When the viceroy refused Archbishop Loaisa permission to hold the council, which he was actually obliged to hold, by the pope's command, the archbishop appealed to the king. By the time the king gave a favorable reply, there was a new archbishop in Lima. Archbishop Toribio waited until he had a clear understanding of the state of church affairs in the New World; then he convoked the council. At the first session, which began in August, 1582, the catechisms in Castilian, Quechua and Aymara were approved and the Jesuit Fathers were commissioned to print them. The second session, instituted a year later, was not yet finished when the viceroy died and the *audiencia* assumed its usual interim rule in Peru. During this session, St. Toribio endured trials enough to sanctify any man. A bishop named Lartaún was accused before the council of unworthy conduct and he had his partisans among the bishops. A friend of Bishop Lartaún's, a turbulent judge named Cristóbal Ramírez de Cartagena, represented the *audiencia*. Aided by the bishops of La Plata and Tucumán, the judge stole the testimonies and the book of resolutions from the session room. Throughout the altercations which ensued, the *audiencia* supported Cristóbal and his recalcitrant prelate friends against the holy archbishop and the rest of the council. All Lima was in a furor over the controversy, but the saint maintained his invincible calm. The only remark attributed to him was: "I confess that I was happier with my Indians."

Besides the earthquake which terrified Lima and Callao, the year 1584 brought a second experience to be remembered: the arrival of the new viceroy, Fernando de Torres y Portugal. His term began tumultuously. He was at odds with the *audiencia* on account of the many protests which he received at their unjust conduct. He was furious, too, at the *corregidores*. Both Spanish Peruvians and Indians were suffering from their greed and now appealed for relief. In the case of the Indians, many were herded unwillingly to the cloth factories or mines. Many who were exempt from taxation by law were forced to pay taxes several times a year. When they took their complaints to court, the judges of the *audiencia* fattened on bribes from the *corregidores* and other lesser officials while they let the cases be drawn out interminably so that the Indians were ruined by the court costs.

While the viceroy sought a remedy for the worst abuses suffered by the Indians, he was also obliged to force an increased proportion of labor from them. Contraband traffic was lowering the revenues derived from Peruvian export and import enterprises; the deficiency had to be supplied by mining and smelting more gold and silver.

These and many other grave concerns absorbed the viceroy's thoughts; hence, he can scarcely be blamed if he was not impressed when he learned in April, 1586, that the wife of a fusilier in his private guard, Gaspar Flores, had been blessed by the birth of a daughter. He wondered exceedingly, though, when he heard that the lady had suffered no pain in childbirth.

"A tall tale indeed!" he muttered testily as he strode away

from his amused informant. "If people must lie, why do they not say something credible?"

As it happened, the report was true. But if St. Rose caused Oliva no pain at her birth, she caused her much pain later.

CHAPTER FOUR

What's in a Name?

ST. ROSE'S life story begins with a question mark: on precisely what day was she born? All but one of the existing testimonies give the twentieth of April. The contradictory testimony was given by Oliva. It is contained in the original copy of St. Rose's *Process of Beatification*, preserved in the archives of the Convent of St. Catherine in Lima. My defense is of the twentieth, and it runs as follows: (1) When St. Rose's mother gave her testimony, she was speaking in general of the end of the month, and the twentieth could qualify as falling near or at the end of the month; (2) St. Rose's father, her spiritual director (Very Rev. Juan de Lorenzana, O.P.), Gonzalo de la Maza and the saint herself give the twentieth as the correct date.

Now, what of the saint's painless birth? Is there any natural factor that could account for it? In Oliva's case, no. She had borne nine children before Rose, and had suffered in giving birth to each one. She suffered in delivering the three who were born subsequently. If there is any doubt on this point, one need only reflect that she would never have mentioned it in giving testimony if the event had not been extraordinary.

As a peace offering to Isabel, whose hypersensitivity and imperious will were making life wretched for them, Gaspar and Oliva named the little girl Isabel. Her grandmother was mollified; the baby was unusually lovely and her presence soothed the grieving heart of the bereaved woman. She was, therefore, somewhat restored physically and more alert than ever when the next controversy broke out. This was the changing of the baby's name from Isabel to Rose. Since several versions of the incident which prompted the change are extant, it will be necessary to weigh their plausibility and choose between them. All revert to Oliva's testimony as their guarantee of authenticity, but they are widely at variance with one another. They fall into two general categories, which might be described as the supernatural and the rationalist approaches to the interpretation of Oliva's words. The first accepts the existence of a miraculous interpretation; the second denies or ignores altogether the miraculous interpretation and produces in its stead an appallingly prosaic one. How can these different points of view be reconciled? Quite easily.

Those who believe that the baby's name was changed as a result of some miracle disagree as to its nature. Some say that the face of little Isabel turned into a rose, while others say that a rose appeared in the air above her cradle. Those who discard the possibility of a miraculous explanation claim that Oliva changed the baby's name simply because Mariana, the adolescent Indian servant girl of the family, exclaimed at the rose-like appearance of the diminutive face.

Long before the baby's name was actually changed, Mariana had often lovingly called her "my little rose," a pet name which the baby deserved on account of her extraordinarily delicate coloring. But no one who has considered the character of Oliva would imagine for an instant that on this account she would have changed Isabel's name. The very fact that it was her humble Indian servant girl who first used it would have been enough to deter her from the thought. We must, therefore, conclude that the name was changed because of that instant in which Mariana saw in the baby's face an altogether overpowering resemblance to a rose, a resemblance which made her cry out to Oliva.

What of the two different versions of the miracle? They can be explained by the different position in which Mariana stood from that of Oliva, as regards the cradle. To the one standing beside the cradle, the apparition of the rose seemed to hang above the baby's face. To the other, bending directly over the cradle, the apparition hid that tiny face altogether. To her it seemed as though Isabel's face had turned for a moment into a rose.

Why should God have worked this prodigy? Why does he work any prodigy? To confer some benefit or show to a doubting world the signal sanctity of one of his children. In the case of St. Rose, this first miracle was worked to impress on the members of her household the fact that she was chosen by God in a special way. The chief doubters of her sanctity were not to be those outside that household but its own members. Later they were to reproach Rose for the miracles that she worked, attributing them to witchcraft.

The boys and Gaspar do not seem to have been present, nor the grandmother, Isabel. Had she been there, the history of the household would have been quite different. However, Bernardina and perhaps Mercedes were with their mother and Mariana when the miracle occurred. From them, the boys were to hear of it as they grew older, for the change of names was continually before their minds until after Rose's confirmation. Despite what the saint later suffered from the members of her family, we may say in all security that without the miracle of the rose she would have suffered more. The vision remained to goad them on towards the truth, although most of them remained wilfully blind to it as long as their sister lived. It may still be asked, why did God choose the symbol of the rose? Why did he choose as the site of the apparition that same ground on which the first roses of Peru had bloomed? The reason is clear. Christian thought has always used the rose to signify charity and self-immolation, the prodigal spending of self for God and one's neighbor. And these two virtues, so intimately fused, were to be characteristic of St. Rose of Lima.

Oliva was seated on a stone bench in the *patio* mending one of Gaspar's ruffs when the miracle occurred. Nearby lay the three-months-old infant in her cradle. Bernardina and Mercedes were sitting on another bench, bent over a picture book of the life of St. Catherine of Siena which their grandmother had given them for the feast of the three Kings. Suddenly Mariana appeared in the doorway of the kitchen, a one-room adobe structure behind the patio.

At the time the Indian girl must have been in her early 'teens, a slim, brown-skinned, graceful maid who carried herself with the natural dignity of her race. Mariana wore her sleek black hair drawn back tightly from her brows and braided in a style peculiar to her tribe, her age and status. If she was of Aymar stock, her braids were fastened with a strip of red cloth to show that she was of marriageable age. Like most Indian girls of her class, she wore a blouse and skirt which were probably of plain undyed homespun linen. The blouse had short sleeves; the skirt reached to the middle of the calf of the leg.

"Well, Mariana, what do you want?" Oliva asked abruptly.

"Will the de Gama's be here for supper?" asked Mariana anxiously. "We haven't a bird's meal to spare for them."

"You will have to buy something," Oliva answered with a frown. "Be sure to save the orange conserve for Thursday."

Mariana did not have to wonder who was coming on Thursday; the whole house had been painted and the kitchen whitewashed for her visit. The archbishop's sister, Grimanesa, was calling with two other distinguished ladies to collect the family contribution to the archbishop's fund for the relief of earthquake victims. There was little enough that Gaspar could spare for the victims, but Maria de Oliva was bent on giving luncheon to the collectors. To her, their visit was of far greater social importance than that of the insignificant guests whom her mother was at present entertaining in the living room.

As she listened to her mistress' orders, the Indian girl's gaze sought the cradle where her cherished Isabel lay sleeping. She reached over to brush a fly from the netting that hooded the cradle.

"Jesús María!" she gasped. "A rose without stem or thorns, where my little one's face was!"

Oliva looked up over Mariana's shoulder.

"No! It is hanging over her head!" she cried. "Do you see it, girls?" She asked her older daughters excitedly.

The children rushed to the cradle, dropping their book on the stones.

"Look! Look at the flower!"

"What's holding it up?"

"I don't know."

Bernardina, who had wriggled nearest to the cradle, reached out to touch it. The rose vanished. Oliva snatched up the baby and rocked her back and forth tenderly.

"Rose! My little Rose! Her name must be Rose, not Isabel! It is a sign from heaven."

Bernardina looked worried. She knew her grandmother's temper.

"But Mama! She is named after grandmother. Will she not be angry?"

"Hold your tongue, Bernardina," snapped her mother. "The baby shall be called Rose."

Grimanesa and her two companions came that Thursday according to schedule and, on being pressed to do so, stayed for luncheon. They swiftly saw that they had stepped into the midst of a family quarrel. Scarcely had they entered the house when Oliva showed them the baby, explaining that although she had been baptized Isabel, they were now resolving to call her Rose. On being asked whether the new name was to be a nickname or her formal name, Oliva answered decisively that it was to be formal. At this juncture, Isabel interrupted her daughter.

"The baby's formal name will always be Isabel," she said. "That is her name according to God and the Church, for she received it at holy baptism."

Paling at these words and compressing her lips slightly, an indication of anger which escaped none of her visitors, Oliva proceeded to tell them of the extraordinary reason for the change. After many murmurs of suitable sympathy which they hoped were being directed vaguely enough to avoid wounding either of their hostesses, the good ladies changed the subject. But it remained painfully uppermost in their minds because all were burning with eagerness to discuss it freely the moment that they should leave. Already their minds were bursting with opinions for and against the authenticity of the miracle. Of the three guests, Grimanesa remained the calmest because she felt convinced that the vision was of divine origin. She liked both Oliva and her mother, so she felt some distress and embarrassment on witnessing the signs of their disagreement. However, she considered the difference of minor importance and was disposed to treat it cheerfully. Of course, Oliva was right in changing the baby's name under such circumstances, and it was natural that Isabel should regret the change, since the little one had been called Isabel in honor of her. But she was a woman of sound common sense and would soon see that there was no need to quarrel. So Grimanesa thought, being of a quite different temperament.

Archbishop Toribio was soon afterwards back in Lima from a brief visitation of some suburban churches, so it was not long before he received a visit from his sister, who brought him the funds collected during the relief drive. As always, he was pleased to see her, although he happened to be especially busy that morning. There was a letter which he simply had to send off at once, so after greeting Grimanesa, he excused himself and continued writing, listening to her with as much attention as he could spare. Her visits amused him, but how she did chatter! What was this that she was telling him now?

"Then the baby's face turned into a rose!"

The archbishop looked up blankly at his sister; the nib of his quill spluttered and a copious blob of ink blotted the signature of his letter.

"I beg your pardon?" he asked.

Grimanesa regarded him patiently. In appearance they were somewhat alike, both having oval faces, slightly cleft chins, rather ample noses and expressive eyes with an almond cast. But, while Grimanesa's complexion was pale by nature and paler by art, her brother's was tanned to match the wood of his desk. Arduous journeys under a burning sun had made him as dark as an Indian. He was lean and wiry, too, while she was inclined to be plump, although she had made the resolution to lose weight, if only because the new style with hoops in the back of one's skirt required that one be slim to be graceful.

"I was speaking of the Flores baby," she said. "María de Oliva was in the patio with her other daughters and the maid when the baby's face turned into a rose. Everyone saw it; it was the size of a pomegranate."

"May God preserve us!"

Don Toribio laid down his quill and leaned towards his sister.

"What can it mean?" he asked. "What else did they tell you?"

"They say that God must have worked the miracle so that they would change the baby's name."

The archbishop smiled.

"What name is so dreadful that God will work a miracle to change it?" he asked.

"Isabel. They named her after her grandmother."

"Isabel," Toribio mused. "Well, this name is certainly common. How is the good grandmother taking this decision to change the name?"

Grimanesa laughed. Toribio knew people.

"She is indignant, of course, but I must say that to me it seems sensible of them after such a sign. Do you not think so yourself?"

Don Toribio smiled enigmatically. He relaxed in his chair.

"I really could not say," he answered. "But I like the sound of it. Rosa de Flores: Rose of the flowers. We shall see what this rosebud will be when she opens in the light of grace."

"Then, you are truly interested?" Grimanesa asked.

"By all means," said the archbishop with a vigorous nod. "Where such phenomena exist, they must be examined and the persons who experience them need guidance. Who can tell? Perhaps this infant will grow up to be a saint."

Far from the humble heart and mind of the man who spoke was the thought that he himself might be one, but his sister knew better. His self-effacing air, the poverty of his worn soutane, the palace stripped of its lackeys should have warned a stranger. The affability of the prelate to the humblest, his utter dedication to work and prayer, the hours of silent vigil before the sacramental Christ should have warned his household. But apart from Grimanesa and her husband, for too many the archbishop's holiness passed unnoticed. Only his servant, who entered his bedroom at midnight to draw the curtains so that Toribio might scourge himself to blood for the sins of his flock, treasured each smile and gesture as one might a relic. And often, while his master's macerations went on and on, the *criado* wept in silence outside the door.

Archbishop Toribio had much to concern him at the moment; so the miracle of the rose soon slipped from his mind and with it the thought of Rose. He was enduring all the agony of a father when his children are stricken with some dread disease. During the past year a cruel epidemic had been raging in and about Cuzco. The Indians, the most cherished little ones of his vast family, were dying in numbers. Now the pestilence had spread to Lima.

The city was still reeling from the effects of the earthquake, as was its suburb seaport, Callao. Ten years would be required to rebuild the flattened town. One could look nowhere without seeing wretched, homeless families huddled in miserable temporary shelters. In Lima, although to a somewhat lesser extent, it was the same story. In these conditions quarantine was difficult and the disease passed swiftly from hut to hut. What hospitals remained were soon filled to capacity. Emergency stations were set up in every quarter but these were not enough. Death hung over the capital and port like an insidious foe.

Like all the mothers of Lima and Callao, Oliva was terrified, and her terror centered on Mariana. More Indians were catching the plague than Peruvians of Spanish blood, so her very presence in the house seemed a threat to the lives of all. Yet, her work was indispensable. Perhaps, Oliva hoped, the maid's youth would be a source of strength to her in resisting infection.

All about them in the city, hundreds of stricken Indians lay dying. Others of Spanish blood were dying too, among them some children. While every householder vied with the civic and royal authorities in devising means of isolating the sick and disinfecting homes and food, the mortality rate kept rising. At the Hospital of Santa Ana for the Indians, from fourteen to sixteen died daily. Ecuador was also being ravaged by the same plague, and while Lima writhed in agony, word came from Quito that four thousand persons had died within a period of three months.

Like the rest of her family and much of Lima's nobility, Oliva was undernourished. The diet which Gaspar's wages afforded was scanty, and prices continued to rise as the number of Indians tilling the land dwindled alarmingly and, as a consequence, the crops decreased. She was forced to close her school, for she dared not risk the danger of one of the children bringing the plague into her home. Moreover, if one of her pupils were to catch the plague, she might well be blamed by the child's frantic parents. With their income so diminished, Oliva and Isabel must sometimes have been near despair as they strove to provide the essential food for the family. Mariana, for all her devotion and sincere efforts to drive the best possible bargains with the Indians at the market, could not do the impossible.

When the Hospital of the Holy Spirit, next door to their home, began taking the plague-stricken, the mother's panic reached a supreme pitch. As an added precaution she began keeping all her children in the house. Their noisy games, quarrels and whining added to her nervous tension. She could not manage them; when she tried to discipline one of them, the culprit fled for shelter to grandmother and usually found it. Bickering between the two women grew fiercer and more frequent. Gaspar found relief from the disorders of his household by visiting the hospitals with other volunteer workers from the Guard, where he cared for the plague-stricken according to the elementary methods in use at the time.

In her state of panic, Oliva did not share his eagerness to be of help to the stricken. Instead, she heaped abuse on him for endangering his family by exposing himself to the plague. After one such reproof from his wife, Gaspar withdrew from their room at the front of the house and installed himself in a small detached room near the kitchen. Somewhat satisfied by this isolation of the potential plague-bearer, Oliva ceased to nag at him but her mood by no means improved. In fact, at this juncture the war between herself and her mother assumed major proportions. The cause of this fresh offensive on both sides was the unfolding intelligence of the baby, who soon discovered that she had two names and began to answer to each with equal docility. For her promptitude and sweetness she was rewarded by sound spankings, although all that she could do was smile and hold out her arms.

It is with regret that we learn that Oliva and her mother both used the baby as target for their rancour. From her infancy Rose suffered a continual persecution from both women. Nevertheless, neither Oliva nor Isabel ever realized the gravity or culpability of their conduct. Both were so blinded by the passions of anger and jealousy that they thought of the punishments which they inflicted on the child as a simple means of training her.

When Rose was about nine months old a crisis came which nearly deprived her of life. She was not yet weaned and Oliva's milk failed. The mother, nervously unbalanced under the effect of so many consecutive shocks and so many conjoined anxieties, seemed to be in a stupor. Under the need of the moment she did not react normally by acknowledging that her milk had stopped, or even by weaning the baby without acknowledging that fact. Instead, dazed by her own physical failure and in dread of her mother's jibes and Gaspar's disenchantment (for he never tired of praising her as a perfect mother) she pretended to feed Rose and risked giving her some liquid porridge.

The next morning Oliva was hopeful. She had eaten more supper than usual, and she had worn Rose's caul all night, pinned to her clothing. Everyone knew that a caul was the best remedy for stopped milk.

Oliva had to shake Rose to make her stir. The infant did not cry, but lay in the cradle and smiled. Her body was swollen with gas; the porridge had not agreed with her. Suddenly, she began to choke. Oliva sprang up and snatched Rose from the cradle. The baby was gasping; her lips drawn back and her tongue protruding from her mouth. The mother plunged her handkerchief into a glass of fruit juice and pressed the dripping linen to Rose's lips. The baby sputtered, then began to suck thirstily. In desperate haste, Oliva drenched the handkerchief again and Rose sucked it. She lay the baby back in her cradle and called Mariana.

"Get me a cup of warm milk!" she exclaimed. "It is time that I weaned the baby."

"With joy, my lady," she said. "It is time for Rose to be weaned. She has been as pale as the moon since you began to feed her that porridge. Some vegetables will do her good."

Soon the crisis passed; Rose thrived on her diet of diluted goat's milk and mashed potatoes, varied with a spoonful or two of mixed vegetables and stewed meat.

Soon, the frightful plague ended; Gaspar ceased his expeditions as a volunteer nurse; the life of the family resumed its natural course; the children were again permitted to play outside with the youngsters of the neighborhood.

Did they play with a certain shy, well-mannered eight-year-old colored boy named Martin, one of the very few mulattos in Lima? He lived near them on the adjoining street called *Espíritu Santo*, after the hospital and chapel. He was the natural son of the distinguished and noble John de Porres. This gentleman was a native of Burgos in Spain, and in the colonial life at the time it entitled him to the greatest respect.

Had Martin been sired by a less illustrious father, the Flores children might have been forbidden to play with him, but John de Porres held a post of importance in Guayaquil, Ecuador, and on his periodic visits to Lima he often stayed with friends of influence at the Court.

That Martin was not excluded from the favor and friendship even of the very great is well known, as is also the fact that he was later a close friend of Rose. We may assume, then, without great risk of error, that their acquaintance began when both were children. Certainly the Flores children would not have been allowed to play at the house of the lovely, dusky Ana Velázquez, Martin's *morena* mother. But, there was nothing to prevent his playing in the large, luxuriant Flores garden. However, he was treated less kindly by some of them at times than one could wish.

Perhaps it was in part the distressing moments that befell him when he was with others of his age that led young Martin to seek increasingly the companionship of God in preference to theirs. He was a quiet boy, much given to helping the indigent and paying long, intimate visits to our Lord in the nearby church of St. Sebastian, where both he and Rose had been baptized.

The Church of St. Sebastian is one of the treasured colonial monuments of Lima. It is spacious, well built, and beautifully ornamented. Although the primitive structure no longer stands, the present church of St. Sebastian is very old. It was begun soon after the completion of the primitive church, and excelled it in every way except perhaps in size. Chronologically, the parish is the oldest in the city after the cathedral. The baptismal font at which Martin and Rose became children of God is in an unusually fine state of preservation.

Martin and Rose were baptized by the same priest: Father Antonio Polanco. The difference in the inscriptions which he made in the baptismal register after these two ceremonies is poignant. When Martin was baptized, he noted that the father was unknown. When Rose was baptized, he wrote, instead of the usual "legitimate daughter," "esteemed daughter."

After her emotional crisis at the time when her milk failed, Oliva seems to have recovered her balance to a great extent. She and her husband seem to have wished to make a peace overture towards Isabel when Rose was about four years old. This softening process must have been gradual, and we may assume that it began shortly after Rose was weaned. However, Isabel did not reciprocate their desire. Since Oliva had no intention of giving up the cherished name of Rose, the war went on. In fact, it even intensified to all appearances as the child grew.

Rose tried to be as good as she could to please everyone. Of course, she could not; when she pleased one, she automatically displeased another. While this was most violent in the case of her mother and grandmother, everyone in the family had to take sides.

The year 1588 brought trouble between Archbishop Toribio and the viceroy, who backed the *audiencia* against the prelate in his struggle to obtain support for his Indian churches and hospitals. The archbishop had been visiting the provinces of Cajatambo, Jauja and Tarma. There he found that church ornaments and vestments, altar linens and other necessaries were lacking and patients in the hospitals deprived of food and medicines. He had not far to look for the cause: the *corregidores* had been withholding the money raised by taxation for these purposes. On July 13, 1588, the archbishop held his own court in Santo Domingo de Sicaya, and the offenders were given fifty days in which to pay the sums owed; but far from paying them, they appealed to the *audiencia*. When the time of grace elapsed, the excommunication imposed by the archbishop automatically took effect.

Two of the persons excommunicated had such fervent support among the judges that the latter demanded the lifting of the censures. The archbishop refused. On January 23, 1589, the *audiencia* ordered the confiscation of the goods of the archbishop, who was still on apostolic visitation. The citizens of Lima held violent views either for or against the prelate. On March 6 the viceroy intervened on the *audiencia's* side. He begged Toribio to absolve the *corregidores* for a year without exacting the payment of the sums fraudulently withheld. He then authorized the archbishop to visit and examine the condition of church and hospital equipment, with the promise that the *corregidores* would be forced to provide what was necessary. The archbishop absolved the *corregidores,* and knowing that distorted reports would be sent to Spain, he wrote a report to the king.

King Philip II was by this time eager to recall the Count de Villar, and the count obediently expressed a desire to return to Spain. The king's response was immediate. He needed a more forceful administrator in Peru to fend off foreign pirates and extract larger sums for his depleted treasury. It seemed to him that he had found such a vigorous man in García Hurtado de Mendoza, who was named viceroy and sailed for the New World on March 13, 1589.

By this time Rose was dashing about the house at breakneck speed, and cascades of Spanish fell from her lips with fluency. Her mind was developing rapidly and she took an eager interest in all that went on around her. She already knew the basic truths of faith and listened raptly when, at bed time, Isabel took her on her knees to add some further item to the child's religious knowledge. There were two pictures of Christ hanging in her parents' bedroom, both of which fascinated the child. It was a heart-warming moment when one of the adults entered the room to find her kneeling in devout prayer before them. One of these pictures was of the Child Jesus, the other of Christ crowned with thorns.

How deep and sincere Rose's devotion to the suffering Christ already was and how she profited from it was revealed at this time through an accident. The child was in the kitchen "helping" her elders prepare a meal. One of them left the heavy lid of the flour bin open and the toddler tried to close it. The lid slipped from her tiny fingers and fell on her thumb. The injury was serious. Two or three days later it was found that a large blood clot had formed under her nail, and the finger was infected. In agitated haste, Gaspar sent Oliva and Isabel to a fashionable surgeon named Pérez de Zumeta. His fees were beyond what the family could afford, but Gaspar's anxiety, as well as Oliva's, made the costly choice instinctive.

The doctor had to reach the clot quickly; a painful operation was performed with no anaesthetic. First, a portion of the nail was removed; then, acid was applied to the rest of the nail and left on it for several days to loosen it. Rose's courage was such that the surgeon marvelled at it. Many years later he was still praising the child's fortitude.

Rose had endured continual unjust punishment all during her short life, day after day. She had never rebelled. Instead, she had continued to offer her mother and grandmother an unspoiled love and trust. When she was put to bed and asked if her thumb did not hurt her greatly, she pointed to the picture of our Lord crowned with thorns.

"That crown hurt worse."

Already she was measuring her own sufferings against those of Christ and finding them small, indeed. It was the only comparison that she ever used.

It was probably while Rose was being kept in the house on account of her wounded thumb that her mother had one of those inspirations which kept life in the Flores family from growing dull.

"I am going to teach Rose her reading and writing," she announced.

"Oliva! She is only three! Use your common sense!" Isabel protested.

"She is my child. If I wish to teach her, I believe that I may do so. Besides, she is more intelligent than most children of her age. I have made up my mind, Mother, so do not waste your time arguing. Bernardina, tomorrow you may buy a notebook for Rose. She shall have her own."

"She *is* rather young, though, is she not, my dear?'" asked Gaspar in a cautious tone. Usually he left the training of their daughters to Oliva.

"This is my affair," said his wife irritably. "Buy her a story, too," she added, turning to Bernardina. "Another copy of that life of St. Catherine will do. The words are simple. It is too bad that your old one is worn out."

"If Isabel is to have her first story book, I wish to buy it for her," said Isabel.

"Rose will be quite content with the one that I shall buy her," answered Oliva curtly.

Bernardina bought the two books and, between household tasks, Oliva began Rose's lessons. However, she did not meet with the immediate success of which she had been certain. Rose, always so intelligent, seemed unspeakably dense when confronted with the letters of the alphabet. After several humiliations and spankings, Oliva thought that the child might be ready for another lesson.

"Now, I have made a letter of the alphabet at the top of each page," she said to Rose. "Go into the bedroom and copy them. It is too noisy here."

Her cheeks aglow with self-conscious eagerness, Rose skipped into the bedroom with her pencil and notebook. Half an hour later she emerged, looking pleased.

"See, Mama; I have done every one of the letters!"

Oliva took the notebook expectantly. This time her praises of Rose's intellect would be vindicated. Then she frowned; she gave the child a push that almost sent her to the floor.

"No! They are all wrong!" she exclaimed.

Rose smiled uncertainly.

"I am sorry, Mama. Please show me again. I shall try hard to do better."

Oliva repeated the first lesson; then she closed the book abruptly. Her voice was hard with determination.

"Now, Rose, go and try again," she said, shaking her finger at the child. "This time, be careful."

Some time later, the small student returned. She sat close to her mother and waited hopefully for her reaction. It soon came. With a cry of disgust, Oliva threw the book across the room; it fell at Isabel's feet.

"You are stupid, hopeless! Get out of my sight! I have no more time to waste on you today!"

Isabel picked up the notebook and rose from her chair.

"Come to grandmother, Isabel darling," she said in a voice dripping with sweetness. "It is time for your catechism lesson. Come; I shall teach you about the Baby Jesus."

Rose's face lighted up; she slipped from her place beside her mother and began to cross the room.

"Rose, stay where you are!" she snapped. "I shall tell you when to go."

"You just told her to get out of your sight, Mother," remarked Bernardina, looking up from her embroidery.

Rose, bewildered, turned first to her grandmother, then to Oliva.

"What shall I do, Mama dear?"

"Go into the bedroom. In a few minutes I shall come and prepare you for your nap." Then as the child began to obey, she added, handing her the pencil and notebook: "Take these with you, too. If you leave them here, they will be mislaid."

Some fifteen minutes later, Rose ran back into the living room.

"Look, Mama! See what I have written!"

Oliva glanced at the page in annoyance. As she looked, she gasped.

"Why, this is perfect!" she exclaimed. "I cannnot understand such a change!"

In sheer amazement, she held the notebook towards her husband. Gaspar began to examine the pages and so did Isabel. While they were still marvelling at the excellence of her work, Rose astounded them even more by what she next did. Taking her story book, she read several paragraphs with ease and rapidity, although a few minutes before she could not have stammered a line.

"How did you learn so quickly, Rose?" asked Oliva when the three-year-old student had finished showing what she could do.

Rose's eyes danced and her smile was endearing.

"I asked the Baby Jesus to teach me, Mama, to save you the work; and he did."

Such is the story of how St. Rose learned to read and write. Oliva attested to it under oath at a time when Rose had already worked many miracles; had already been long venerated in Lima as a saint; when her relics had been enshrined near the high altar in the church of Santo Domingo and throngs visited her tomb continually and received favors from her. There was no need, then, for her mother to exaggerate a particular incident in a life already blazing with glory. Besides, although growing old when she gave her testimony, Oliva still possessed a clear memory and she was at that time practicing the virtues with edifying proficiency.

The problem remains, however, as to the interpretation to be placed on Rose's words. Are we to conclude that the Infant Jesus appeared to the toddler and taught her in visible form? Not necessarily; in fact, the brevity of Rose's words would seem to show that he did not. Surely, if she had seen the Child in a vision, she would have added some description of him. Nor are we told that she ever referred later to any such vision, although she was very open and simple in the descriptions that she gave of those that she did receive.

What did Rose mean, then, when she said that the Baby Jesus had taught her to read and write? Simply that, in answer to her trusting prayer, addressed to the Infant, he infused into her mind a sudden comprehension of what Oliva had been teaching her. Later, she was to receive many such graces when looking lovingly at holy pictures; for this reason she always used them for her devotion, no matter how sublime her prayer.

To put the matter briefly, we have in this case not the revelation by God of a field of knowledge until then completely outside the child's grasp by reason of its nature and her opportunities to master it, but an answer to her prayer. Rose's prayer was inspiringly selfless. She asked the Infant Jesus to teach her, not to save herself the labor of learning or for fear of the punishment meted out on failure, but to save her mother the work of teaching her. That is what she said and that is what she did.

Don García proved to be one of sixteenth-century Peru's ablest and best known viceroys. However, if we can credit his critics, he craved fame and flattery. What might have caused this is now problematical, but it had its repercussions on Peruvian literature, for it became the fashion to laud him in poems and even the theater. In addition to this, he showed an extraordinary attachment to points of honor.

One of the new viceroy's first announcements brought tremors of apprehension to the people of Peru, especially those living on or near the coast. The colonists were already aware of the pitiable state of Callao's defenses, but to hear them denounced as useless by the viceroy was not reassuring. He produced plans for better placed bastions and work on them proceeded as quickly as possible.

The war in Chile also received prompt attention from García. In turning to the problem of raising reinforcements for the Chilean colonists, hard pressed by the Araucanian Indians, the viceroy found that he could not proceed without facing sharp opposition. To deplete Callao's land forces, insufficient as they already were, seemed madness, but Chile needed help and Peru was the logical place to find it. García insisted and the troops eventually went.

A partial victory followed at Mariguenu, but in the midst of the war the Governor of Chile left his post without permission and sailed for Spain. The fierce though sporadic war was to deprive Peru of many of her bravest men. Indeed, Gaspar would one day give to Chile perhaps the finest of his own sons.

Despite his failings, García was a man of rectitude. His lasting claim to recognition is chiefly his effort to reform the *corregidores*. When he arrived on the colonial scene, they were still scandalously busy fleecing their flocks. He demanded that such dishonesty cease. The offenders fled to the king for support, and when García asked Philip II for authority to begin the reform, he was told that the time was not opportune.

It would have been greatly to the benefit of the king to heed the viceroy's advice. The colonial receipts were dwindling, but a few years' honest administration in the provinces would have swelled them exceedingly. It is not easy to estimate the sum that was kept back annually by corrupt civil servants in the New World, but within four years the Governor of Chucuito had sent 60,000 pesos to Spain for safekeeping as a retirement fund for himself, although his salary was only 3,000 pesos a year. King Philip II had desired a strong viceroy to curb such embezzlement and increase the royal receipts. Now, when he had the man for the task, he failed to support him.

In the Flores family the first years of García's administration passed without incident, if we except an ear infection which Rose developed at four. She bore it and the surgeon's treatment as heroically as she had borne the injury to her thumb the year before. Once again the passionate solicitude of her mother showed that Oliva's usual severity with the child was due to vehement and jealous love, fearful of losing ground before Isabel's possessiveness. However, Oliva's desire to reach a truce with her mother was beginning to bear fruit. Without relinquishing the cherished name Rose, which would have done much to end all acrimony, she still wished to offer Isabel some sign of love and confidence. Isabel had begun to seek spiritual help from the Jesuit Fathers and was continually praising their wisdom as confessors. So, when Rose reached the age of five and could make her first confession, Oliva let Isabel choose the church where she should go. Soon Rose was going regularly with her grandmother to the church of the Jesuits.

Rose lost no time in petitioning the priest who heard her confessions for a privilege that she had been coveting since she learned to read. In her story book on the life of St. Catherine of Siena she had learned of the existence of a vow of virginity. She determined to make it herself. The step was, in Rose's eyes, the decisive step in her life, by which she fixed her resolution to live for Christ alone.

Astoundingly, she received permission to make the vow. She presented her plea with such grave dignity and intelligence, such purity of intention and firmness of will that the priest saw in her a truly chosen soul. There would be no harm in letting her make the vow and much good might come of it. If at any time she changed her convictions as to the state of life in which God wished her, she could be freed from her vow.

Doubtless the priest did not give his consent without first resorting to prayer, reflection and the taking of counsel. Whose counsel did he ask? As a Jesuit, that of his superior. Did his superior in turn seek counsel? We do not know. If he did, it is possible that he consulted Archbishop Toribio. It is a charming possibility. If Rose made her request as early as March, 1601, Toribio was absent from Lima. If she made it later in the year, say in July, the archbishop was back in the city. In that case, the Jesuit superior could have consulted him and may well have done so. It was an unusual case and one that no prudent priest would settle lightly.

After Rose made her cherished vow of virginity, prayer grew sweeter than ever to her. She had been thrown into the arms of God from infancy by the constant rebuffs of her mother and grandmother. As her sisters, Bernardina and Mercedes, were so much older than herself, Rose was thrown on her own resources very often. While her young brothers and the children of the neighborhood enjoyed themselves in games, Rose slipped off to play in some corner, alone. This play usually ended in prayer. She would pretend that she was St. Catherine of Siena in seclusion at home.

Rose often played with her brother Fernando when he was not with his brothers or the other young boys of the neighborhood. Fernando was two years her senior, a pleasant, care-free child who loved to tease. He was extremely fond of Rose and played willingly with her, although at times he grew too rough for her liking. To a greater extent than any of her other brothers and sisters, he was Rose's confidant, auxiliary and sometimes accomplice.

Their favorite retreat was a banana tree which Fernando had trained to grow against the garden wall so that it formed a kind of hut. Under the inspiration of Rose, the two children transformed it into a quasi-shrine. Anything that could be culled from the family discards was purloined for its adornment.

One day, Rose called Fernando with a conspiratory gesture.

"Come to the hermitage," she whispered.

He wondered what was afoot, but had not long to wait. As soon as they were hidden in the leaf hut, she knelt and took off her veil.

"Oh, Rose! What a sight you are! the boy cried, strangling with laughter.

His little sister's hair hung about her face in short, jagged clumps. Only the very front fringe was unclipped.

"I left this part long," she explained gravely, "so that when I have my veil on, no one will notice that my hair is cut. As so many girls go to hell on account of their pretty hair, I have decided to keep mine short. Now I look ugly and no one will want to marry me."

Fernando continued to rock with laughter.

Rose's tonsure went undetected until that evening. Despite Isabel's protests that they were too young, Bernardina and Mercedes were learning to dance. Oliva insisted on it; she had learned young, she said, and it had done her good. If they learned now, by the time that they reached an age when they could attend balls, they would be experts. She herself was teaching them, just now.

Rose was curled up on a huge hassock near her grandmother's armchair, watching the deft movement of her knitting needles. She was making a pair of lacy black stockings for Bernardina, throwing the thread over her needle twice each time she made a stitch to create long, diamond shaped stitches.

"Come, Rose! No more pouting in the corner! You will learn to dance, too!"

"Oliva! Do not be ridiculous! Isabel is only five years old!"

"Rose will dance if I tell her to do so. She is too quiet; she should be livelier at her age."

Rose stood hesitantly in the middle of the floor.

"Please, Mama, do not make me learn!"

"Do not be a stick! Come now; no more arguments!"

Oliva reached over and caught Rose by the end of her veil. The treacherous square of linen came off, revealing her downy head topped by the deceptive fringe of long hair at the temples. The mother's scream was soon drowned in a chorus of cries.

"Rose! What have you done to your hair?"

Rose smiled. Now everything would be well; when she explained her reasons, Mama would understand.

"I did it because it is so dangerous for young girls to have long hair," she said. "And to keep souls from being caught in my hair and dragged down to hell. St. Catherine cut her hair too, so that must be best."

Oliva stood stunned for an instant; then she began to shake Rose violently.

"Stop, Oliva!" cried Isabel, rising shakily from her chair. "You will make my Isabel ill! It is no more than a childish prank; her hair will soon grow in again."

"Leave me alone!" said Oliva savagely. "Mother, I have borne enough of your interference. I shall punish my daughter when she deserves it, and I am going to give her a spanking that she will never forget."

CHAPTER FIVE

Rose With Thorns

THE YEAR 1591 closed gloomily for the Peruvian people, the Flores family included. King Philip II's Christmas gift to them was the deflating word that the money raised by them and their fellow-colonists of Ecuador was not sufficient to meet the royal needs. Peru was still suffering from the double blow of the earthquake and plague, yet she had given generously to the king's war fund. Now, a fresh sacrifice was asked of her.

In Spain a commerce excise tax of ten percent had long been collected on every commercial transaction except articles of primary necessity. So far, this tax had never been exacted in Peru. Faced by the fact that his duty demanded it, García gave notice that it should begin on January 1, 1592. In view of the ravaged condition of Peru, he lowered it to two percent, but even that was too much to ask of an already impatient people. It seemed likely that a revolution would break out.

During the night of April 23, agitators were thronging the streets. It was an anxious time for the Flores family and all shared the tension which was probably increased by the absence of Gaspar, who was most likely at the palace, ready to answer any emergency call. It must have been with a heavy heart that Rose's father looked forward to the morning. If a revolution did break out, he would be faced by the alternative of deserting his post of honor and fighting with the insur-

gents, or shooting down his fellow-citizens for whose grievance he doubtless felt a strong sympathy.

The following day brought nothing more violent than the
expected verbal forays when the corporation met. After
many discussions, it was decided that a civic envoy should go
to the king to ask for exemption from the tax. Jerónimo de
Guevara was chosen for this hopeful journey. He must have
been a man of high persuasive powers, for the city felt that
his words might well sway the king to listen favorably to its
claims.

Meanwhile, in Quito the imposition of the tax was hotly
contested. Some of the *regidores* were imprisoned and the
people sacked the prison. On October 1, the viceroy received
a plea from the judges of the Quito *audiencia* appealing for
help. In response to this plea, García sent General Pedro de
Arano with sixty picked soldiers via Guayaquil to enforce the
tax there. But as events proved, he would have done better to
send the men to Quito at once. One night a man was shot
near the houses of the *audiencia* and a revolution ensued.
The insurgents raided the *audiencia*, making attempts on the
lives of the judges. The revolution in Ecuador, if unchecked,
might well stir up the malcontents of Lima to armed revolt.

During the angry turbulence Rose was old enough to interest herself in praying and making sacrifices for peace. Perhaps
she prayed, too, that the tax might not be imposed if God so
willed, for she was surely well aware by this time of the poverty of her family and country. Then, too, she had an additional reason for following the revolution in Ecuador with her
anxious prayers. Martin de Porres, their neighbor and play-
mate, had gone to Guayaquil with his father and little sister,
Juana.

Undoubtedly the revolution in Ecuador and the conse-
quent deaths of prominent persons consoled Oliva for her
husband's inconspicuous post. She would not have been her-

self had she not envied Juan de Porres his appointment in
Guayaquil. Now she began to see dimly that success can cost
so much that it spells calamity.

If the year 1592 began with a political upheaval, it saw the
end of at least one struggle between the Church and the administration. In this, too, Rose had her hidden part in prayer
and sacrifice, for it involved many persons in whom she was
affectionately interested. Archbishop Toribio had begun
building a church for their beloved Indians, just outside
Lima. He gave it an image of our Lady called *Nuestra Señora
de Copacabana*. This was a copy of the original statue carved
by a devout Indian, whose work evidently so pleased our
Lady that she performed many miracles when petitions were
addressed to her before the image. The original statue stood
in a chapel on the shore of Lake Titicaca, where a pagan
shrine had once attracted thousands.

Archbishop Toribio, having built his Indian church with
diocesan funds, suddenly found to his dismay that the viceroy
wished to take it from him. The latter, partly through natural preference for his brother, a Jesuit who had come to join
the Peruvian foundation, and partly because of the situation
of the new church, wished to have Archbishop Toribio's favorite parish administered not by diocesan priests but by the
Jesuit Fathers. Moreover, he ordered that many Indians who
had moved to this district of San Lázaro near the river should
move to the town of Cercado, which was a Jesuit parish.

The archbishop fought this civil interference in what
should have been his domain, but without success. The viceroy's version of the issue went to the king and was duly given
royal support. In the end, the prelate was forced to cede his
church to the Society of Jesus, which may not have particularly wanted it. The Society did not enjoy its position as the
pet lion of Viceroy García. It was a role that came with too
many leashes attached.

The Flores household undoubtedly found itself on the blade of the knife during the Copacabana controversy. The family belonged to a diocesan parish, St. Sebastian. Gaspar worked for the viceroy. Isabel and Rose went to the Jesuit Fathers for confession and spiritual direction. It was perhaps this embarrassing situation that caused Oliva to frequent increasingly the Dominican church of Santo Domingo. It was actually a more logical choice than St. Sebastian from the point of view of distance.

This change proved of lasting importance in the life of the six-year-old Rose. Her mother and grandmother began to visit the chapel of Our Lady of the Rosary in the Dominican church and Rose felt her soul drawn towards it as to a magnet. In this chapel she was to receive some of the most striking favors of her life, which was already so rich in the promise of heaven's blessings. Soon it became the established custom for Oliva to take Rose each afternoon for a visit to the Blessed Sacrament in the church of Santo Domingo and a long, ardent colloquy with Our Lady of the Rosary. Undoubtedly these colloquies would have been much longer than they actually were, if Rose had not had an impatient Oliva tugging at her elbow. Actually, it was greatly to Oliva's credit that she made the effort to take Rose for this daily visit, pressed as she was with such a multiplicity of duties at home.

The statue of Our Lady of the Rosary for which Rose's favorite chapel was named is still one of Lima's most revered images. It is a charming statue, in which an oval-faced, smiling Madonna with a rosary in her hands holds a chubby, benign Infant Jesus who blesses with one hand and holds a small, cross-topped world in the other. The expression on the face of the Infant is particularly loveable. Although not smiling, he seems about to burst into a cascade of infantile glee. It is a statue which would naturally attract any child, and

Rose was no exception. What she heard of the miraculous interventions of this Madonna in the history of Lima fired her imagination and fervor.

To this venerated image the populace of Lima has flocked in time of peril since the early days of the city's existence. Favors uncounted have been granted before this Madonna and Child. More than once the whole assembly of the faithful has witnessed the animation of both figures. On account of the many miracles attributed to the history of the statue, both the Madonna and Child have been officially crowned by the Church.

It was a providential coincidence that brought Rose into contact with Our Lady of the Rosary at the very time when the disorders in Lima and the bloody revolution in Ecuador held a special place in her prayers. The crisis proved a passing one, but while it lasted the danger of revolution in Peru was real. The episode formed the child's mind in a certain thought pattern that recurred throughout her life. She entered fully into the trials and calamities experienced by her city and country, her archbishop and Church. Her prayers and sacrifices, and as she grew older, her penances were focused on these great intentions of her time.

If the statue of Our Lady of the Rosary was miraculous, that of Our Lady of Copacabana was no less so. The Indians had kept their copy of the original statue in a poor hut, but someone destroyed the hut one night, leaving the sacred statue exposed to the elements. Archbishop Toribio held a procession of the Blessed Sacrament in reparation for the deed and ordered special prayers in all the churches of Lima. When the solemn procession carrying the statue reached the cathedral, the sacred image began to sweat abundantly. The miracle continued for four hours; two chalices were full of liquid when the phenomenon ceased. The whole city ran to witness the marvel, the Flores family certainly included. Soon the sick and afflicted were begging for a few drops of the miraculous liquid, and with the effect for which they hoped.

Deprived of the church that he had built to house this miraculous statue, the archbishop now sought for some means of enshrining it worthily. A chapel was built for it in the cathedral, where it continued to work prodigies.

Besides the miraculous images already mentioned in these pages, Lima boasted others which attracted many to chapels of pilgrimage. These images, too, were reputed as miraculous. Rose grew up, then, in an atmosphere of miracles. Miracles were almost taken for granted in the Lima of her time. One must bear this fact in mind if the casual attitude taken towards them by the saint herself and by her family is to be understood. When she began to work miracles, Rose paid al- ·most no notice to them. The time was to come when the very flowers and trees would dance at her bidding and bees and birds join her in psalmody. Yet she saw in this a fact no more extraordinary than their creation. To her, life was all faith; she never descended from the supernatural, and what might amaze others was of little account to her. As for her family, which was incurably prosaic, the time was to come when its members would find Rose's miracles as common as bread and butter and sometimes more so. Because of this very prodigality of God, their hearts remained blinded.

For Mariana the wonders worked before the image of Our Lady of Copacabana were a profound and necessary preparation for her strange partnership with Rose. This partnership began soon after the child's First Communion, when her spirit of love and sacrifice sought new outlets and she needed a friend's assistance. Mariana was solidly founded in the faith, more so than many of her people, but she needed first-hand experience of the miraculous in order to be of help to Rose. She needed to take the extraordinary with supreme impassivity. She could not show herself unduly impressed by Rose's lavish spiritual gifts without peril to the child's humility and simplicity. Moreover, she could not approach the role which the saint was to assign to her without overcoming her purely natural love, which shrank from seeing Rose suffer. More than this, despite her love, she herself would have to make Rose suffer.

Beyond these qualities, Mariana had to have something else which her racial origin supplied, while piety raised it to a supernatural level. That something was the understanding of the severest Christian ascetical practices, their toleration in Rose and a willingness to help her hide them. Being an Indian girl, Mariana had been raised in poverty and want. She was used to being despised, ill-treated and neglected. She knew what it was to see her loved ones flogged, robbed, forced into every servile occupation. Yet she knew, too, from personal experience, that true honor and dignity are not lost under unjust treatment. She knew that when such treatment is rightly borne, it can enhance the honor and dignity of the bearer. Such was the preparation of Mariana for the intimate part that she was to play in Rose's life.

Besides the controversy over the Indian church which he had built, Archbishop Toribio was embroiled in other troubles with the viceroy. Rose's prayers for him, faithful from the first, were then applied in a special way to the solving of these issues. For this reason it will be of interest to treat them at least in summary.

One controversy which would never have sprung up, had it not been for García's tenacious insistence on a point of honor, concerned the archbishop's desire to enforce the constitutions of the Council of 1567. The viceroy had been prejudiced against the archbishop even before meeting him. He wrote to the king that he had not yet visited the archbishop because he was never in the city, but was going among the Indians "*comiendoles la miseria que tienen.*" Later he called him *"incapaz"* (incompetent) and advised King Philip II to summon him to Spain.

Toribio's resolution to carry out what had been decreed by the Council regarding the new Mass rubrics promulgated by St. Pius V aroused the viceroy's hostility further. It had become customary in Peru for the deacon of the Mass to leave the altar to give the kiss of peace to the civil authorities; that is, the viceroy and president of the *audiencia*. Instead, the *"pax"* should have been given by an almoner dressed in a surplice.

Archbishop Toribio had the constitutions read in the pulpit of the cathedral on December 18, 1590. The viceroy was furious and ceased attending the cathedral services on Sundays and great feasts, as he had previously done.

Rose must have heard much at home of this, for Gaspar had always attended these services with the viceroy and was now subject to the latter's whims. From one holy day to the next, he could not predict with certainty where he would be or whether he could reach home by mealtime. Sometimes the viceroy's peregrinations took him far afield. Anything seemed preferable to Mass at the cathedral.

After his formal protest and plea that the customs remain as they had been, García began to feel confident that in time his presence might be resumed there without loss of dignity. Surely, the archbishop would cede him the accustomed honor. He, therefore, let it be known that he would attend the High Mass at the cathedral on the first Sunday of Advent, 1592. Toribio had, in the meantime, received an order from the king to leave the customs as they had been, but he was not to be deflected from his duty. To save the viceroy's face, he sent Father Juan Sebastian, the Jesuit Provincial, to warn him. The choice of intermediary is significant. At that moment, the Jesuits alone held the key to the viceroy's heart on account of his Jesuit brother. However, they were careful not to turn it often, for they realized that the favor which they enjoyed was a perilous one.

Father Juan Sebastian did not succeed in mollifying the viceroy, despite his explanations. Don García refused to attend the cathedral Mass. To the chagrin of Gaspar and his other guards, as well as his suite, he went to the town of Surco on the pretext of a message received by courier.

Another dispute which exceeded this in intensity was that of the diocesan seminary. In 1591, the archbishop bought some houses designated as seminary buildings, to which he admitted a fixed number of students. Over them he placed as their rector Francisco Guzmán. The archbishop placed his seminary under the patronage of St. Toribio de Astorga and organized its operation according to the customs of the Major College of Salamanca, where he had been a student. Finally, he had his episcopal coat of arms placed over the main entrance.

All this might seem innocuous or even praiseworthy on the part of the archbishop, but García thought differently. On learning that the prelate had had the temerity to have his coat of arms placed over the main doorway of the seminary, the viceroy's temper exceeded itself. On the claim that the presence of the archbishop's coat of arms violated the royal patronage of the seminary (a patronage which extended to all such institutions), he ordered a captain of his Private Guard and some soldiers to chip off the coat of arms and leave no trace of it. To expedite the work, they were told to take several stonecutters with them.

But García was dealing with a man who had long ago shed all interest in such points of honor and refinements of insult, although the gesture of contempt would not have escaped him. The archbishop who refused the services of a valet, although they seemed indispensable to men of his class, whether prelates or laymen, was a poor target for the viceroy's

malice. He who had stripped the archiepiscopal staff of all but
a residue of servants and who dressed much more humbly
than the least of his domestic prelates and curates, was not
apt to fuss or fume at such pettiness when it was directed
against himself. To put the facts tersely, García shot wide of
his target because he was aiming not at a haughty nobleman
but a meek and humble servant of Christ.

Don García had written the king a tart report of the incident, as a result of which he hoped for the archbishop's disgrace. In the meantime, he had also taken exception to the
prelate's choice of rector and staff members for the seminary.
As the interference came only two months before the seminary was due to open, Toribio had no time to plead with
Madrid. He was forced to capitulate for the time being; but
he too wrote to the king, setting forth his case with restraint
and charity. Philip II received these conflicting reports and
let the matter ride for almost a year, probably in order to obtain information from some impartial sources in Lima. Then
he wrote to the viceroy, who by this time must have been
feeling assured of the victory.

To his humiliation, the king ordered that Toribio be permitted to govern and administer the seminary college and
name the members of the faculty. This was in accordance
with the dispositions of the Council of Trent and the Council of 1583. Moreover the king, who was by no means insensi-
tive to his royal honor, was sufficiently clear-sighted to see
that the imposition of Toribio's coat of arms on the seminary
doorway was no insult to himself. He therefore ordered that
the archbishop be permitted to have the coat of arms replaced, giving due precedence to that of Castille.

This decree, which reached Lima early in August, 1592,
must have been a source of relief to most of the city's citizens. However, as close observers such as Gaspar must have
remarked, the viceroy did not forget the public snub to him-

self implied in the royal decree; on the first opportunity, he would take his revenge.

That opportunity came even sooner than he had hoped. Archbishop Toribio, straitened on every side by the civil interference in Peruvian church affairs, and having no one in Peru who could help him, wrote to the pope. He must have foreseen that he would suffer when his act came to the king's knowledge, but he saw it as his duty in conscience to do so. Personal affronts he would bear with equanimity; so, too, he would patiently await the untangling of endless red tape each time he sought permission for some necessary official act. But he could not tolerate abuses detrimental to the dignity and power of the Church; so he set before the pope the nature of those abuses which, in Peru, cried out loudest for remedy.

As the archbishop expected, the pope took up the complaints with the Spanish ambassador at Rome. The latter exposed the scandal to the king. A prelate who owed his mitre to the royal favor had dared to denounce customs approved of or tolerated by His Catholic Majesty! It would be difficult to say whose temperature ran higher, the pope's or the king's, but it was the king's anger that prevailed. On May 29, 1593, he wrote to García, detailing the public humiliation which he was to administer to the culprit. It was a command which the viceroy lost no time in obeying.

During 1592 Oliva had another pregnancy, during which her health seems to have shown no marked defects. Late in the year she gave birth to a son whose physical soundness was a cause of rejoicing to all his family. When she and Gaspar began to discuss possible names for their newborn son, both parents found that they shared a desire which until then they nourished in secret. This was to choose a name that would give pleasure to Isabel. To be sure, they had no intention of going back to the use of Rose's baptismal name, but there must surely be some choice that they could make for her baby brother which would be a gesture of peace. There was; a name that combined four advantages and would do much to salve the hurt feelings of his grandmother. This happy choice was "Francisco." In giving their son St. Francis as patron they would do homage to Isabel's favorite saint and be able to name him for both his grandfathers. Moreover, they would arm their son with a patron who would be a powerful defense to him all his life, who would see him through all vicissitudes. The name, Francisco, was a respected one in Peruvian history. In short, the idea seemed an inspiration and it was.

Under the warming rays of domestic unity, little Francisco began his course. The whole household welcomed him with joy, but no one felt a keener delight in him than Rose. She who had been deprived of the maternal pleasure which her playmates found in dolls now enjoyed the possession of a baby brother whom she could fondle, rock, play with and sing to sleep. Her heart, already alive to the world about her with the fresh generosity of childhood, expanded with this first experience of growing up. She was no longer the baby of the family; Oliva found less time to devote to her training and Isabel revelled in the daily unfolding of the newcomer's loveable qualities. Another child might have reacted to the changed situation by conceiving a dislike for Francisco; not Rose. She was grateful for the baby and the atmosphere of love with his advent brought to her home. If she was left more to herself from this time on, this too made her happy. She had extra time to spend in prayer.

Now the leaf hut, with its improvised altar, where she set her cherished holy pictures between candle stubs begged from Mariana, became for Rose a dear retreat. Here she found God and poured out her soul to him. Here she planned for a life of solitude and charity like that of St. Catherine, whom she had taken as her spiritual mother. Here she confided to the Virgin Mother and her adorable Son her anxieties lest her parents insist that she marry. Already the child's incredible beauty was drawing the praises of all who saw her; already Oliva was speaking to her of her future husband. When she taught Rose to care for little Francisco, when she showed her how to knit or embroider, it was always with the remark that this skill would serve her well when she was a wife and mother. Above all, when Oliva dressed Rose for some *fiesta* where persons of distinction would see her, she impressed on the child the necessity of pleasing them. She must make her friends among those of the noblest blood; she was destined for greatness.

When Rose made her vow of virginity at five years of age, she made it without telling anyone. Indeed, her confessor had imposed this condition as the sole one on which he based his permission. Rose was sorry that she could not share her joy with her mother, but as she grew older she realized that this could not be. Had she consulted her mother or told her of the vow, Oliva would have been very angry. As it was, she had no inkling of its existence and consoled herself daily in her poverty that Rose would wed illustriously.

It was the custom even for little girls to wear veils that covered most of their hair. When mothers dressed their daughters for some feast, they circled their brows with wreaths of flowers set over their veils. It was a charming and delicate tribute to their beauty which enhanced it fragrantly. The Incas, too, had crowned their maidens and even their warriors with blossoms. Peru, and especially Lima, glowed richly with exotic blooms well suited for weaving into wreaths. But not even the wife of the viceroy possessed lovelier flowers than Oliva grew in her garden. A profusion of flawless Castilian roses were hers: the first in Peru. She made the most of them. For every signal occasion she plucked the loveliest for Rose's crown; the less showy flowers went to Bernardina and Mercedes.

We know nothing of the appearance of Rose's two sisters, but we may gather from the effusive compliments received by Rose from all who knew the family that they were less winsome than she. Mercedes was probably too thin to look well, and too pale for the brilliant hues of dress material then in use. Above her fragile face, already wan with the first manifestations of her fatal illness, roses would have seemed overpowering. As for Bernardina, perhaps she had something of Oliva's air of severity and her rather pointed chin. Rose's face was a smooth oval, set off by unusually large and expressive eyes. Her brows were thin and highly arched, her nose straight and sensitive with small nostrils. Her mouth was narrow, the curve of her lips deep and gently sloped. The indentation above her upper lip was well marked. Her expression was thoughtful, gentle and sweet. The corners of her mouth turned up endearingly when her countenance was in repose. But, supremely comely though she was, Rose received most of her compliments on account of her complexion. Her cheeks and lips were still flushed with the same translucent rosiness that had been theirs in her infancy. Her skin was fair, finely textured and softer than suede.

Oliva clothed her older daughters in cut-down dresses of her own, but for Rose's dresses she bought new material. Then as now, one could often buy costly remnants of yard goods cheaply, and as it was the fashion to combine different shades and materials in the same garment, it was easy for her to make Rose magnificent costumes. It was a gratification to Oliva and her mother to frequent the expensive shops on the *Calle de los Mercadores* where merely to meet the wealthy ladies who happened to be there raised one's reputation. Several wealthy ladies of their acquaintance developed a habit which also made it easy for her to dress Rose opulently. Quite captured by the child's loveliness, her humility and simple dignity, they often gave Oliva what was left of the material that they had bought to have dresses made for themselves. Then too, they sometimes gave Rose lengths of fine linen or lace of the rarest quality. It gave them pleasure to see the child wearing clothes that resembled theirs.

Oliva could find no occupation that seemed sweeter than to spend weeks at work on some costume for Rose that would bring her a torrent of praise on the next great feast. But, understandably enough, she looked for a reward. This reward was twofold: the gratitude and show of love that Rose should give her for all her work and special care of her dress, and the delight that the little girl would feel in receiving and wearing what her mother had made for her. But Oliva received only gentle protests. Rose did not want a new dress and veil; her old satin shoes were fine enough. It was shameful for her to be so well dressed when the family was so poor. She ought not to be dressed more finely than her older sisters. She did not enjoy feasts and celebrations where one met so many persons. Please, could she not stay at home this time with Mariana?

But if Rose, who was always so cheerful and obedient, suddenly grew glum just when her mother looked for a sign of enchantment, and if she sought out every argument to escape these fine clothes and entertainments, her actions grew most disappointing when Oliva came to put a crown of roses on her head. She did not like wearing roses; when she did, everyone paid her too many compliments. She would rather wear some other flower so that no one would notice her. The roses were so sweet; would it not be better to give them to the sacristan at Santo Domingo's? Let Jesus have them, or Our Lady of the Rosary. Rose did not want them.

Preparing for a *fiesta* was always an hour of strain for Oliva. She had the responsibility of seeing that all her children were immaculately groomed, and the cruel certainty taunted her that, when the family reached its destination, some of them would look like ragamuffins. She had the exhausting task of keeping them in order and close at hand when the time of departure should come. In addition, she had the testy observations of her mother to cope with. Isabel, who was extremely set in her tastes, seldom approved of her daughter's decisions. Finally, when she came to dress Rose, there were the inevitable arguments and altercations.

Isabel agreed with the child; it was ridiculous to make her wear such a showy crown. The roses were too large; or they were too fragrant. It was not good for Isabel to be breathing such a strong scent. Fundamentally, of course, the grandmother's motives were always the same in this periodic fray; without fail, when Rose entered a room wearing her crown of roses, someone would make a graceful play on words, bringing in her name. Then would come effervescent flattery addressed to Oliva for having chosen to call the little girl Rose. It was most humiliating to Isabel.

How shall we explain Rose's conduct concerning her mother's choice of costumes for her, her aversion to parties and compliments, the repugnance that she showed to wearing a crown of roses? It was not from ingratitude; neither was it because she did not appreciate beauty in things and persons. It was not due to any anti-social quality in her nature. She loved people. If she had not, they would not have been so attached to her. Physical charm alone does not win and hold esteem such as Rose found wherever she went. It was the delicacy of her soul, her refinement and gentle humility that made her the object of such lavish attentions. And it was precisely this same delicacy of soul and this humility that made her shrink from the clothes and gorgeous roses that drew all eyes and hearts towards her.

Rose had been practicing virtue seriously according to her capacity since she first began to learn the truths of faith. Virtue appeared to her the only beauty worth seeking, since it made her more like the Child Jesus. When showered with applause by the great ladies, Rose felt an inward movement of complacency in them. Instantaneously too, the assaults of temptation from devils were added to torment her. Her pure will revolted against these insinuations and against these natural movements of pride that spring unbidden from the deep-rooted egoism that all human beings possess to some degree. She fought and won the victory; yet, to her mind this was not enough. She had to fly from these occasions of temptation.

In short, out of spiritual self-defence Rose had to protest against these pretentious costumes and roses. She had to plead to be excused from attending gatherings where she was certain to meet flatterers. She had to oppose the mother whom she loved and revered, and whose will was law to her in every other matter. It hurt Oliva very much, for she never understood. Good Christian though she was, her thoughts were on a different level from those of her daughter. This divergence grew wider and deeper with the years, causing incredible pain to both. Their love for one another, under these conditions, was their heavy cross.

Rose had chosen St. Catherine of Siena as her spiritual mother. She was old enough now to reflect systematically on her model's life and to begin to imitate her as well as she could. She therefore began to utilize such opportunities as came her way: Holy Mass, confession, prayer, the Blessed Sacrament, and as soon as she could obtain permission, frequent Communion. Then, too, she noted happily that like St. Catherine she had a large family. She could seek out ways of being of service to them. St. Catherine had deprived herself of sleep to go about the house gathering up soiled laundry and washing it. She had worked in the kitchen with her mother's cooks and maids. Here, Rose had the advantage over her model, since her family was so poor. It would be easy for her to find occasions for hard and humiliating work. Mariana already had too much to do and her mother knew it. At times she herself had to don an apron and help with the cooking. Finally, Rose had penance. This was an avenue that she had scarcely yet explored. It was to prove the way that she would take to heaven.

As matter for prayer, Rose had many intentions at this time that resembled those so dear to her patroness' heart, although they were by no means identical with the ones that had absorbed her during life. Every day at dinner, she heard conversations that brought tears to her great, wondering eyes. A ship had docked at Callao with news from Europe: news of the trials of Spain and of the Church. St. Catherine had prayed, done penance, and engaged in diplomatic missions for the welfare of state and Church. The Church and the state had been her two great loves. Rose too would love Spain and Rome, the Church and the fatherland, and her own dear home, Peru. St. Catherine had consoled the Holy Father, warned and guided him. Rose would pray and work and do penance for the Vicar of Christ in his afflictions. St. Catherine had exhorted and reformed many priests and prelates; Rose would spend her days and nights in the service of the Church. She would work and pray all day and then, while her family slept, she would pray and work.

All this was high planning for a little girl of seven, but Rose was undaunted. St. Catherine had not done everything at once; she had gone about it gradually. Rose too would begin in a small way, since she was small. The rest would come when she grew older.

One of the first signs of what Oliva took for selfishness in Rose was her persistent plea for a room by herself. It was a plea that seemed unreasonable in so crowded a household, where no one had a private bedroom. It seemed egotistical, too, for when asked why she needed a room to herself, Rose only replied: "So that I can be alone." This was not an answer that went unreproved, for Oliva soon made it clear that she thought Rose proud.

"Who are you, that your sisters are unworthy to share a room with you?" she asked indignantly. When Rose replied meekly: "I am no one," she continued scornfully: "That is right! You are a no one who must have a private room!"

To this, Rose had only one more argument: St. Catherine had had a room to herself. She did not add that her mother had taken it from her for some time on discovering that her daughter kept vigils and slept on boards. Nor did she add that these very penances were what she coveted and that the reason why she wished to have a private room was to give herself up to them. She had asked her spiritual father for permission to rise during the night to pray and he had said that she could for a short time. However, as long as she slept in her sisters' room she could not use this permission. He had said, too, that she might make her bed uncomfortable if she wished, provided that she was able to sleep. But while she slept with Bernardina and Mercedes this was out of the question, for they noticed everything.

Long before Rose obtained the private bedroom for which she was campaigning, she began to cause Oliva concern by her frugality at table. The child had excellent health, except for the occasional fever; and in Lima this was common. She radiated good health and Oliva was resolved to keep her so. But this was easier said than done. Rose began by refusing desserts, especially those of which she had once been fondest. She continued by taking smaller servings of vegetables and fruit. Finally, to her parents' discontent, she turned to refusing meat, of which she had always taken a good portion. When coaxed, she would accept some, setting most of it aside and toying with the rest until the next course was served. Then she would eat a mouthful or two hastily.

Oliva and Gaspar worried over this apparent loss of appetite; their parental hearts were already grieved by Mercedes' consistent decline. Now, the health of Rose, their favorite, seemed threatened. Isabel shared their anxiety. Something had to be done to encourage Rose to eat. Oliva taught Mariana to prepare more delicate dishes; whenever Gaspar could afford it, they invited guests to dinner. Then, quite unaware of their ruse, Rose ate what was placed before her.

In other ways, Rose's developing character and talents pleased her parents exceedingly. In an age when blind, instant, unquestioning obedience was demanded by parents, Rose's parents could find no fault with her obedience. Only Oliva complained wryly that Rose was too obedient. She had to take great care in phrasing her commands, for the child would carry them out whatever the cost. Even when, for some reason, one of them proved impracticable, she obeyed without objection.

Rose knew what kind of obedience her mother wished; and she gave it. She was happy when Oliva made these wry complaints, for she knew that her mother was actually proud of her obedience. That Rose had not understood ill the sort of obedience which her mother required is shown by more than one of Oliva's training tactics. Undoubtedly she tried to teach all her children the Christian virtues; but seeing that Rose took an unusual interest in virtue, she used her ingenuity in testing hers. For example, she made Rose ask for permission to drink water between meals. As for eating between meals, there was no question of that, except in case of illness, in a household where food was so precious.

Intent on self-denial, Rose would often wait two or three days before asking Oliva for a drink of water that she felt she needed. Oliva, not realizing that the child was already waiting a long time before seeking permission, wished to teach her that virtue. Accordingly, she often refused to let Rose take the drink she asked for. The child never explained or complained; it was only many years later that Oliva learned how she had deprived her unwittingly of the water so necessary to the system in hot weather.

Oliva also undertook to test Rose's obedience in another area: this was needlework. For at least the past three years, the little girl had been showing talent in drawing. She was often found sketching a flower or a scene; sometimes she tried to copy abstract patterns from her mother's book of embroidery designs. Oliva hoped that this talent would develop into a skill that would add much to the family resources. If Rose learned to embroider as well as draw, she could perhaps earn some money by working to order. Oliva and Isabel had long ago begun to do this and it was lucrative for them because of their outstanding talent. But before beginning to teach Rose, Oliva wished to give her a sound lesson in humility and obedience.

One day she summoned the child from her nook in the garden and told her that she would teach her how to embroider. Rose was enchanted; she had been watching her elders as they worked for a long time and thought that she already knew how. She remarked as much to her mother; and, with compressed lips, Oliva resolved to show her that too much confidence in a beginner was not a virtue. Without the slightest trace of amusement or any sign that she was testing her daughter, she proceeded to show how a flower should be worked; but she stitched it inside out! Rose knew what was amiss but said nothing; she followed her mother's example and in due time produced what would have looked like a flower, had the embroidery been turned over.

Rose took her finished masterpiece to Oliva, but her mother was busy, teaching Bernardina and Mercedes how to trace an embroidery design on a length of plain material. Seeing that her mother could not just then pronounce her verdict on the sorry effort at needlework, the child skipped to the *patio* and embroidered another flower like the first. Then, she sought out Oliva. The latter took Rose's work with more than usual interest, then cast it on the table and threw up both hands in feigned horror.

"But these are not flowers!" she cried.

Rose's ready laugh rippled out.

"I could see that they were wrong, but that is how you showed me to do it, Mama, and that is how I have done it!"

The year 1593 brought no special events to the Flores household, unless it was that the old bickering was renewed oftener. The first months after Francisco's baptism had been cordial, but now the glow had died. Isabel's hurt feelings reasserted themselves. Oliva was exasperated at her mother's refusal to admit that she was an adult able to make her own decisions. As always, Rose found herself caught in this vicious circle. To provoke a quarrel, all that she had to do was answer when called.

Mariana, too, felt the effects of Isabel's rancor. The Indian girl had begun to call Rose "her little Rose" even before the miracle in the *patio*. Isabel, without realizing it, transferred some of her resentment to Mariana and treated her coldly, sometimes even harshly. Rose felt this keenly, for she was devoted to the Indian maid who had always shown such a warm love for her. In an effort to soften her grandmother's bitterness, she often spoke to her enthusiastically of Mariana's great love of God. It was her way of imitating St. Catherine, who had striven so to bring peace to her world. She tried at the same time to bring her mother and grandmother closer together, speaking all the good that she could to each of the other in her absence. All the while, she suffered and prayed; for she felt in some way to blame for the rift between these two women who were both so dear to her.

One day late in June 1593, Gaspar came home in the evening in a furious temper. Oliva tried to calm him, but with no success. When asked the reason for his mood, he could only say: "Pray for Archbishop Toribio. The viceroy is going to give him a shocking humiliation." Like the rest of the family, Rose was filled with apprehension at these words and the anger of her father. When the meal was finished she went to Gaspar who had been left alone in the *patio* at his own request. When Rose went up to him he stamped his foot at her.

"Who sent you here to annoy me? Leave me alone, I am not fit to speak to anyone!"

Rose put her hand gently on his shoulder.

"Father dear, I have come to ask if you would not like your *capa*. It is cool and you have just been out of bed for a few days."

Gaspar had been confined to his room with an annoying ague. At Rose's words, he managed a short laugh.

"Yes; bring me my *capa*. You are more sensible than I. You would make a good nurse, Rose. You must learn to take care of the sick. That is what young Martin is going to do, and I admire him for it. I was so angry when I left the palace that I forgot to tell you that I met him today in the plaza. He has come back with his father from Guayaquil; they left little Juana with an uncle who lives there. Martin says that he will be apprenticed to a barber-surgeon. Of course, you cannot be a barber-surgeon," he added with an affectionate smile at his daughter, "but you can learn to treat illnesses. In a household as large as ours, it will always be useful. And later, when you wed. . . ."

He broke off as he saw the shadow flit across Rose's face.

"Do not worry, little one, we shall not wed you to an Indian. Would to God that I could give you a decent dowry!"

Rose hesitated, half ready to tell him of her vow. Then she remembered her director's words. He had warned her to keep her vow and resolution secret; and she must obey. Answering her father only by a smile, she ran to bring him his cloak. When she returned with it, he had rejoined the family and was speaking to them of Martin, in whom they were all interested.

"I have been telling Rose that she should learn to care for the sick," he added as the child entered the room. "You see how quick she is to think of what others need."

"It is true; she is not so bad sometimes," said Oliva good humoredly. "I have been thinking of teaching her a few things myself and of having Mariana show her how to make medicines. It is easy; one just measures out the dried herbs and boils them. They would be useful when someone is ill; one cannot always afford to buy them."

"I should love to learn!" cried Rose in delight. "Perhaps too, we could give some to the poor."

"Excellent, if you can make more than we need!" beamed Oliva. Rose was thinking already like a great lady. Most of the wealthy families in Lima gave bread daily to the poor, but the Flores could not afford to do so. This had often been a source of humiliation to Oliva. If Rose and Mariana could make decoctions from herbs that they had grown in the garden, this was one charity that they could afford.

Doña Isabel frowned. She disliked the project as a whole because it involved Rose spending more time than ever with Mariana; she seemed to be passing half her days in the kitchen of late. Quite apart from this, the fastidious lady imagined a daily lineup of unwashed, infected people in their *patio*. Let Rose give the extra medicine to the friars at the Convent of the Holy Rosary. They distributed food and medicines to the poor each morning.

Oliva saw her mother's lips about to open in protest; to avert a fresh quarrel she turned swiftly to her husband. Gaspar caught his mother-in-law's frown and his wife's meaningful glance, and nodded decisively.

"Yes, you are right, my dear."

Then, turning to Rose, he added: "Rose, you must plant your own herb garden next spring and tend it yourself. At the end of the season we shall see whether you have any herbs to spare; if you have, you may certainly give them to the poor. God knows," he continued, taking Isabel into the orbit of his gaze, "we all know how little we can spare for charity. Let us do what we can, for it is our duty."

Doña Isabel, seeing herself vanquished, for once gave in gracefully. Perhaps it would do Rose good to work outside in the garden. She stayed indoors too much. And, of course, Gaspar was right: it was fitting that those of noble blood should set the example of kindness to the lowly.

Like a number of people in Lima and in the Indian reductions on the outskirts of the city, Rose slept fitfully that night. She prayed much for Archbishop Toribio as her father had bidden his family do. When she did fall asleep, she had a recurring nightmare in which the viceroy, dressed in full armor, ran his sword repeatedly through a prostrate Toribio. When García ran him through, blood covered the glory of the archbishop's vestments and Rose wept. Suddenly Martin de Porres appeared on the scene, grown very tall. "I shall have to operate," he said in a sonorous voice. But before he did, Rose passed him a container of medicine that she had made, and he poured some into Toribio's wounds.

When Rose woke up from this nightmare, she heard her father letting himself out of the house. She sat up in bed and leaned over so that she could pull back the window curtains and look outside. As she peered through the barred window she saw that it was dawn. In a few minutes her father passed, leading his horse quietly to the front gate. In the semi-darkness she could see his dark silhouette, topped by his great cocked hat. She was surprised to see that he had brought his horse home; still, he usually did when he had to be at the palace very early, before it was safe to walk the streets alone. But even riding his horse, he might meet with ruffians who would waylay him, so Rose prayed for his safety. Don Gaspar needed prayers just then, for he had a painful day ahead of him.

While Rose wept over his wounds in her sleep, the archbishop knelt motionless on his *prie-dieu* in the deserted silence of his private chapel in the episcopal palace. Around him the shadows flickered eerily with the flame in the lamp of wrought gold that burned before the Blessed Sacrament. He had been kneeling there since the departure of his sister and brother-in-law some few minutes before midnight. They had come to warn him of what he already knew: on the morrow he must appear in disgrace before the viceroy and the whole tribunal of the *audiencia*. The viceroy had received a royal decree wholly concerned with his humble person. What was in that decree? Don Toribio did not know; and that was the cause of his present anguish.

He had weighed well the possible consequences of the act that had brought his life to this present crisis. As it seemed to him, he stood a strong chance of being recalled to Spain and retired from the episcopate. But which was the greater evil, to bring this humiliation on himself or go on bearing the torments of conscience that a continued silence caused him? At first he had thought that if the abuses had been accepted by tacit permission of the pope, he might close his eyes to them. But gradually the fear had begun to grip him that they might not come to the attention of the Holy Father. Finally, knowing well that his work in the New World meant more to him than life, so long as it meant the fulfillment of God's will, he had risked its termination in order to write to the pope.

But now that he had the certainty of knowing that the whole matter lay before the Supreme Pontiff's gaze, his first sense of relief had vanished. In its place a sense of misery had swept over him, permeating his soul with bitter affliction. This see had been a spouse of blood to him from the first moment in which the king had singled him out for it, but it had also brought him the greatest joys of his life. His labors with the semi-pagan Indians, his care of the African slaves and the noble, decimated race of the Incas had been supremely precious to him. Then there was the administration on the Spanish parishes and the establishment of the seminary which was vital to the future of the colony. His relations with his bishops, though sometimes stormy, had borne good fruit for the Church in the New World. His struggles to reform the *doctrineros* and parish priests of his vast archdiocese were still incomplete, however. Would his successor spend himself as fearlessly as he felt was necessary?

These anxieties, painful as they were, were not unmingled with personal feelings of shame. He had brought his sister and brother-in-law with him to Peru; to their growing family, as well as to themselves after all these years, Peru was the homeland. Don Francisco was a man of honor and ability; he had done great service to the colony as Admiral of the South Sea and *Corregidor Mayor* of Lima. As he was not only his brother-in-law but also his first cousin and their intimacy was well known, would not Francisco also be disgraced?

Moreover, what of his own debt of gratitude to the king? Philip II had chosen him as Archbishop of Lima while he was still a simple layman. Before the unreserved confidence which the king had placed in him, no obstacle had seemed of import. But now, instead of appealing to the king and exposing the doubts and scruples of conscience that tormented him, he had gone over his head to the pope. It was true that the very abuses which concerned him were in no way, probably, unknown to King Philip II. For example, there was the custom of new bishops taking possession of their sees directly on being nominated by the king, instead of waiting for the pope's approval. Perhaps if he had explained his views of the abuses to the Catholic King, he might have put a stop to them. As it was, the king was possibly in the pope's disfavor on his account.

The sorrow of Archbishop Toribio as he thought of this can scarcely be understood. He had a saint's love of country and he had only one greater love than this; that was his love of the Church. Now, Toribio turned anguished eyes towards the tabernacle where Christ silently shared his hour of extremity. Could he, as his Lord had done in Gethsemane, say: "Father, if it be possible let this chalice pass from me; yet nevertheless, not my will but thine be done"?

The saint raised his head. Over the altar hung the crucifix; was he not, in his priesthood, another Christ? Was he not, in his episcopate, filled with the spirit of the priesthood? Still kneeling on his *prie-dieu* he stretched out his arms in the form of a cross. His large, sorrowful eyes sought those of the Savior on the crucifix; suddenly, they flashed with joy. His lean, brown face wrinkled in a smile.

As Rose lay awake in her child's bed murmuring: "Jesus be blessed; Jesus be with him!" Toribio also spoke. In his voice was a ring of triumph.

"Father, into thy hands I commend my spirit."

Those who were to write of him later would say that he bore this trial with all his usual invincible calm.

At the appointed hour, Archbishop Toribio took his place in the assembly room and listened patiently to the viceroy while he read in tones of unmistakable relish the king's message. "Let him hear," the latter had written, "what an unworthy thing it has been for one of his state and profession to write such things to Rome! Tell him in the same manner (publicly) that it would indeed be just to command that he be called to my court so that this business might be treated of more pointedly and (so that I might) make of the case a great demonstration which his excess deserves. I omit it because of what his Church and flock might feel during such a long absence." Around the viceroy sat the great men of Lima, many of whom stared coldly at Toribio. About the room stood the noble guards, Rose's father among them.

Like Christ, the holy archbishop spoke no word in his own defense. When pressed for a comment, his only remark was: "Our king is offended; so for the love of God let us satisfy him. Let us satisfy him." The repetition of this last phrase is our sole clue to the vehemence of the saint's emotions and resolution. It opens before us the vision of what lay behind his controlled and restrained exterior.

Toribio felt the full bite of the king's rebuke and the pointed publicity with which it was delivered. But he was grateful, too, that in spite of his anger Philip II had not recalled him or removed him from his see. And for this we must give the king credit. He had his faults; he was an absolute monarch in the full sense of the word, and he had an imperious temper. Archbishop Toribio had placed him in a most awkward position in regard to the Holy See. However, despite this and the many criticisms that he had been receiving from Peru that might have led him to conclude that he had erred in raising Toribio to the episcopal dignity, he never seems to have considered withdrawing him from that see. At most, what he mentioned was a trip to Spain to explain his conduct.

How can we account adequately for the king's leniency, compared with the rigor that he might have shown? He had undoubtedly already learned that the prelate's letter would evoke no action from Rome. This fact certainly must have softened his anger. The year 1591 had seen the death of Pope Gregory XIV and the election of Pope Innocent IX. During the conclave preceding the one held at Pope Gregory XIV's death, Philip II had exerted undue pressure on the cardinals. He had openly designated some names as acceptable to him and had excluded others. Now he had grown less impetuous and sent instructions to his representatives at the next conclave to the effect that this procedure should not be renewed. When Pope Innocent IX died, he restricted his efforts to a profuse outpouring of pensions upon the cardinals. This tragic death had taken place on December 30, 1591, leaving the Holy See vacant for the fourth time in a little more than a year.

At the conclave of January 10, 1592, great strife arose among the cardinals, so much so that many feared a schism. The Spanish cardinals had supported Cardinal Santori. Such confusion filled the hall of the conclave that the votes could not be counted. It was thought that Cardinal Santori had been elected, but when comparative calm was restored to the assembly and another vote was taken, he had only thirty out of fifty-seven ballots. The Spanish cardinals now began to support the cardinal whom they had placed last on their unpublished list of acceptable candidates, but with some reserve. To put it plainly, they did not like him. When informed officially that King Philip II had named this cardinal as his "last resort" candidate, they were forced to support him openly. At noon on January 30, more to their amazement than delight, he was elected unanimously as pope. He took the name of Clement VIII.

The new pope was quite aware that he had been a postscript on King Philip II's *papabili* list, so it was natural that the king should wish to obtain his good graces by a show of docility. He was counting on his mediation to conclude an agreement with France which would free him from the fear that she would help England against him in the forthcoming war. At the time when the pope received Archbishop Toribio's letter, he had not yet sent his ambassador to Madrid. It would not look well for the king to remove Toribio from his see for having written to the pope, nor would such an act endear him to the Holy Father.

However, King Philip had many abuses to account for, greater than those denounced by Toribio, and he knew it, although he did not acknowledge them as abuses. If the pope were to begin correcting all of them he would be inconvenienced and humiliated. The most effective means of preventing such an all-embracing action on the part of the pope was to send humble explanations to Rome in answer to Toribio's charges.

Pope Clement VIII was a holy, dedicated pope. His faults were few, but one of them was irresolution. On receiving Toribio's letter he acted in character by simply asking for the Spanish ambassador's version of the cases in question. Neither he nor the cardinals who advised him wished to make an issue of them, for papal relations with Spain had been recurrently painful during each pontificate in King Philip II's lifetime. Besides, he had much graver issues to settle with Spain at the moment. Shortly after the new Papal Ambassador arrived in Madrid in February 1593, a law was published by the king which was in marked violation of the jurisdiction and freedom of the Church. All the energies of the nuncio were concentrated on obtaining a modification of this law. Archbishop Toribio's letter was consigned to the archives, as of much less import. The pope accepted King Philip II's explanation.

Such were the motives on both sides that led to the leniency of Toribio's punishment. If we look farther than the proximate causes of this leniency, we see in it the providential work of God. Toribio had long years of labor in the Indies still before him. His influence for good on all the Spanish colonies of the New World was incalculable. If we consider

St. Rose's life alone, we shall see that this influence was of far-reaching significance.

Rose had other motives for gratitude now besides the fact that Archbishop Toribio had not been called back to Spain. The viceroy seemed to be intent on doing as much as he could for the Indians. The year before, he had just founded a college for the *caciques*, that is, sons of Indian chiefs, of whom there were many. The soutane of the students and professors was of dark blue, the *beca* worn over it of light blue bearing a royal crown. Rose's delight at this foundation cannot be described. It reached its peak when her mother learned that the ceremony of the opening was to take place in the adjacent Dominican church. It was to be a brilliant assembly: the viceroy and his suite, his private guard, including Gaspar in his most resplendent uniform, the *audiencia* and doctors of the University. Oliva and Isabel could not miss it, nor did they have the heart of stone that would have been needed to force Rose to stay at home. It was a day that she never forgot.

At about this time Rose made her First Communion. She was much younger than the age customary then, but her precocity and ardor forestalled all opposition. Her confessor soon granted permission for Communion during the week. Soon she was receiving four times a week and asking for daily Communion. Oliva took her to church at Santo Domingo's, less than two minutes' walk from their home. It says much for her own fervor that she was willing to do so.

In the spring, Rose began her cherished project of the herb garden under Mariana's supervision. She tended it diligently and it yielded beyond their hopes. She learned to make mixtures from the dried leaves and members of her family drank of them with beneficial effects. At the end of the year she had enough of the dried leaves left to undertake their distribution to any poor persons who presented themselves at the Flores' door. Soon, every morning a small queue formed in the *patio* and was greeted lovingly by Rose, who doled out portions of the medicines on request. Oliva stood by at times and measured out the doses for the child; and when she was otherwise occupied, Isabel did her this service. Later, as Rose grew older she was to be permitted to do it alone. It was one of the joys of her life. The following spring she was allowed more space for her herbs and added a few flowers to them. She tended each plant as though it had been an infant. In time she became an expert gardener.

Now, when her frequent Communions and direct contact with the suffering members of Christ's Mystical Body sent her charity soaring, she began to practice mortification. In her childish enthusiasm she enlisted Mariana as her ally. The Indian maid was to insult her, kick her, spit on her when others were not there to witness it. Mariana fought this harsh assignment with all the strength of her attachment to Rose. When she saw that it would really bring the child pleasure to be mistreated by her, however, she relented. Still, we may be sure that her cooperation was less wholehearted than Rose could have wished. Rose was still, and would always be, "her little Rose."

Since she knew that Mariana loved her with the same devotedness as of old, Rose found the maid's insults and rough treatment less of a mortification than she had hoped. She reread daily her life of St. Catherine and pondered on the gross insults heaped on the Son of God. She was determined to show her love by the only true proof of love: imitation. Consequently, she renewed her pleas for a private bedroom. Without this, she could not practice any of the penances that she coveted. Oliva and Gaspar continued to treat these pleas as the whim of a selfish child until something occurred which led them to think of them more kindly. Rose had been continuing to cause an unpleasant scene every time Oliva dressed her for some feast or party. Above all, she had argued and wriggled uncooperatively when Oliva put on her crown of roses. Suddenly, she ceased to argue and lowered her head to receive it with all docility. The abrupt change did much to soften Oliva's mood, even though Rose still asked to be left at home whenever the plans for any outing were discussed.

If Oliva had known the reason for Rose's change of attitude towards the crowns which she had formerly resisted, she would have been horrified. The secret was this: the child had learned how to turn these crowns into instruments of penance. How did this come about? Probably someone stuck a pin through her scalp by accident one day as the crown was being fastened on, and Rose had an inspiration. Next time, she herself arranged a pin in her veil in such a way that it dug into her scalp with each movement of her head. Hence, while the beauty of her person was being extolled by the kind ladies, Rose felt the sharp pain that this pin caused her. She had suffered much more acutely at three years of age from the injury to her thumbnail and four from an infected ear, so that the pain of the pin, pressed by the weight of the crown, seemed slight in comparison.

If Oliva had known of Rose's stratagem, she would have punished the child and forbidden her to repeat it. That would have put an end to the act of penance, for Rose would not disobey her mother. But she managed to use the pin without being noticed, so she continued her act of self-affliction.

One may well ask how it was that Rose's director gave her permission for such an act. The answer is probably he knew nothing about it. If Rose had asked the priest for permission to run a pin through her scalp, his answer would have been a shocked "No!" However, she *was* a child. Although she had been receiving spiritual direction for about four years, this direction had been concerned with prayer and the ordinary practice of the virtues in keeping with childhood. There had been little focus on penance.

It is true, nevertheless, that her director may have allowed her to ask for Mariana's help in humiliating herself. Such a permission would have been quite in line with the spirituality of the age, which leaned heavily on humiliation, especially if the penitent was of noble family. The fact that Rose desired humiliations would have been a valuable indication to the priest as to the degree of humility that she already possessed. But the insertion of pins in the child's scalp was quite another question, and had Rose asked him for permission to turn her crown of roses into a crown of thorns he would have refused emphatically. But most likely Rose did not ask him; her inexperience made her think that it was an ordinary penance. She had read of the severe penances practiced by St. Catherine but no mention was made in her book of the permissions first sought and obtained for them. Under the illusion that Rose had become more interested in personal adornment, Oliva began to think of asking Gaspar to have a room built for her. When she did, she learned that Gaspar, too, wished to do so. He had often been struck by a quality in Rose which none of his other children possessed to the same degree. This was the full realization of her dignity, combined with a humble and eager desire to be of service to others. He thought now that it would be well to encourage this sense of dignity in her. Oliva agreed.

As soon as he could afford the small outlay involved, Gaspar had Mariana make the bricks. It was an easy matter; one mixed mud and straw in a given proportion and placed the mixture in a mold to dry. The Flores boys added their willing help and Rose was not outdone by them. In no time the bricks were ready.

Now came the work of digging the excavation, and for this

Gaspar hired Indian laborers. Rose's room was built detached from the other rooms, and probably it had only one door, so her privacy was assured.

The inside of the room was finished as plainly as possible and furnished with a minimum of expense. One item which Rose must have asked for was a bed with curtains, as was the style. When drawn, these curtains gave complete privacy to the occupant of the room. They were essential to Rose's program of asceticism. She had been given permission by her confessor to make her bed uncomfortable, provided that she could still sleep. Her ingenuity soon found a way. With Mariana's help she placed several logs in the mattress. A shorter one she inserted in her pillow.

At this time, to her measureless gratitude, Rose's parents allowed her to fast several times a week. She was communicating that often and it was the custom of the age to perform some outstanding act of penance on the day before receiving. However, Rose still found great difficulties placed in the way of her desired abstinence from meat. As her health seemed not to suffer, her parents reluctantly permitted her to abstain when the family was dining alone, but they insisted, like her director, that she take her portion whenever there were guests.

At about this time, Rose ceased to go to the Jesuits for confession, although she continued under the same spiritual father. The reason for this is not obscure; it was usual to confess before receiving Communion, but it would have been inconvenient for Oliva to go three or four times a week to the relatively distant church of the Jesuits. The church of the Dominicans, therefore, provided a natural solution; and although Rose's devotedness to the Jesuit Fathers in no way diminished, her attachment to the Dominican friars increased rapidly.

The first contacts with the priests who were St. Catherine's spiritual brothers strengthened Rose's attraction for the church of St. Dominic. Before long she asked for permission to give some of the flowers from her garden to the sacristan. Her conversations with him enabled her to learn something of sacristy work, and it now became her dream to tend the altar in the chapel of Our Lady of the Rosary, a dream which still had to wait some years for fulfillment.

CHAPTER SIX

Rose Transplanted

ARCHBISHOP TORIBIO was no man to grieve over a reverse. Soon after his return to his palace after García's reprimand he was light-heartedly setting his affairs in order. He had a fresh project in view: his second pastoral visitation. This was the work that he loved most, for it brought him into contact with the poor, the humble and despised.

This was his precious opportunity to draw near to the hearts of the children when he administered the sacrament of confirmation. He could speak to them of God, of the prodigality of Christ's love for little ones, and above all of his desire that they unite their souls to his in Holy Communion. This was his opportunity, too, to reach his beloved Indians, to listen to their sorrows and to correct as many of the injustices as he could.

Where would he go first on this visitation? If he were to begin packing that evening or tomorrow at the latest, he could leave the next day after Holy Mass. First, he would visit la Magdalena and Surquillo, then come back to Lima. When he had attended to what work awaited him here, he would go to Lurigancho; then Callao, Santo Domingo de Mama and Choclo, with more pauses in Lima between visitations; finally, the provinces, beginning with Chancay and ending with Amazonas. Then would follow the visit to Canta, beginning in the town of Quive. Quive! A shadow passed over the archbishop's countenance. Here was an angry and turbulent populace with a grievance. It consisted mostly of Indians who had lost the lottery of the *mita* and been herded to the silver mines. He would find little piety among them, for they were estranged from their *doctrinero*. He had received many complaints of late from this area, some of them from the priest himself, a Mercedarian named Francisco González. As mediator he would have much to do and suffer in the province of Canta, especially in the town of Quive.

Despite his optimism, Archbishop Toribio had at that moment many men ranged against him, wielding a power which thwarted God's work. He had, for example, been forced to open the Council of 1951 without solemnity on account of the viceroy's absence. García had ignored the day like a pouting child. Knowing that the deliberations of the Council would be scrutinized by hostile eyes, the archbishop had restricted the questions to be discussed to purely disciplinary and canonical matters. Nevertheless, despite this and his added precaution of sending a prelate to the king as his spokesman, he had failed. Toribio could not now implement the decrees of his Council without incurring serious inconveniences.

Here in Lima, the tenacity of the religious orders in refusing to give up *doctrinas* administered by their subjects, even though they were incompetent, wrought many evils to the souls of Indians throughout Peru. Archbishop Toribio's efforts to place competent diocesan priests in the *doctrinas* were of little avail. The Franciscans alone were willing to give up the *doctrinas*, thus delivering their friars from the solitary and spiritually perilous life of a *doctrinero*. Toribio approached these and other frustrations of his just desires in a lively spirit of faith, acknowledging that God permitted them for his own ends. Although it pained him exceedingly to see the harm done to souls, he could only go on doing his utmost to overcome them, trusting divine providence to bring good out of evil.

In the following year, during one of his brief intervals spent in Lima, the archbishop was able to establish two foundations which were to prove of invaluable help to his priests. The first was the Confraternity of St. Peter, established at the cathedral for the aid of needy priests; the second was the Hospital of St. Peter for the care of sick priests who were without means. Some months earlier, after many delays, a home for abandoned children had also been opened. Pitifully small and inadequate though it was, at least it was a beginning and gave promise of future expansion. Curiously, this expansion, when it came some years later, was to be the fruit of a poor man's charity: in fact, the charity of St. Martin de Porres. Archbishop Toribio had confirmed him not long before, in the church of St. Sebastian.

At this time, Rose began to take an interest in music and poetry. Her parents were delighted, for spontaneous banter in the form of verse was the most prized type of drawing room wit. They obtained copies of some contemporary Peruvian poems to feed her talent. They also had her learn the guitar, and often she sang these poems to her own accompaniment. As new popular ballads came into vogue they taught her these, too; soon she showed real skill in rendering them.

Many of these ballads were soldiers' laments; others were melancholy love songs. As Oliva listened to Rose singing them, she smiled complacently. This new occupation would soon awaken in her daughter an interest in marriage. The mother noted how often, of late, Rose sang these love songs when she was alone in her leaf hut. That was a good sign, thought Oliva. Of course, prayer had its place in every life, but Rose tended to exaggerate. These songs were more in keeping with her age.

Had Oliva guessed Rose's thoughts as she sang these love songs, her pleasure would have turned to chagrin. When she sang them, Rose thought of Christ, to whom she was espoused by her vow of virginity.

> Alas, my only true love has vanished;
> From his favor I am banished.
> Gone that smile which flashed so bright,
> Gone my heart's once radiant light.
> How could he leave me?
> Did his promise deceive me?
> Ah, no! He will return.
> Soon, soon my heart will burn!
> Come thou, my pleasure,
> And I shall love thee without measure!

Was Rose already experiencing aridity in prayer? It appears that she was. How else can we explain the appeal that such songs of abandonment had for her? Still, these times of spiritual dryness could not have lasted long, though they left Rose stunned and bewildered. She had surely done something to displease God, but what? How could she correct her fault if she could not find it? She began to torment herself, going over and over her least hesitations in responding to grace. Then she remembered what she had read of Christ's agony in the garden. Being in an agony, he had prayed the longer. She asked her mother for permission to pray more during the day; when this permission was refused her on the grounds that she was needed to help with the household duties, she asked to be allowed to pray in the garden in the evenings. After some hesitation, Oliva consented.

"Very well; I do not see any harm in it, if you are not nervous. I could never stay out alone in the dark!"

Rose's interest in poetry was intensified by the fact that one of Peru's greatest poets was a member of the community of friars nearby, attached to the Church of St. Dominic. This was Diego de Ojeda (sometimes spelled Hojeda), who had taken his vows in 1591. He had come to Peru while still very young, without his parents' consent, and earned his living as a peddler until his entrance into the Order. His poem, *La Cristiada*, would prove to be one of the finest religious epics produced by colonial Peru. To St. Rose, the poems of this gifted friar were an inspiration and a challenge. She too began to write poetry; some of it was childish and immature but gradually she learned the rules of versification and produced poems of real literary worth. This was a hobby that she was to develop until the close of her life.

Often now, as she knelt in the garden, she sang songs of her own composition to the Christ Child, to Mary and the saints. When the presence of God made itself sweet to her consciousness, she knelt long in wordless gratitude; then she sang songs of thankful love to him, accompanying herself on the guitar.

Both Oliva and Gaspar were delighted and charmed by this newly unfolding talent of Rose's. Often they spoke of it and marvelled at the whimsical beauty of the thoughts that the child expressed. This was one more augury of the brilliant future that they foresaw, not only for Rose but for her whole family, which would share her fortune. After all, Rose might yet marry before Bernardina; as for Mercedes, neither of the parents dared mention her. By this time both knew, although they would not say it, that she would not live to reach maturity.

The viceroy had been ill of late, a fact which in no way sweetened his temper, and it was probably no surprise to Gaspar when he learned that García had asked to be relieved of his post. It was a request which he did not have to repeat. By this time, King Philip II was eager to find some pretext for recalling him, for his autocratic and intolerant ways had won him enemies. They denounced him tirelessly to the Council of the Indies, and to the king himself. To the general relief, the king named as García's successor not the man designated by him but Louis Velasco, at the moment acting as Governor of Mexico.

Velasco was named viceroy of Peru on June 6, 1595. He entered Lima on June 23 and was received magnificently. As his private chaplain he brought with him a Franciscan friar, Father Juan de la Concepción. Like other Peruvians who had the opportunity to study the new viceroy at close quarters, Gaspar was swift to decide that in choosing him, the king had given Peru of his best. Although he had been viceroy in Mexico where the field was still wide for official graft, Velasco was a poor man. He was upright and of sensitive conscience, yet of the practical turn of mind essential in an able administrator. He was an experienced and loyal servant of the crown; the king could depend on him to implement his desires without fear or favor.

The Chilean war was one of the first problems to claim Velasco's attention. On April 25, 1597, he was able to send a contingent of reinforcements. The raising of this contingent had occupied the preceding months. Again in October of the same year he sent further reinforcements. Rose was old enough to appreciate fully the dangers into which these men were going, and to share the anxiety of her parents and all the people of Peru. However, by this time her family had moved away from the excited capital, so that they were more distracted from the crisis than they would otherwise have been. The miners of the province of Canta had been growing more unruly than ever and Velasco thought of sending a member of his private guard to supervise the mines near Quive. His eyes fell on Gaspar, a poor man like himself and one deserving of some special notice. He was offered the post and accepted.

Although life in Quive offered few social opportunities and

the climate was colder than that in Lima, Oliva and Isabel were both happy to leave the capital for the time being. The war with England was imminent; attacks on Callao and Lima were expected. The assignment in Quive, some twenty miles inland from the city, took the family into a district that was comparatively safe from the enemy.

It was towards the close of the year that the Flores family found itself transplanted to the mining town, a populous and thriving settlement in which they were the leading citizens. There were a few other Spanish families living there, so that some mutual interchange of hospitality could be enjoyed. As administrator of the silver mines, appointed by the new viceroy, Gaspar enjoyed great prestige. Oliva and her children shared it, as did Isabel.

The trip from Lima to Quive (sometimes spelled Quivi), was probably made by donkey cart, in several stages. As Oliva would never have left the closing of the house in Lima to Isabel, she undoubtedly sent her mother ahead with the older children. Finally, on the last of their moving days, she herself left Lima with Gaspar, Mariana and little Francisco, who had by this time been joined by a baby sister, Juana. Did Rose go with her mother and father on this last journey, or earlier with her grandmother? Knowing the rivalry which existed between Oliva and her mother over the affection of Rose, we can have no doubt on the subject. Rose went with her mother.

Their trip was made unpleasant by the fact that Rose was plunged in disgrace. Oliva had discovered Rose's penitential bed and her recriminations filled the house. She scarcely spoke to Rose during the trip to Quive, except to make some remark barbed with angry sarcasm. Her reaction is easily understood; she was afraid that Rose might injure her health by doing penance of such a kind, and she was hurt and grieved because Rose had done it without her consent. When the girl

assured her that her director had said that she might make
her bed uncomfortable, Oliva countered the defense sharply.

"He did not say that you could ruin your health!"

At this, Rose said nothing. At any rate, she was not to have
a private bedroom at Quive; the house was too small to make
this possible. So she would have been forced to relinquish
her penance in any case.

It is certain that the departure of the Flores family from
Lima was a heavy cross to Rose. She no longer had the spiritual counsel of her director each week; she could not visit her
beloved chapel of Our Lady of the Rosary. Her Dominican
confessor was no longer available to her; she had no herb garden from which to harvest medicine for her family and her
beloved poor. She was forced to leave the leaf-hermitage
where she had passed so many tender hours in prayer. Finally,
in Quive she was not to pray after supper in the garden as she
had in Lima. The Indians of the *mita* there were too restive;
it would not be well for her to go out alone after dark, even
in their own garden.

The house where Rose's family took up residence in Quive
is still to be seen; but because of the distance of the town
from Lima, it is visited by fewer pilgrims than one could
wish. The building as it stands is not in the same condition as
it was in St. Rose's day; undoubtedly it had several *adobe*
rooms at the back, which have vanished with the passage of
time. When identified as the Flores house, it was in ruins, although it was one of stone, for the town had long been almost
abandoned. If the stone structure had fallen into a ruined
state, how much more the rooms of unkilned *adobes!* We
cannot, therefore, ascertain the precise number of rooms that
it contained when Gaspar and his household occupied it.
However, we know for certain that while it sufficed in size for
the members of the family and Mariana, who now had to live

in, it was too small for house guests to be entertained there with suitable dignity.

Around the corner almost opposite the house, stood the village church. Like the Flores home, it was of stone. To Rose, it's nearness to her home in Quive was one of the few consolations that she enjoyed in her years there. Her family was invited to the homes of the mine officials and also went on a few sight-seeing tours of the surrounding district. Sometimes they visited the mines, which were of interest to the boys especially. But Rose never joined them either in these tours or visits; during the whole period when the town remained their place of exile, she never left home except to go to the church. Oliva continued to take her there daily for a visit to the Blessed Sacrament.

Although every effort was made to encourage Rose to go out with her family, she pleaded so well for the privilege of staying at home that Oliva and Gaspar relented. There came a time when Mercedes too began to ask for the same privilege; social gatherings tired her. Rose enjoyed her companionship and together they had many intimate talks. Like Rose, Mercedes thought often of God and of heaven; she must have known that she would soon be leaving this life. When she grew too weak to leave her room, Rose often came to read to her or sit beside her with her embroidery. When she was occupied elsewhere in household work, she made it her custom to pause frequently at her sister's side to ask if there were anything that she needed. At last, to the distress of Rose and her whole family, Mercedes grew too ill to leave her bed and had to be anointed.

Her peaceful death soon came. It was a tragic separation for all, but Rose felt it most keenly. She had grown very close to Mercedes. Now, to the other prayers which she found time to say daily, she added many for the repose of her sister's soul. However, Mercedes had lived a retired life and had died while only fourteen. It was unlikely that she would suffer long in purgatory, if indeed she went there at all.

Soon after the Flores family moved to Quive, an event took place which was to have a violent influence on their lives. The pastorate of San Damián in Huarochiri became vacant and a zealous priest, Francisco de Avila, was named to the parish. He was already qualified to work among the Indians in virtue of his fluency in the Quechua language. He was soon to immerse himself in the study of Indian customs and culture, in order to make himself as useful as possible to his flock and his archbishop. It was this priest who would later make the most appalling discovery in colonial Peruvian history, a discovery that rocked the clergy and people to the depths of their being and caused all Europe to tremble either with wrath or confusion. It would send Rose's penance skyrocketing until it passed the bounds possible to nature, and would create a chasm between herself and her family that would be closed only on her death-bed.

But before these events would transpire, Rose had much to do and much to endure, and Quive formed the setting of the second scene. Soon after Mercedes' death, Rose began to suffer from cold and numbness in her hands and feet. The malady gained ground until she could no longer walk; the movement of her arms and hands also gradually grew impossible. She was bed-ridden, a total invalid pronounced incurable by the doctor.

The grief of Oliva, Gaspar and Isabel can be imagined, as also the depression experienced by the older children. They had just lost one sister; now it seemed that they were to lose another. They began to realize what the sunny and obliging presence of Rose about the house had meant to them; all showed their sympathy and love in a thousand thoughtful ways. Perhaps the most pained was Fernando. He had always been closest to Rose, except for Mercedes during her last months. He often came and sat beside her bed, summoning some semblance of his usual droll wit to encourage Rose. But to his amazement and edification he found that she needed no encouragement. In all her pains and the numberless trials which her paralysis entailed, she had only one regret: she caused her family extra work. So, when Fernando's turn came to make a sacrifice for Rose, he was ready. He made it generously.

Somewhere, Oliva heard of a remedy for paralysis which consisted in binding an uncured animal hide on the paralyzed limbs. Perhaps it was an ancient Indian remedy, but whatever its origin, Oliva resolved to try it on Rose. Gaspar and Isabel agreed that she should, for they had nothing to lose and everything to gain by the attempt. As it was, Rose seemed doomed to total helplessness and an early death; perhaps the hide might restore her health.

For many years, Fernando had nurtured the boyish dream of owning a llama. Due to the recklessness with which the herds had been depleted by the *conquistadores* and colonists, the once common beast was now a rarity. But Gaspar was able to buy one for his son, and it gave him pleasure to do so. Fernando was in raptures over his llama; he fed her himself and coddled her like a child, sheared her wool as proudly as though it had been of gold, and spent hours in training her to respond to his commands. While Mariana milked her he fussed like a mother hen lest the maid startle or injure his pet. Now he was asked to give up his llama for Rose.

The boy agreed promptly as soon as he learned that his sister might possibly be cured by the hide. The gentle beast was slaughtered and skinned. Most of the carcass was salted and the rest prepared for immediate consumption. The hide, freshly removed from the scene of the holocaust, was carried to the house where Oliva awaited it eagerly. As she had been told to do, she took it to Rose while it was still warm.

"Here is the skin of a freshly killed llama," she said to Rose. "They say that it will cure paralysis. I am going to bind it on you tightly; when the proper time has passed, I shall come and take it off. Now, do not loosen these strings no matter how it feels. If there is any virtue in this skin, you must have the benefit of it."

Rose looked up at her mother with great, startled eyes.

"I do hope that this is not the skin of Fernando's llama that you have brought me, Mama; for although I am grateful that you wish to try so costly a cure, I should feel very badly if Fernando has had to give up his llama. He loves her so."

"He loves you more, daughter," said Oliva firmly as she bent over her daughter's wasted body to tie a knot more firmly in place. "Now, put Fernando out of your mind and go to sleep if you can. Perhaps, God willing, when you waken you may be well."

Distracted by her many duties, Oliva forgot the time. When at last she remembered, she ran to Rose.

"How are you, child?" she asked anxiously. "I am sorry that I forgot you; I have had so much extra work to do."

"The hide has not cured me, Mama," answered Rose with a weak smile. "But I have not unbound it or loosened the strings since you put it on."

"That is good; you are obedient," said Oliva as she cut the knots. "Now, we shall see what effect it has had. Perhaps the extra time has been all to the good."

As she spoke, she lifted the hide from Rose's back. Then, she shrieked. Great pieces of the young girl's flesh came off with the hide; her back was ulcerated and her body covered with a rash.

"You must have been in agony, Rose! Why did you not tell me? Why did you not loosen the strings?"

"But, Mama! You told me not to loosen those strings or

unbind that hide until you came to take it off. What could I do but obey you?"

That Sunday at Mass an unexpected announcement was made by Father González. In three weeks Archbishop Toribio would come for the visitation of the parish and to administer the sacrament of confirmation. Would the parents of children ready for the reception of the sacrament kindly make their names known?

"Did you hear that announcement?" Oliva asked her mother as they left the church after Mass.

"Of course I heard the announcement, Oliva," snapped Isabel as she made her way through the ragged, unwashed Indians, drawing her veil and mantle protectively about her. "After all, I am not deaf!"

Oliva smiled within the folds of her veil. Her mother was indeed deaf, but it would do no good to show that this favorite expression was now more amusing than caustic.

"Rose should be confirmed," said Oliva as they reached the edge of the road. "She is ready; but of course Archbishop Toribio will have to come to the house. I am sure that he will make no difficulties; he is so obliging. At least he will not have far to walk."

"Let us have Gaspar speak to Father González. It will do no harm to ask."

But it was not to be as the women planned. Don Toribio did not come to the house to confirm Rose; she was quite well by the time that he arrived in Quive. What caused her cure, which was certainly a marvel? Not the llama skin, which only made her worse.

Rose had been resigned to paralysis and death until she heard of the coming confirmation ceremony; but her intense desire to receive the sacrament revived her interest in living. Her humility and modesty made her shrink from the thought of having the archbishop confirm her in her room, so she began to pray ardently for her cure. This is half the story; the other half lies locked in St. Toribio's heart. He who was a man of prayer as well as action would have been praying especially for the children whom he was to confirm in Canta; he would have been begging almighty God that all who were of the correct age should be instructed in the catechism and receive the sacrament.

The conjunction of these fervent prayers of two of his saints was too much for God's paternal love to withstand. Besides, he willed Rose to be well and to live for many more years on earth. So the sick child grew suddenly better. Warmth and life returned to her paralyzed limbs; by the time the archbishop came to Quive, she was cured.

Undoubtedly Quive received Archbishop Toribio with festive formality. The mines would have been closed for the ceremony of his reception and all the Indians ordered out to throng the streets. The Spanish citizens, dressed as elaborately as possible, waited for him in rank according to their dignity at some conspicuous spot, probably before the church. Some of the less prominent men would have ridden out beyond the town to meet him and escort him to the church.

In Lima this duty would have fallen to Gaspar as a member of the guard, but in Quive he was one of the noblest and most honored citizens. He therefore waited in unruffled dignity before the church. One could not say on the church steps, for there were none, so humble was the structure. Oliva and Isabel, with the other noble ladies, awaited him elsewhere, probably in the home where he was to lodge. There a reception would have made him acquainted with the dignitaries of the region.

On being introduced to him, Oliva could not have failed to remind the prelate of their repeated meetings at such receptions in Lima and of the fact that she knew his sister, Grimanesa. Doubtless Rose's parents inquired as to the

health of her husband, Francisco de Quiñones. More reinforcements sent to Chile had failed to rout the Araucanian
Indians and this noble-hearted gentleman had offered to
finance another expedition. It had been placed in his hands,
and he had earned the title "Admiral of the South Seas." But
despite emergency troops sent from Spain, the expedition was
proving a failure. Humiliating defeats piled one on another,
weighing down the spirit of the man who was bearing all the
cost. Finally, Francisco's health gave way, and he was confined to bed in a helpless state.

"My brother-in-law pleads in vain for his release from this
terrible task," Toribio told Rose's mother and grandmother.
"We fear that he will die without having obtained it. Pray
to God for him, that at least he may have the consolation of
dying in the midst of his family."

Oliva and Isabel promised to pray for Francisco's recall. It
was a double joy to do this, for Toribio himself had asked
them to obtain the favor for him and they shared the general
high regard for Francisco de Quiñones.

When Oliva remarked that her daughter, Rose, was to receive confirmation at his hands, the archbishop recalled all
that Grimanesa had told him of the Flores family and of
Rose. It was, therefore, with unusual joy and interest that he
waited for the moment when he should meet her.

Archbishop Toribio had to make certain that his candidates
knew their Christian doctrine before confirming them. Ordinarily, questions addressed to candidates by bishops on this
subject are merely perfunctory, but in Peru at that time it
could not be so. Don Toribio could trust only a handful of
his many *doctrineros* to see that the children were adequately
instructed or answer his inquiries truthfully. The rest were
not to be relied on; those who were neither dissolute nor em-
bezzlers were incompetent and bent on hiding the fact. The
saint, therefore, had to conduct a personal test of the candi-

dates in most of the *doctrinas* which he visited. This test could be no brief question or two asked during the confirmation ceremony. It had to be comprehensive and revealing.

The visitation progressed rapidly, like everything done by Archbishop Toribio where he had a freee hand. First, he went to the church and prayed long and fervently for the people of Quive. Then he was forced to spend half an hour in a reception line which he would have wished to escape. As soon as he could, he returned to the church and began taking the inventory of its goods. He made the visitation of the church, noting the condition of the building and pointing out a few possible improvements and repairs that were needed. All this he did with great care and deliberation.

Had Quive been a larger center, he would have then proceeded to visit the monasteries, confraternities and other pious places, but there were no other sacred buildings in this mountain town. All spiritual life centered on the church. Hence, the archbishop was soon free to speak to the people who presented themselves at the house where he was staying, and to preach special sermons to all groups and classes. In the midst of these occupations he found time for an interview with the confirmation candidates. As they were only two in number, he asked them to come to the home of his hosts. Accordingly, at the pre-arranged time, Oliva and Gaspar took Rose to this favored house.

After the first pleasantries, the archbishop's secretary led Rose into the next room where her confirmation companion was already waiting. In the meantime, Toribio was asking Oliva and Gaspar how long Rose had been studying the catechism and how it was that she had not been named after some saint. The fact that he already knew the story of the miracle of the rose in no way deterred him from asking this; he had no intention of letting Rose's parents know that it had been common gossip at the time. The moment that he asked, Oliva told him in detail of the apparition. Then she and Gaspar added a few words concerning Isabel's refusal to accept the change of names. Without entering into details, they conveyed the impression that a feud existed in the family.

What were Rose's emotions as she waited for the archbishop whom she had venerated since babyhood and for whom she had prayed so often and ardently? Her soul was flooded with consolation. His utter simplicity, threadbare cassock and fatherly kindness had already disarmed her of her natural reserve. She knew her catechism thoroughly; she had no cause for anxiety as to the questions that he would ask her. Her sole cause of embarrassment was the presence of the youth who was also to be confirmed on the morrow. He was the son of one of the mine officials; her parents considered him an eligible match for her. Happily for Rose, she was spared the embarrassment of speaking to him alone. Convention bade the archbishop's secretary stay with them until the prelate entered.

Archbishop Toribio examined Rose and her companion with equal care. His manner towards both was identical, as prudence and charity demanded. The only unusual circumstance was that, as he had only two candidates to question, he was able to speak at leisure. But his passion for time saving urged him to give to the interview no notable length, as also his discretion. Later in Lima he was to show his predilection for Rose, but not here. Quive was a busy-tongued, inquisitive town. Moreover, any show of favoritism would hurt Rose's companion; any undue questions would have made him uneasy. He was a youth of ordinary spiritual knowledge; his self-consciousness was increased by the fact that Rose was listening to his answers. Out of compassion for him, then, if for no other reasons, Toribio did not prolong the test uselessly.

However, although the time that he spent with Rose was brief, to him it was unforgettable. The Holy Spirit had already endowed him with the charism of the reading of hearts. When he gazed paternally on this young girl he saw beyond her incredible beauty to her more incredible beauty of soul. He saw in her a budding saint; one vibrating with the purity of supernatural life. When the time came for him to pass from this life, she would be reaching adulthood; her life would be spent in support of his successor's work as a kind of prolongation of his own.

As for Rose, once Toribio began to speak to her and her fellow-candidate, she was enraptured. She had met a few persons in her lifetime who loved God as she did: her Jesuit director, the friars at Santo Domingo. But none of them had been like Archbishop Toribio. When he questioned her, his accents were so lively and tender, so charged with charity toward God and herself, that she felt her soul kindled with fire. If she had believed before that her archbishop was a saint, now she knew it by the unction of his words and the phenomenal effect that they had on her soul. Her love of God and the Church, which he personified for her, increased so much during that one conversation that she could scarcely understand herself. It seemed to her that for the first time she was truly dedicated, ready to fight all God's battles for no reward other than himself.

Later, Rose knelt at the altar rail with her confirmation companion. She gazed adoringly at the tabernacle, then inwardly at the Jesus of her soul. She raised her heart to the Holy Ghost who was coming soon to her so that he might increase in her his seven gifts, together with the infused supernatural virtues. Finally, with awe-struck gaze, she watched Archbishop Toribio move along the flower-strewn way from the altar to the altar rail. Gone was the paternal smile, the shabby soutane and shoes; now he was magnificent in pontifical vestments and grave of countenance.

Rose's turn came first out of deference to her father's dignity in Quive. Don Toribio laid his brown hand gently on her head. After this came the murmured ripple of Latin and a small sign of the cross on her brow with the warm chrism. It was time for him to speak her name. He paused; this was one of the moments that change lives. What did he see and hear? Did his sister's voice, re-echoing, float across the years to him?

"The baby's face turned into a rose. . . . They call her Rose. Doña Isabel is indignant."

Did the carefully phrased words of Rose's parents regarding the family feud return to him? Did the scene before him fade? In its stead did he see in an instant all the multitude of other scenes that the changing of Rose's name had evoked? Did he feel sweeping through him the victim's agony and bewilderment, her heroic patience, her sweet spirit of forgiveness, her doubts and fears lest her love for this nickname spring from vanity? We do not know. All that we know is what he said. When the instant's pause was over and his words burst forth again in a torrent, he called her Rose.

Seated near the altar rail, Isabel heard his voice. A shock ran through her whole being. She leaned towards her daughter and whispered in the utmost astonishment: "He did not say her right name! He called her Rose."

"What do you mean, Mother?" answered Oliva. "Rose is her right name!"

Isabel began to protest; suddenly she stopped. A revolution took place in her heart; she smiled and looked complacently up at the archbishop. He must have been watching for that smile as he turned from the altar rail and walked majestically back to the altar.

"Well, after all," the old lady went on in a piercing whisper which perhaps even Toribio heard, "since the archbishop has called her Rose, I suppose it is right. I have always thought that it suited her; but I wanted to do the correct thing before God and the Church."

The final prayers had been concluded. The archbishop turned from the altar; his eyes swept over the multitude before him. This was to be his last blessing upon them before his departure. He would pour into it all the love and yearning compassion of his soul. He raised his right hand in the ritual sign, but he did not make it. Instead, he uttered an anguished cry. Tears filled his eyes.

"Miserable ones!" he exclaimed. "You shall not exceed three!"

What was the cause of this cry? What was its meaning? It became clear only after he had left the town. In a flash of interior light, the saint had seen the spiritual state of the whole populace. In this town of three thousand souls there were only three families with Christian sentiments. But that was not all; God had reached the limit of his patience. He would disperse this ungrateful people. The town would fall into ruins; it would shrink to almost nothing. One or two, sometimes three families might remain there, but never more than three. It was no wonder that St. Toribio wept.

Rose wept, too, when she learned the meaning of his cry; but her affliction was doubled on learning what happened when her hero left the church. Still half blinded by tears, he made his way along the street with his secretary. He was accosted by a group of grimacing Indians. Some of them began to clamor coarsely at him, accompanying their cries with mocking sounds.

"Big-nose! Big-nose!"

The saint looked about him at the hostile faces in bewilderment; then he lowered his head. Without a word he passed through the jostling crowd into the house that sheltered him. There he gave vent to his grief; he wept and scourged himself far into the night in expiation of the sins that he had seen upon the souls of the people of Quive. He desisted only when his secretary urged him to spare some strength for the morrow's journey. Then he collected himself. Like a man awakening from a nightmare he gazed around the room. His half-packed luggage lay spread on the bed and chairs.

"Our duty," he said. "Ah, yes; we must do our duty."

Toribio Mogrovejo left Quive an old man; a few days before, he had been in his vigor. In that town where he had found the soul of a saint, he had loved and lost three thousand souls. To bring any one of them to Christ he would have gladly given, like the Savior, his blood and his life.

Since their earliest days in Quive, the low moral status of the place had been apparent to all the adults and older children of the Flores household. Mariana, too, had remarked on it almost at once. She made no friends among the Indians there, for despite her race she had almost nothing in common with them. Her piety and loyalty to the hated Spaniards made her suspect in their eyes. She kept away from them as much as possible.

As for Oliva and Isabel, there were only a few homes where they felt themselves at ease, for such society as they found elsewhere in the town was too dissolute for their taste. They were nervous for the sake of the children, so impressionable, so prone to adopt the airs and views of others. For this reason they were not confounded by Archbishop Toribio's revelation. Only Rose, who had seen next to nothing of life in Quive due to her illness, was broken by his words.

Was Rose's family one of the three just families found in this town of three thousand? Very probably. In an age when marital infidelity was appallingly frequent, Gaspar and Oliva were refreshingly faithful to their marriage vows. In an age when every man seemed bent on padding his purse and often cared little what laws he broke in so doing, Gaspar was honest. Many a man would have made his fortune as mine administrator in Quive; Gaspar emerged from his term poorer than ever. He could have connived at the abuses of lesser officials and so cut his slice of the spoils; but he did not do so.

While the Flores family lived in Quive, Spain suffered two blows. The first was wholly unexpected: the defeat of the so-called Invincible Armada. It was a crushing defeat, all the more humiliating because Spain had just reached the peak of her glory. Now, like the rest of the colonies, Peru's coastal population held their breath. If they had feared the English attack even before the war, now their fears flared up to giant size.

King Philip II did not live long after the loss of his Armada. He died on September 13, 1598, in San Lorenzo del Escorial. He was in many ways a great and noble man, worthy of his high state. If he was suspicious of his advisors and appointees, only too often it was with reason.

But his will was inclined to a rigidity which showed itself above all in his zeal as a Catholic. Unfortunately this zeal, intense as it was, had in it a strong admixture of personal ambition and pride. He assumed a dictatorial air towards the popes and the college of cardinals, under the illusion that he could see the true interests of the Church more clearly than they. Yet he was venerated by many of his vassals and idolized by his family. He did much for the extension of the Spanish Empire.

The news of his death did not reach Lima until March 10, 1599. Although no instructions were received with regard to the mourning, the viceroy and *audiencia* agreed at once that it should be as solemn, ornate and courtly as possible.

All this the Flores family missed, for in Quive little could be done. The town and its citizens were draped in black and solemn services were held in the church, where Gaspar and his wife figured prominently. But they shared none of the excitement that stirred the capital.

There was some anxiety regarding the new king. He had a reputation for simplicity and good-heartedness, but this was combined with more impulsiveness and less prudence than King Philip had boasted. How would he fare in the complex intrigue of international politics? With his off-hand, sweeping decisiveness, would he study situations and questions in the detail demanded by his absolute power? All this lay uneasily at the bottom of Peru's national consciousness. Even Rose, young as she was, could not have failed to catch something of the mood of her elders.

Rose's experience in Quive, most of all her presence in the church which was the scene of Archbishop Toribio's frightful revelation, left her at first in a state of shock. But her deep trust in God soon raised her spirits and she began to pray more insistently than ever for this suffering people. As her health was restored, she began to mortify herself again in ways approved by her director.

Her mother had objected to the logs confiscated when they moved to Quive, but on being told that Rose had her director's permission for a hard bed, she had not forbidden it. Rose, therefore, assumed that she had no objection to the continuation of the penance, provided that smooth logs were used. She found a smooth log and inserted it in her pillow case. However, as soon as Oliva found it, it went the way of the others, despite its smoothness.

At this time, Rose's parents allowed her to begin taking the discipline. She had had the permission since before their departure from Lima, but first Mercedes' illness and then her own had prevented her from starting. The discipline which she now made for herself was nothing terrifying: it was of light rope strands twisted together at one end to form a handle and left free at the other. It was waxed; the wax served to stiffen and give substance to the rope.

In Rose's time, the use of the discipline was more common among the laity than it is today. It was also ordinarily used by religious and by many of the secular clergy. However, in the sixteenth and seventeenth century it often took a much more severe form than that just described.

Sometimes disciplines of chain were used; more commonly, a cord scourge was equipped with metal points. All this sounds gruesome, and it is; but so was the passion of Jesus Christ. Such extremes of penance are wholesome only when adopted by those who share the Redeemer's thirst to save the world, who can endure the effects while performing their duties of life, and are permitted to punish themselves in this way by their spiritual directors.

This brings us to a question of the highest importance to anyone wishing to understand the psychology of the saints, and especially one like St. Rose. That question is: why corporal penance? There is one basic motive for corporal punishment, whether inflicted by the state, parents or teachers, or by individuals on themselves as an act of religion: to satisfy for some offense. Guilt is punished by God in this life, in purgatory and in hell. Self-punishment in this life reduces the debt owed to God for sin, so that one's purgatorial cleansing is shortened or cancelled. Moreover, it chastens the senses so that one's propensity to sin is weakened and the life of grace safeguarded. When performed solely from the preventive motive, self-punishment is usually called mortification.

But Christians form one spiritual body: the Mystical Body of Christ. As the prayers of one member may assist all, so too may his penances. God accepts this vicarious satisfaction on behalf of the souls in purgatory. As the ancient Dominican Tertiary Rule stated: "Charity overcomes even death." More than this, the living can also receive help and grace through the penances of others, not only those who are faithful to God's grace, but also the unbaptized and Christians who have fallen from grace. These latter receive actual graces which they would otherwise not enjoy, although God always gives every soul sufficient grace to do his will.

Theologians teach that as supernatural charity grows in a soul, the other infused virtues grow in identical proportion with it and one another. The measure of charity is the measure of each and every virtue. Applying this to the virtue of mortification and again to penance, we see that our charity is the measure of our spirit of penance. We can, therefore, expect to find in souls approaching sanctity a thirst for penance. In the saints, this thirst becomes a craving which is satisfied only by the limits imposed by obedience.

Soon the Flores family was relieved to know that Gaspar's work in Quive would end. All the members of the family were eager to leave this unfavorable location which had brought them so much sorrow, with the possible exception of Bernardina, who may have found a suitor there. The sole regret of the family on moving away from the town was having to part from a small mound marked by a stone cross in the little cemetery. They well knew that in their poverty they would probably never see it again. The trip to Quive cost too much.

The impressions of Rose on returning to Lima were vivid; she seemed overwhelmed. With its crowded streets and grand buildings, it made her feel very small and unimportant. Little did she dream that the day would come when her statue, borne through those same streets on a gaily decked float, would be acclaimed by the whole populace each year. She was now a lovely young girl of fourteen, poised and mature for her years. Wherever she went, she drew all eyes upon her by her captivating beauty, modesty and sweetness.

As she had done at Quive, Rose wished to bury herself at

home, but her mother's friends and acquaintances pressed their attentions on her. Often—too often for her liking—the great homes of Lima welcomed her as a favorite. On her mother's pleading, she had let her hair grow; and as of old, Oliva tenderly but firmly placed elegant veils and wreaths of roses on her head. Rose did not resist, although the adornment pleased her less than ever. For the sake of peace, she let her mother fuss over her, but she continued piercing her scalp with a pin each time that she had to wear one of the wreaths.

Rose found a few changes at Santo Domingo's. The most astonishing was the discovery of Martin de Porres in the convent. During the absence of the Flores family in Quive, he had finished his apprenticeship and had begun the practice of medicine and barbering. In his spare time he had frequented the church of St. Dominic. As he prayed there and sought the spiritual guidance of the friars, his attraction to the Order had grown. Convinced that he was answering the call of God, he applied for admission as a tertiary or *donado*.

Martin's application had been accepted by the new Father Provincial, a learned and zealous priest named Juan de Lorenzana. Not long in office, he had already proved worthy of the esteem of his brethren. His office as provincial brought with it automatically the exacting post of inquisitor.

This Father, who spared himself no exertion or inconvenience when it was a question of helping a soul, was to be a major influence in Rose's spiritual formation as well as Martin's. For both, though in different ways, he was to be a guide and protector. His counsels and examples were to lead them to glorious heights in the imitation of St. Dominic and St. Catherine of Siena.

The prior of the convent and a majority of the chapter members had seconded Father Lorenzana's approval. As a tertiary, the young barber-surgeon had been in seventh heaven, but his illustrious father now objected to his lowly position. He felt that the family dignity demanded a higher vocation. In his opinion, Martin should have entered the priesthood or at least the lay brothers of the First Order.

When Rose heard from Martin of his joy and peace of soul as a *donado* and his father's demands, her heart brimmed with sympathy. She too knew what it was to have her vocation thwarted by parental designs, however well intentioned. Every day her mother spoke to her of marriage and plotted meetings with eligible young men. Rose dared not circumvent these plans lest she cause a storm. Yet, in her heart she felt confirmed in her childhood resolution to give her love and life to Christ.

Although Rose understood Martin's wish to correspond with what seemed to him to be God's will, her high regard for his virtues made her wonder whether some day he might not be raised to a greater vocation that that of tertiary. As such, he enjoyed many spiritual advantages of the Order, but in a way suited to his humility. Yet this very humility, marked as it was by composure and recollection, revealed him as a soul of prayer. Rumor had it that he cured by miracles those whom he could not cure by medical treatment. Whenever he went abroad through the city, he was at once surrounded by a group of poor and afflicted persons. His deft dark fingers busied themselves hour after hour with the sick and wretched; homeless waifs followed him like a father. Persons of high position came to the convent to recommend themselves to his prayers. His superiors looked on him with paternal pleasure. As the months passed and Rose met him frequently on her visits to St. Dominic's, especially in her sacristy work, she began to look on him as a friend. She often spoke of his virtues to others.

From the first, Rose sensed in Martin a holiness like that which she had felt in Archbishop Toribio. She could speak openly to him of her inmost desires and most intimate thoughts on the subject dearest to her: God and his love. Martin, on his part, thought himself unworthy to speak to her, but when occasions came his way, he never failed to do so. He found her always the same: gentle, pleasant, interested in his life and problems, ready with a consoling word or a frank disclosure of her own.

Besides their devotion to the Order of Friars Preachers and their fervent desire for sanctity, Rose and Martin had other interests in common. As soon as the household routine was established in their Lima home, the Flores family had opened its charity once more to the sick poor. With the approval of her parents and grandmother, Rose had resumed the free distribution of her herb medicines. The increased age and beauty of the donor combined with her kindness to lengthen the queue; soon Rose found herself being asked to tend wounds and give advice far beyond her capacity.

She had already mastered what her mother could teach her of nursing, but from experience she knew that Oliva's knowledge was apt to prove wanting in a crisis. More than once she had suffered from these gaps which all her mother's nervous energy and good will could not fill. The most recent was the application of mercury to Rose's scalp, which had become infected with a kind of scurvy. After this agonizing treatment, which reduced her whole head to one wound, she could not place reliance on Oliva's advice. She had to look to someone who knew how to diagnose and treat the diseases which she met most commonly among the poor who crowded the *patio* of her home each morning. That someone was Brother Martin.

Martin was eager to share his knowledge with one as interested as Rose. He let her use his precious medical books and case notes. When Rose had finished her work in the chapel of Our Lady of the Rosary, they went over the points that were difficult for the young student.

In time, Rose became a competent diagnostician and learned how to treat many diseases. Her medical work gradually increased in volume until it encroached on her time of prayer. It took her from the household duties which pressed upon her. It began to assume the earmarks of a profession, if not a lucrative one. As the months and years passed, it was to disrupt Oliva's careful routine and threaten the peace of the family. But for Rose it was always a joy beyond measure. Through it she became known as "mother of the poor."

Just now, however, Rose's principal domestic duty was the care of her baby brother, Antonio. He had been born soon after her confirmation, just before the family's return to Lima. Bernardina was busy preparing her trousseau, for she had set her heart on marrying a certain youth who seemed to her parents quite beneath them. Nevertheless, once Oliva found that her daughter refused to think of another suitor, she consented to help with the sewing. She had married for love and her marriage had been happy. Although Bernardina's choice was disappointing, she would help her make the best of it. Isabel, too, took part in the preparations, despite her deteriorating health. In the months that followed their return to Lima, Rose found much of the management of the home falling on her shoulders. She was grateful to her mother for the confidence that she showed in leaving so much to her judgment. Oliva, on her part, eagerly seized the excuse for shifting these duties on Rose. It would place her daughter in a favorable light when potential suitors saw her so capable and experienced in household affairs.

Not long after her return from Quive, Rose obtained permission from her Jesuit director and her parents to receive Holy Communion daily. This meant that she was obligated to a life of strict fasting and other corporal penances. Actually, the change was more theoretical than factual as far as her diet was concerned, but her hours of prayer had to be prolonged and this meant subtraction from her hours of sleep. Her quota of household work had swollen to such an extent that the most she could achieve by way of daytime devotions was a short visit to the Blessed Sacrament and Our Lady of the Rosary. While she worked she tried to recall the presence of God by ejaculatory prayer. When possible, she recited the beads while she worked, and in order to have them always at hand when a free moment came, she began to wear the rosary over her right shoulder.

With the practice of daily Communion and its concommitants—fasting and vigils, prolonged disciplines and the wearing of instruments of penance—Rose's life acquired a basic routine which it never lost. Her days consisted of a drab, familiar round of hard work in noisy, confused surroundings hostile to a life of prayer. She never complained. By a good intention she kept her work on a supernatural plane. By renewing her good intention as often as she could, she kept her heart united to God. It was not a dramatic life nor an eventful one to outward appearances, but inwardly it was eventful indeed. The longest journeys are made by the heart; this was Rose's conviction and discovery. The more she retired from worldly ambitions, the more closely she approached heaven. God was her goal—for herself and others.

"The kingdom of heaven suffers violence and the violent bear it away," said our Lord; and he added: "The kingdom of heaven is within you." Rose's violence was turned within herself against her passions and concupiscences so that she might subject her soul to the reign of Christ. In this battle she used every weapon she had and made no truce. How she seized the kingdom that she might open it to the wretched as a haven and home is one of the most stirring stories in Christian history. That she triumphed over all the obstacles posed by fear and human weakness is a tribute to her nature as well as her grace. She was not a soldier's daughter for nothing.

CHAPTER SEVEN

Growth

~~~~~

WHEN THE Flores family returned to Lima, it found Archbishop Toribio again embroiled with the civil powers. The time had come for the prelate to hold another Council and, as always, he wished to do his duty. He must have known from experience that there would be opposition, but perhaps not from the forces which now swung into action.

Rightly fearing that the Council would wish to reduce their privileges, some of the religious orders of men in Peru aroused civil opposition to its convocation. Their fear was that the *doctrinas* would be placed under the direct supervision of the archbishop—a move which might have done much to improve their administration.

While on visitation, Toribio had received a letter from the viceroy bidding him abandon his plan of holding the Council. This letter was followed later by a royal decree. But Archbishop Toribio had already summoned the bishops with the king's permission. The Bishop of Cuzco arrived in Lima, but the other bishops delayed. Apparently they had been forewarned of the prohibition. Believing that the Council would not be held without them, the Bishop of Cuzco went home to his diocese. Then the Bishop of Panama arrived. The Bishop of La Imperial was already there, so Archbishop Toribio called the other bishops. But the Bishop of La Imperial was in no mood to attend the Council. He was in Lima for the purpose of obtaining a more important see, not on Toribio's petition, but that of the viceroy and the *audiencia*. Therefore, he refused to attend, appealing to his patrons for support. They gave it willingly. So encouraged, the deluded prelate wrote an impassioned letter to the king, stating his willingness to bear with a good heart whatever inconvenience might come his way, for the sake of justice in the service of his king and lord who had raised him up from the dust of the earth. Doubtless, he hoped for a high appointment by return mail.

While these events were in progress, Toribio wrote to the bishops of Quito and Tucumán, telling them to come in haste. They reluctantly arrived in Lima by April, 1601. On April 11 the Council opened in the throne room of the archiepiscopal palace. The viceroy and his judges, who should have been present, were conspicuously absent. To them, the mere opening of the Council seemed near treason.

These grave cares of her beloved Archbishop Toribio would have served alone to make Rose push her hours of prayer far into the night. But soon a new one was added which dwarfed them in comparison. Both for herself and Toribio it brought spiritual crucifixion. Yet, to say this is to point only to the back of the design.

Rose, like the archbishop, had been praying with fervor for the new king. Like some of her contemporaries, she had hoped that his good will and eager nature might cause a change in royal policy, leading him to act in favor of the Indians. They did. With a thump of the fist and a thrust of the quill, he swept into play a whirlwind of forces that soon surpassed his control. His intentions were pure, his act noble and fearless; but living a life of royal luxury and prodigal spending, he had no conception of the poverty and avarice of the lords of Peru. He read with pain and indignation of the state of the Indians in the land of gold and silver that had once been theirs. The viceroy had written him a lurid account of their sufferings; he had called them intolerable. Very well;

if they were intolerable, then the king would abolish them.

On November 24, 1601, he abolished Indian personal service, not only in Peru but in his other New World domains as well. He forbade the *encomenderos* to exact any service as tribute; those who did were to be deprived of their holdings. He forbade Indians to work on the sugar plantations. Negroes (five times stronger than Indians physically) were to serve there as laborers. *Mestizos* (half Spanish and half Indian) could also be used in this work.

All this struck a death blow to colonial rapacity. But the king went further. The *yanaconas*, who under the Incas had been a servant class, were theoretically free under the Spanish rule, but in practice those who tilled the soil were held on the lands where they had been born. The custom reduced them to slavery in fact, if not according to law. Now the king proceeded to remind large landholders of that law. The *yanaconas* were to be considered free and in no way bound to the land. Infraction of this order would be gravely punished.

Some months passed before the king's decree reached Lima; when it did, the effect was explosive. The brave and generous act was branded as imprudent. They fought against the decree by fair means and foul.

The first means was debate; the second, delay. The evil hour of enforcement was deferred until men would rally to defend their rights. A petition was sent to the king, signed by prominent persons, both clerical and lay. Let him reconsider, for it was not the time to put the decree in force. When that time was likely to come, they did not say.

The viceroy, whose vivid exposition of the Indians' distress had moved the king to abolish their personal service, marshalled all the protests that he had received and set them forth in order. To read his appeal, one would never dream that he had once planned a change in the existing abuses. In fact, he probably had not; like his predecessors, he had been shocked by what he found on his arrival in the New World, but prudence had warned him that no real reform could be pressed on the Peruvians from without.

As an opening shot, he hurled at the distant ruler the charge that the Indians would not work unless forced to do so. How was this charge to be proved or disproved? It was impossible for the king to do either. He could only take the viceroy's word as truth. But it was a revealing indictment of what had once been a most industrious people. It revealed the horrors of their present working conditions more than any fault in themselves.

Next, the viceroy claimed that it was to the Indians' advantage to keep them as they were. If left to the disposition of the *caciques* or chiefs, their fate would be much worse, he said. How much truth lay behind this statement? There was some, to be sure. Once the advent of the Spaniard brought the use of money into the national economy, the *caciques* were as grasping as any white official. But to say that the fate of the Indians would be worse when employed by them than when herded into forced labor in the mines and fields was to say too much. If we wish to learn what the Indians themselves thought of the mines, especially the mercury mines at Huancavelica, we need only turn to the testimony of history. They called them "the jaws of hell." To many, suicide seemed preferable to a term there as *mitayo*. The devils would torment them less than the Spaniards, they believed.

Thirdly, the viceroy reminded the king that the distribution of Indians was held as a trust by the *corregidores,* who assigned them according to the needs of those who asked for them, on the approval of himself. If the king wished, he could investigate the use of Indian labor, but it was certain that few Indians would hire themselves out voluntarily. There was a shortage of hands to work the mines. It would be of no use to substitute slaves for the Indians as miners, and the cost of hiring Spaniards would be prohibitive.

Here, one feels like taking the good viceroy by the shoulders and turning him squarely towards the facts. Originally, black slave labor had been introduced into the Spanish New World colonies precisely as a replacement for Indian labor in the mines and other work too strenuous for the Indians. The suggestion had come from a Dominican prelate named las Casas, a man of sensitive conscience and an outraged sense of justice. He had made that suggestion, not because he approved of slavery in itself, but because the Africans were five times stronger than the Indians. Taking slavery as an institution that had existed from earliest times, he simply suggested using Negroes as a more humane practice than the use of Indian forced labor.

What had so changed the face of things that it would be "useless to substitute slaves for the Indians as miners"? Two facts alone: first, the available slave labor was already absorbed in the sugar and other plantations and in various municipal public works; second, if slave labor were removed from its present assigned roles and replaced by paid Indian and white labor, the pocketings of the great landholders would have been sliced. In short, it was the impassioned partisanship of vested interests that made the *audiencia* cry out as one man that to enforce the king's decree would mean a great detriment to the country and perhaps its ruin.

Besides the drastic reforms already mentioned, the king had specifically ordered that Indians no longer be used to carry packs or to run with the mail as couriers. It should surprise no one that these decrees remained more or less on paper. Actually, there was no other alternative to the use of Indian couriers, and this for two reasons. The inhumane treatment of the African slaves had made them unruly, wildly immoral and incapable of filling posts of trust. They had to be used in chain gangs and closely watched by armed guards. Couriers ran the mail route alone, over mountains and through forests. They carried loads of official mail. African slaves were the last people in Peru at the time who could have been given it safely. As for using Spaniards to run the routes, it would have been sheer murder. Besides, with the rarest exceptions, the Spaniards of whatever social and financial status who lived in Peru at that time were too proud for such work. Most of them preferred to live on the borderline of starvation rather than lower themselves to tasks which seemed fit only for a subject race.

Finally, in case the king might expect some improvement in Indian affairs through the action of the viceroy, the latter added a backhand thrust in his own defense. It was scarcely feasible to guard the Indians by means of the laws already passed because they had to be put in force by ministers who "had little mercy and were very greedy."

What stand did Archbishop Toribio take in this conflict in which the human and perhaps the supernatural life of a whole race was more or less at stake? Knowing his intense paternal love of the Indians and the vehemence of his many defenses of them in the past, we need not wonder. The king's abolition of Indian personal service was the answer to his prayers and petitions of twenty-two years. It would have served as a beginning in the rehabilitation of the race on a level of decency, a vital preparation for the reception of spiritual truths. From the outset of his episcopate, he had found this reform thwarted in Spain by the Council of the Indies and the king who headed it officially. Now both Council and king had spoken in favor of justice and Christian mercy.

But the anguished prelate found even in his own household a nest of traitors to his espoused cause. The dean of the cathedral and his own vicar general backed the *audiencia*.

Numbers of priests followed their opinion. Some went so far as to say that it was not morally wrong to employ Indians in the mines even though they died as a result of it. As an absolute monarch, they claimed, the king derived his power from God and had the right of life and death over all his vassals. No one could live for more than three or four years in the mercurial vapors of Huancavelica. It was simply necessary to make the choice as to who was expendable. No matter who died in consequence, mercury was needed for refining.

Not all priests adopted this point of view. The Jesuits and the Franciscans notably took the opposing stand. Gradually the latter worked out their case on a sound basis and presented it to the public in pamphlet form. But this was not until after St. Toribio's death. In the tempest of the early 1600's he stood almost alone.

He could not know it, but in the humble house near the Espíritu Santo, Rose was watching with him. The tenderness of her heart and the dilation of her love were the chief instruments of her suffering, but her knowledge of the archbishop's suffering was likewise a source of pain. In a moment of confidence, Grimanesa had confided her burden of sorrow to Oliva; and she, in turn, had brought it home to Rose.

For both of these saints, the one nearing final maturity and the other still in the springtime of her life, the force of their woe was the twofold pull of their love. Their hearts were on the rack. Archbishop Toribio had long since pushed his share of austerities and prayer to the limit, so there was no other outlet for his zeal. St. Rose had scarcely begun to run the race, so she could add much to hers. To discover the means of so doing and to exploit them to the full now became her chief immediate intent.

But just when she felt urged as never before to fill up in her flesh what was wanting to Christ's sufferings for his Church in Peru and the entire New World, Rose found to her dismay that she had become accustomed to the mortifications and penances that she had been practicing. She had reached a plateau, like many before her, on which she might have loitered indefinitely; but now she began to raise her eyes to the mountains. The saints before her and her beloved archbishop had shed their blood for the souls so dear to Jesus; she would do the same. As soon as she could, she confided her wish to her director and asked him for permission to add metal tips to her discipline. The priest understood and he himself gave her a handful of the sharp steel points. At that moment Rose was especially grateful for the fact that her spiritual father was a Jesuit. As such, he saw the issue of the king's decree in the same light as herself.

Is it astonishing that the priest should have given Rose these points so easily? No; as an experienced guide of souls, he knew that she was prepared to share to this extent in the passion of Christ. Her motive in wishing to endure this suffering was unsullied, sane and mature. Her body was accustomed to pain as a result of her childhood and youthful sicknesses and her past mortifications. She would not prolong the flagellation beyond the time he set, for she was obedient. That time was short, very short in the beginning. Only when it grew clear that the penance was not more than her strength could bear, would he permit a few more strokes. When she had grown used to it, Rose took the discipline with points for perhaps five or ten minutes at the most. She found that enough, at least, then.

We have no record of any words spoken by Rose to describe what this penance cost her, but we do have the words of another saint who is near to our time and our hearts—St. Thérèse of Lisieux. At about the same age as Rose, she began to use a discipline with knots, points and a spiked metal ball as a penance in her Lisieux Carmel. Her confidence to her fellow-Carmelite sister, Celine, voiced the views of all saintly souls who have used this severe form of penance since the early days of Christian asceticism.

Celine candidly admitted her aversion to this discipline of the Carmelite Rule, adding that she stiffened instinctively to ward off the self-inflicted blows. St. Thérèse gazed on her with amazement, then revealed her own way of acting and its motive. Since her object in scourging herself was to feel pain, she wanted to suffer as much as she could. Although tears filled her eyes, she made herself smile. Thus, her face expressed the joy of her heart in suffering with Jesus for souls. Surely this was also the outlook of St. Rose.

This does not mean that all Christians are called to practice the heroic corporal penances of St. Rose or St. Thérèse, but it does mean that even today, as Pope John XXIII pointed out, corporal penance does have a vital role to play in the lives of all Christians and especially in the lives of priests and religious. It is well to emphasize, as St. Thérèse has done, the inner self-discipline which safeguards the virtue of penance and all the other virtues. It is well to recall that penance unseen is penance least exposed to vainglory. But we must be on guard lest we lose our sense of proportion and discard what has been the practice of the most perfect Christians until now. If not, we risk settling back in our complacency and becoming what T. S. Eliot calls "stuffed men."

Let us now look more closely at St. Rose and her discipline. It is strange that a saint who lived only for the love of God and of souls should be remembered more for her penances than for her love. After all, it was love and not penances which made her a saint. Severe as they were, her penances rank with those of the happy St. Francis of Assisi, St. Clare, St. Teresa of Avila and many others. We shall see how strikingly she resembled the Poverello.

Basically, the challenge of St. Rose so far as we are concerned today may be reduced to two things: first, that we love God and souls as ardently and selflessly as she, so that we shall be willing to suffer for them as she did; second, that like herself we submit this desire to obedience.

To Rose, her latest permission for penance was some consolation; but it did not seem to her that she was doing enough. In the crisis that held Peru in its grip, she must spend herself to the utmost. Therefore, she sought and obtained permission for a private vow to abstain from meat for the rest of her life and to fast on bread and water. However, like every private vow, it was subject to the interpretation of her confessor. Foreseeing that in certain cases Rose would not be able to adhere rigidly to her vow without causing undesirable comment, he conditioned his permission on obedience to her mother in regard to its fulfillment. This meant that on an instant's notice Oliva could command Rose to eat meat or any other food without causing her to break her promise to God.

In practice, this vow brought little change to Rose's diet, but it made her acts of penance more meritorious. Offered for the grave intentions that had elicited it, it brought down more abundant graces on souls. Despite its limitations, it represented something profound in her life—her longing to consecrate her whole being to God by the religious vows of poverty, chastity and obedience. More and more clearly she saw that the cloister seemed to offer the opportunities for prayer and penance in obscurity which allured her. In a religious community, surrounded by nuns who shared her aspirations to sanctity and self-sacrifice, she would find her fulfillment.

As though Rose needed something more pressing to pray about, the long-expected English arrived in New World waters. The Dutch were with them. After a pause at the Island of St. Mary, the ships divided. For many months the Dutch passed themselves off as Flemish, thus obtaining provisions from the Chilean colonists; but the Araucanians were less hospitable. When news of the existence of English ships reached Lima, the viceroy lost no time in acting. A new galleon was readied in Callao, manned by eight companies of infantry formed in Lima. They were commanded by Franciso Alderete y Maldonado.

Rose's two older brothers, Gaspar and Matthias, went with this expedition. The expense of outfitting them, plus the cost involved in Bernardina's wedding, was already more than Gaspar could spare, but he borrowed money and for the time being all passed easily. However, as the day approached when he had to pay his creditors, he grew alarmed. His pay was as meager as ever and Oliva's needlework had been diverted from the lucrative orders on which he had counted. For months both she and Isabel had been working constantly on Bernardina's trousseau; now, all the clothing of the family needed mending and renewal. What money Bernardina would have earned by sewing had, of course, vanished, as also the slight contribution made to the family income by his two sons. At this time of supreme anxiety something occurred which Gaspar never forgot. It brought him his first inkling of Rose's power over the heart of God.

"You need not lay a place for your father," said Oliva to Rose one evening as the latter began to set the table for supper. "He will not be coming to the table."

"Oh, Mama!" exclaimed Rose in alarm. "What is wrong? Is Papa ill?"

"He has gone to bed," said her mother in a muffled voice. "His fever has come back."

"May I go to him?"

"Yes, child," answered Oliva. "Go as soon as you have set the table. Cheer him a bit if you can. Take some of your medicine to him; he has a headache."

"Thank you, Mama dear," said Rose. Then she looked at

her mother questioningly. "Mama, are you worried about something else?"

Oliva laughed grimly.

"Ask your father. Inquire about those men who called this morning."

When she had finished her task, Rose prepared the medicine and went to the front bedroom. The door was firmly closed; she knocked timidly.

"Papa, may I come in?"

Gaspar opened his eyes and turned his head in her direction.

"Well, daughter, what is this?" he asked, summoning a slight smile.

"It is something to help you get rid of your fever and headache, Papa. I am so sorry that you are ill," she added gently, placing her hand on his forehead. "And Mama is worried about something else, too, but she would not tell me what it is. She said that I should ask you about the gentlemen who called this morning."

"Your mother said that?" asked Gaspar, sighing and pressing his hands to his temples. "Well, then, she must want me to tell you. I owe a great debt, Rose. I must have the money by ten o'clock tomorrow."

Tears gathered in Rose's eyes.

"Poor Papa! Will you go to prison?"

"God knows," said Gaspar. "Now you see why I have a fever, little one. It is the end."

"Oh, Papa, it cannot be the end!" exclaimed Rose. "God our Father will take care of us. Why, we are like little birds in his hand. Did you not tell me so?"

Gaspar smiled ruefully.

"This little bird had better go and have her supper," he said. "Eat now; who knows what you will eat tomorrow!"

The next morning dawned implacably. Oliva could not leave her husband to take Rose to Mass, and Isabel was in a state of semi-shock. She had been told of the impending doom. Therefore, Fernando had to go with his sister to Santo Domingo's. He agreed to do so, but with less good humor than usual.

Rose understood. As they hurried along the silent street, stepping with care to avoid the great pools and muddy patches that daubed it, she let her brother know that she shared the secret.

"Fernando, we must pray very hard at Mass this morning," she said, as though she had noticed nothing surly in his mood.

"You know, too?" he asked, glancing at her in surprise.

"Oh, Fernando! You must not worry! God our Father will not fail us! You will see. Papa will not go to prison."

"Do not make me laugh," said the youth. "Perhaps the viceroy will pay his debt," he added as he let her through the door.

Rose flushed but did not answer. Mass was already beginning.

After her Communion and the last Gospel Rose shortened her thanksgiving. She sensed Fernando's restiveness and sacrificed some of those precious moments to please him. But she felt the continued presence of Jesus in her soul as they left the church. It seemed to her that he reassured and strengthened her with loving promises. As she reflected silently on the words that formed themselves in her mind, seemingly from him, she was startled to feel Fernando's hand barring her way. A well-dressed stranger stood before them. He smiled and asked if he were addressing the daughter of Gaspar de Flores. On learning from Fernando that he was, he inclined his body in a graceful salute.

"I have this package of money for the *señorita*," he said,

adding while she and Fernando stood tongue-tied: "Give this
to your father for his present needs."

In an instant, he lost himself in the crowd in front of the
church.

"I take it back," said Fernando when they had walked a
little way in silence. "From now on I shall believe anything.
Teach me to pray like that."

Soon after this consoling incident, Rose began to suffer in-
teriorly. Perhaps her scruples were caused by the devils, angered at this evidence of her favor with God. Perhaps they
came as a mental reaction to the tension she felt over the
coming battle in which her brothers were to fight for the first
time. Whatever their cause, they came on a day which made
them most painful to her. It was early in the week; she had
just been to see her director and could not return until the
end of the week without having to reveal her inner state to
her mother and grandmother. Ordinarily, she would have
done so spontaneously, but it happened that the question
tormenting her was the very one that she dared not mention
to either of them. That was the question of her name.

It was true that Archbishop Toribio had given her "Rose"
as her confirmation name, but "Isabel" was her baptismal
name. Should she not be called Isabel? She had intended to
take our Lady as her patroness at confirmation but Archbishop Toribio had changed all that. Then she felt such pleasure in being called Rose. Surely in letting herself be called
Rose she was falling into the sin of vainglory!

Could she have done so, the troubled young girl would
have sought out Brother Martin and confided her doubts to
him. But she had just been deprived for two years of his wisdom and understanding. Don Juan de Porres had returned to
Lima on business and had insisted that Martin enter the First
Order of St. Dominic instead of living in the monastery as a
mere tertiary or *donado*. Determined to have his son's future

settled before leaving Lima, he had gone this time to the provincial, the decisive and energetic Father Juan de Lorenzana, who admitted that Martin was surely worthy to be a friar. Sympathy for Martin's convictions as to God's will for him had kept the provincial from suggesting that the young man join the First Order. Armed with this remark, Juan had insisted until his son gave in. His one plea in the face of his father's demands had been that he was unworthy to be a friar.

Having gained the first point, Juan did not rest until he had spoken to the prior of Holy Rosary. His permission was needed before Martin could enter. The prior knew Martin's sentiments of humility, and while he consented to call the chapter so that the community might vote on the youth's admission, he opposed the father's desire that Martin advance to the priesthood. Therefore, Martin entered the Order of Friars Preachers as a postulant and began his formation as a lay brother. During the time which had to elapse before he pronounced his vows, he was not as free as formerly and Rose would not have easy access to Martin's counsel.

Rose, therefore, found herself in complete isolation in her trial of scruples. Cut off from human help, she still had God and our Lady. Accordingly, she turned to the Virgin of the Rosary. After Mass one morning, when the worshippers had left, she knelt before the beloved statue of Mary and the Infant Jesus. Her heart pounding, at first Rose found herself wordless. Suddenly she saw that the Virgin's head seemed to nod reassuringly. The little Jesus smiled broadly as with his right hand he began to play with his Mother's beads. Rose's breathing grew quiet; she was no longer in anxiety. She would ask her question and Mary would answer.

"Please, good Mother, is it wrong for me to be called Rose? I was baptized Isabel. I am afraid that it is out of vanity that I like the name."

Mary seemed to glance maternally at Rose while the Infant Jesus shook his head. Then, Rose heard our Lady's voice. "This divine Infant approves of the name of Rose," she said. "But he wishes you to add to this the name of his Mother. From now on, you will be known as *Rosa de Santa María.*"

Rose looked up at the Virgin through tears of joy. "Oh, good Mother! Good little Jesus! How can I thank you?"

As she whispered this, Fernando came up the aisle and touched her arm. "Come, Rose," he said impatiently. "You have prayed enough."

As soon as they reached home that morning, Rose hurried to tell her mother what had happened. Oliva listened stormily until Rose told her what our Lady had said. Then a smile of triumph sent her frown flying.

"Go and tell your grandmother what you have just told me!" she cried. "Now we shall see who has been right about what is the will of God!"

So Rose began, with the consent of her family, to call herself "Rose of St. Mary." Our Lady's whisper was to echo around the world from age to age, from household shrine to cathedral altar. Its fragrant syllables set Rose's soul aglow with joy and peace.

Ordinarily, beginners in the practice of virtue must pass through a first stage of purification called the active purgation or purgative way. Because of the purity and fidelity of Rose's life since infancy, it seems that she was spared this purgation. As soon as her spiritual life began to manifest itself clearly, she enjoyed the prayer and experienced the trials of those in the second stage of the interior life, the illuminative way. To understand Rose's life from this time on, some idea of this state of prayer and these trials is needed. All that can be done here is to give a brief survey of this vast and profound subject.

Like all those who are in the illuminative way, Rose

showed signs of her state. The divine Thief had stolen her heart and the theft was manifest. She sought him tirelessly; she found no pleasure in anything but him. Like an empty chalice, her soul waited to be filled and consecrated. It was to be a cup of Communion for Christ, the eternal High Priest.

However, like others in this state, Rose still had imperfections, notably a fixed determination to obtain her own way in matters of devotion and a certain hastiness which at times caused her to act impulsively. At prayer, she could still be distracted. Despite these weaknesses, it is a fact that Rose did not fall into the more serious faults which often occur in souls advanced in the illuminative way. Suffering had purified her affections. She was not overly attached to spiritual communications. She can be convicted neither of spiritual pride nor of an autocratic manner. She did not judge harshly those who failed; neither was she lax in her own standards.

In short, Rose still needed some purification before she could enter the unitive way, the highest stage in the spiritual life, but she needed less purification than most souls making progress in the illuminative way. Therefore, we may expect to see her enjoying unitive prayer from time to time even before definitely entering the unitive way, and that at a comparatively early age.

The ordinary prayer of Rose during these years of her adolescence was made in darkness, for the knowledge that she received was stripped of all accidents and images. Her soul rested tranquilly in God; gradually, the darkness became suffused with divine light. Still, it was not the light of day but the translucent pre-dawn sky that seemed to surround her. Her place of prayer, preferred above all others, was the quiet garden mottled with shadows. They and the star-pierced dome of heaven or the luminous mists of the Rímac River, according to the season, symbolized her inner state.

Light came to her from God in various ways outside the

time that she gave to formal prayer. Usually it was a sudden deepening of the understanding on a truth of faith. She read or heard something quite by accident; it penetrated her soul. Such lights passed quickly, but they left her with a clearer vision of the truth. Occasionally, light came to her over a longer period on some aspect of the spiritual life or the application of some phrase from the Gospel to a daily problem. These prolonged lights flooded her with the purest joy.

Some souls are instructed by God in symbolic or allegorical visions impressed on the imagination. These compare with the visual teaching found so practical on the natural level by modern educators. St. John Bosco and St. Frances Cabrini are two saints whom the divine Educator taught in this way. But the Holy Spirit used a different method with Rose, a method rather common among souls classified as mystics. This method is instruction by visions and apparitions accompanied by locutions. These locutions, being produced by God, produce great fruits and effect deep changes in the souls of those who hear them, and Rose was no exception to the rule.

Her visions were mostly of our Lady and the Infant Jesus or of her guardian angel, but since she had chosen St. Catherine of Siena as her spiritual mother, this charitable saint did not neglect her. As the months and years passed, St. Catherine often admonished or consoled her charge. Rose benefited from these visitations and referred them to her spiritual father, who questioned her minutely concerning them and passed his judgment on their origin. By her candid descriptions of these intimate workings of God in her soul, Rose saved herself from several pitfalls open to pious souls. By relying on his judgment she avoided the snares of self-deception and diabolical illusion. She practiced humility and obedience. She escaped the fate of those who, as St. Augustine says, run well but off the course.

Naturally open and submissive to her mother, Rose often

spoke of her experiences in prayer to Oliva. It was sometimes her impulsiveness that led to such disclosures; but sometimes it was her mother's questioning. Gradually, Oliva learned to detect every sign of joy or sorrow that passed over Rose's face and jump to her own conclusions as to its cause. If those conclusions were sometimes wrong, it is not surprising; but since they changed her attitude to Rose, they are important. In time, they made relations between herself and her daughter painful. At last they grew unbearable. Then the only solution was separation, and Oliva welcomed it. Such was the grief towards which Rose was rushing, borne unawares on the swift-flowing stream of events.

Oliva's tantrums were resumed as soon as Bernardina left home. Having married off one daughter, although to a poor man with no special mark of distinction, she now warmed to the task of settling Rose. If she had shown favor to the project before, she now exerted all her vigor to conclude it. Suitors were not wanting, thanks to Rose's attractions, but the young girl was bored by them. Their comings and goings aroused no comment at all, save a protest when some outing or *fiesta* was being planned. Then, knowing that every detail would be arranged in order to encourage the young man included in the party, she would try to stay at home. Absence was her best defense. Sometimes she pleaded, too, that it was against charity to give him hope, but these pleadings were of no use.

"You will come to your senses when you are too old to find a suitor, or when you have driven them all off. Now, do as I say."

Such were Oliva's words, sometimes uttered in shrill tones. Rose said nothing in reply but went on seeking ways of evading parties. Sometimes prayer obtained for her what protests could not; at the last moment she would be atttacked by fever or beset by sick persons needing her help. However, she did not always receive such timely deliverance, and in the desperation of the hour she sometimes acted hastily. Once she went to her parents' bedroom and rubbed Oliva's eyelash cosmetic, a lead compound, into her eyes. Inflamed and swollen, they soon presented such a spectacle that her mother shrank with horror from showing her to society. So Rose stayed at home. In her fury at what seemed to her waywardness and folly, Oliva punished Rose violently. Snatching up Gaspar's heavy knotted stick, which he reserved for his son's castigation, she beat the young girl until her strength failed.

Soon after this incident, as soon in fact as Rose's eyes were again presentable, another party was planned. As usual, a gallant young *caballero* was waiting in the wings. Once on the scene, he would exert his charms on Rose. Hoping to be spared this embarrassment, Rose asked to be left at home. A blow was Oliva's reply. Still, Rose was not defeated. She was working in the kitchen and had removed her shoes; as if by accident, she stepped on the hearth. It was aglow with hot coals and her foot was burned. Her ruse succeeded, for she could not appear in company with bandages. But her brother, Francisco, had seen her look down as she stepped on the coals. He was by this time at the obnoxious stage, a spoiled and self-important eleven-year-old. Seeking to re-instate himself, for he had just been caught devouring a piece of candied fruit intended for the meal, he clamored to his mother.

"Mother, Rose stepped on the coals purposely. I saw her look at them before she burned her foot!"

Instantly, Oliva's annoyance at what she had taken for an accident changed to rage. Seizing Gaspar's stick, she pounded Rose until Isabel interfered. Diverted into a quarrel with her mother, Oliva stopped the beating and Rose limped silently to her room. She had won again, for she stayed at home that day; but Oliva did not forget the ruse. From that hour, she grew severe and caustic with Rose even when there was no reason. Her attitude was sharpened notably by her discovery, at the close of one *fiesta* which she had forced Rose to attend, that an extra pin had mysteriously made its way into her scalp. Recriminations and another beating were Rose's lot, but she took them serenely. Besides the fact that she felt the rift between herself and Oliva keenly, however, she had one other fact to face that caused her regret. She could no longer use this extra pin in her rose crowns, for her mother forbade it.

For some weeks she bore this deprivation without comment; then, one afternoon when Oliva was in a mellow mood, she confided her secret.

"Mama, I shall tell you why I put that pin through my scalp," she said. "I am sorry that I have displeased you so by doing it, but I am sure that when I explain my reason you will approve. After all, it has done me no harm."

"If it has done you no harm, that is not your fault. An infection might have set it. But tell me your reason, I am sure that it is curious."

"Well, Mama dear, you know that when I wear those crowns of roses, your friends give me many compliments. These compliments inflate my pride and vanity, causing me painful struggles. I had an accident one day which gave me the idea of making a little mortification for myself during parties. This detracts from the force of my movements of vanity by distracting me from them. I unite the slight discomfort I feel from the pin with the torments of Jesus crowned with thorns. So, it is useful for souls, too. Now, are you so displeased?"

"Well, perhaps not. But it was a dangerous thing to do. That rusty pin might have made you ill. Did it not give you a headache?"

Rose smiled.

"I admit that it did, Mama, but as you know, I have

suffered before from pains that were far worse. So I do not mind this."

"You need not put it in the present tense!" exclaimed Oliva. "You are not doing it now! And you need not insinuate by your remark that I have made you suffer so much by treating your scurvy with mercury. It is an approved remedy; I do not understand why it went wrong in your case."

"I was not thinking of that at all when I spoke, Mama," answered Rose hastily. "I was recalling at the moment the pain I suffered from my ears and the attacks of migraine I have. I am sure that your treatment did me good. After all, the scurvy has not come back, has it?"

Oliva shook her head, somewhat mollified.

"No; that is true." Then, seeing Rose about to speak again, she added: "Well, perhaps I shall not make you wear the roses any more. Some less showy flower may not draw so many compliments upon you; still, I do not know. Perhaps I am mistaken to give in to your whim. After all, it may be more a temptation to disobedience than vanity."

Rose looked at her mother with sorrowful eyes.

"Ah, Mama! You know that I obey you willingly in everything except the question of parties and suitors."

"And costumes. But what were you about to say? I could tell that you were planning to ask me something. I know that calculating look."

"I was going to ask you, Mama, whether I could not wear a penitential band, since you do not approve of my using the pin. It would have the added advantage that I could use it oftener, and the discomfort would be evenly disposed."

Oliva frowned.

"You do enough penance; but if your director permits it, yes. On condition that you go on wearing the roses."

Rose smiled.

"Thank you, Mama! With pleasure!"

Oliva, who had no idea that Rose meant a head band, broke off the conversation abruptly.

"You thank me when I give you your own way. Do you call that submission to the will of God?"

Rose laughed and laid her hand gently on Oliva's shoulder. Then she hurried to find her grandmother, so that they might go to the college to find her director. Armed as she thought with her mother's permission for a head band, she could not wait to ask him for his approval. Already she had it all planned in her mind. She would have to make the band herself, for they were so much rarer than arm or leg bands that they were not manufactured for sale. It would be a plain silver band adjustable at the back so that she could tighten or loosen it at will, and three rows of nails driven inward through it. Nothing would appear through her veil.

"Ah, my Jesus," she whispered, "now I shall be able to keep you company in the midst of frivolity. I shall have your crown of thorns to wear for the souls you have suffered and died to save; your souls and mine. I am so happy!"

Rose's director gave her permission to make the head band, but restricted her use of it to several times a week. To safeguard her against infection, he ordered that she rotate the position of the points so that some time would elapse between days when they touched a given spot on her head. But Rose could not as yet afford the silver band and nails, so she set to work with fresh zest at her gardening. By selling extra flowers she hoped to save the money that she needed, without contributing any less from this source to the family income. While she worked she prayed, and her patience was amply rewarded. She noted with gratitude that her flowers kept blooming beyond the usual time. As the days passed into weeks, this phenomenon drew comments and orders from persons who had never come to her before. Soon she was able to buy the silver band and nails and make her penitential band. When she wore it, she felt considerable pain but found it bearable. Whenever she was tempted to vanity she pressed it as though to adjust her veil, and the temptation fled.

Rose wore her head band for several months without anyone knowing it. As she thought that Oliva understood its general nature, she did not show it to her. Perhaps in this there was a certain self-defense, for she knew that even though she had given permission for it, her mother was apt to reverse her decision when confronted by the band itself. However, Oliva did see it, and under circumstances not apt to increase her approval. She had thought that Rose intended to buy an arm or leg band such as were in common use. The idea of her daughter wearing a head band had never entered her mind. As far as she was concerned, the contraption had only one feature to recommend it: it was made of silver and so would not rust. The danger of Rose suffering from infection as a result of her penance was, therefore, less than it would otherwise have been, had she obtained a band of some other metal.

The discovery came about due to a disrespectful remark of Francisco's. Don Gaspar reached for his stick to belabor him and the boy fled. Rose stepped between him and her father to intercede for him. Don Gaspar had raised his stick and begun to bring it down with force; when he saw Rose before him he could not stop the blow from striking her. It fell on her forehead and instantly three streams of blood trickled down from beneath her veil. Her father, horrified, tried to restrain her but she ran from the room. She needed every instant, for Oliva was in pursuit of her. Before she could stop the blood from flowing. Oliva reached her bedroom. This time there were no cries or recriminations; her mother simply took the head band from Rose without a word and stalked away. It was this confiscation that Rose had feared; whether or not she anticipated Oliva's next act we do not know. That was to go straight to her director with the head band, still stained with blood.

"Reverend Father, is this the kind of instrument of penance that a young girl should wear? My daughter tells me that she has permission for it. It is far too sharp; it has caused wounds all around her head."

The priest took the band from Oliva with a shocked expression. He assumed that the nails inserted in it would have been filed off flat. To his chagrin he saw that they were sharply pointed. Because Rose had wanted a silver band, she had gone to the silversmith for the materials. He had made the nails to order, shorter than pins but pointed like ordinary nails. The penance which Rose had performed in wearing her head band was, therefore, much more severe than her director had intended.

When he had explained this to Oliva, he pulled a bell rope that hung near the door of his office. A lay brother entered and with a single sweep of his downcast eyes, he saw the bloodstained head band and his Rector's hand shaking with emotion.

"Brother," said the Rector firmly, "bring me a file."

When Oliva left the college, the points of Rose's head band were no more. The nails, filed flat and smooth, could still be felt by Rose, but they opened no wounds. The small discomfort which her band now caused her was for Rose the severest penance of all. She wore it that way the rest of her life, more in memory of the time when it had caused her suffering than as an instrument of penance. Even when she tightened the band as much as she could, it could not fit close to her head because the nail stubs held it off.

To Rose's joy, the threatened battle with the Dutch and English did not take place. The galleon bearing her brothers sailed back to Callao unscathed. However, the two young men did not return to live at home. The taste of independence and adventure had whetted their appetites; the inactivity of former days now seemed insipid. Don Gaspar understood and sympathized with their craving for freedom. He himself had left home as a mere stripling and had never regretted it. He therefore made the sacrifice of their companionship and money which had at least taken the edge off the family's poverty. His act was unselfish and his sons were grateful to him for it. Oliva's distaste was definite. She feared for their moral and physical safety; still more, she needed the pittance they had earned. At times she really lacked the necessaries to put on the table.

It was a crisis such as this that led to Rose's first miracle, which should have drawn the family bonds closer but served instead to strain them.

There came a day when there was nothing to serve for supper but soup and bread. Mariana had reported that even the honey, a cheap staple food in Peru at that time, was finished, and Oliva went down the cellar ladder to verify that it was. By the light of a lamp she and the maid searched every nook of the storage room for another crock. Their search was futile. With a heart pierced with grief the mother climbed the ladder again and went to the patio to cry. She could not go to her own room because Gaspar was sick in bed. She did not dare let him see what his illness was costing. Isabel was confined to her room; the children were playing at a neighbor's; Rose and Fernando were at Santo Domingo's, finishing her sacristy work. Andrés had gone to the center of town; a position as bookkeeper was open and he was applying for it.

"Where is the supper, Mother?" asked Ramón in surprise. He had taken a short cut through the dining room and found nothing on the table but a double plate of bread.

Although his question was innocent enough, Oliva flushed with anger.

"That is enough from you!" she cried with tears in her voice "Is it my fault if we have no money? You are not the only one who is hungry." Then, seeing the look of consternation on her son's face, she added more kindly: "Ramón, go down to the cellar and look in the honey crock. Perhaps there are some scrapings left."

Ramón obeyed; but a few minutes later he returned scowling.

"It is perfectly dry!"

"Well, we shall have to make the best of it," his mother answered. "Thank God, we are invited out for tomorrow."

"Is this all that we have to eat?" asked Andrés with a disgusted glance at the table.

"Mariana will bring the soup in a moment," said Oliva placatingly.

"Is there nothing else, Mother?" asked Fernando.

"There is nothing else," she replied, "unless you want to eat the two oranges that Mariana is taking to your father and grandmother."

Fernando lowered his eyes to hide the moisture gathering in them, but Oliva caught a glimpse of them and her heart softened in contrition.

"Since Francisco is so clever, let him go down and look in the crock for himself."

Francisco left the table to look. Soon he was back, glowering.

"It is as dry as a bone!"

"Mama," said Rose in a small voice, "if you tell me to, I shall take my turn and go down in the name of the Lord to see whether there is not some honey."

'What is the use?" asked Oliva. She looked at Rose, who returned her gaze pleadingly. "All right, Rose. Go down and see."

Rose left her place, picking up the honey jar from the sideboard as she walked to the door. The family sat gloomily at the table, waiting for their soup. Ramón offered the bread ironically to Andrés.

"Oh, no thank you, brother," said Andrés with an elegant bow. "I am waiting for the honey."

His remark ended in a gasp. Rose appeared at the table carrying the honey jar, full to the brim.

"There is a new barrel there beside the crock, Mama," she said.

"There is not!" exclaimed Andrés angrily. "The crock is right against the wall, and I stood on the other side in the only empty space."

"He is right!" cried Ramón and Francisco at the same time.

"What nonsense!" Oliva answered with a frown. She knew that a miracle had been worked by God to set a crock of honey where a few minutes before there had been none. She knew too, that Rose had obtained this miracle in answer to her prayer. But she did not think it well to say so.

"If Rose says there is a fresh barrel of honey beside the empty crock, she is telling the truth. I suppose this jarful that she has brought with her is only an illusion! Use your eyes for a change!"

Her words cut them. To be accused unjustly was more than they could bear. Resentment swelled bitterly within them.

"I have used my eyes, and there was no barrel of honey in the cellar!" cried Ramón, springing to his feet. "And I am going down to see where Rose got that honey!"

"No one is going to make a liar out of me!" roared Andrés, rising from the table too. "Wait for me, Ramón. I am going with you!"

"Me too!" piped Francisco petulantly. "I looked and there was no honey. I just don't believe it!"

One by one, those present climbed down the the ladder and made their way to the storage room. By the bright light of the lamp that was carried by Mariana they gazed in silence at the large barrel with its inner pottery lining and bright binding of braided straw.

"Well, my intelligent sons, are you satisfied?" asked Oliva. "Now, let us go upstairs and eat. Thanks to Rose, we have something for supper."

The family trooped up the ladder and gathered once more around the table. Oliva passed the honey to Andrés.

"No, thank you, Mother," he said coldly. "Like our saint, I am going to fast on bread and water."

Oliva looked sharply at her son; then she turned to Rose, who had broken a piece off a slice of bread and was beginning to eat it dry.

"Eat some honey tonight, Rose," she said quickly. "After all, it is you who have found it."

The rest of the meal passed in silence, but much thinking was in progress. When they had dispersed, Andrés called Ramón aside.

"Well, what do you think?" he asked.

"I do not like it," answered Ramón, scowling. "But it is too soon to say. Let us see whether anything else happens."

So, Rose's brothers, with the exception of Fernando, began to spy on her. Her slightest evidence of piety brought forth jibes and censure. She was going to excess in her prayer and penance. It was plain that she was opening her soul to delusions. Deceived by the devil, she would disgrace them all.

Soon their mistrust and resentment was increased by a second miracle. This time there was no bread, and Rose found the cupboard full, although the others had seen it empty a short time before. They ate; then, with the taste of this bread still in their mouths, they conferred secretly.

"Believe me, this will come to a head! She will end in the chambers of the Inquisition!"

This prediction, overheard by Francisco and repeated by him to his mother, filled Oliva with terror. From that moment she too began to doubt by what spirit Rose was led. She considered it her duty to watch her with tireless vigilance and to contradict her, try her and subject her to intense discipline. In her apprehension, Oliva looked with dread on the least manifestation of Rose's favor with God. The continual presence of flowers blooming out of season in her garden drove her to exasperation. They attracted great ladies from all over Lima who came to gaze and left to gossip. In anguish, she curtailed Rose's gardening time. Henceforth, she was to give almost all her daylight hours to needlework, excepting those which could not be spared from other duties. Rose obeyed. But her family's doubts undermined her sense of security. Soon she began to be assailed by fears and sorrows so heavy that in the darkness of the garden she lay prostrate beneath them.

"If it be possible, Father, let this cup pass from me," she prayed. But the cup did not pass. On the contrary, when she had drained what it held, she found it filled anew.

In the meantime, Archbishop Toribio was approaching the last phase of his life. His sadness over the refusal of the viceroy and *audiencia* to enforce the decree abolishing Indian personal service may be imagined. The controversy dragged on, each week producing its quota of disputations. In the midst of his fervent prayers for the king he received his reward from him in the form of a letter. Dated in Valladolid on October 7, 1602, it reached the archbishop early in 1603. It was almost as harsh as the rebuke which he had received publicly a few years before.

In this letter the king censured him for his outlandish act

in having held a Council without the presence of the viceroy and *audiencia*. He ordered him to give an account of all that had motivated him and the reason for ending the Council so abruptly.

Still, the archbishop had his consolations. Not the least of these was the opening of a new monastery for the Poor Clares. The foundation of this monastery was a project dear to his heart—so dear, in fact, that his heart was enshrined there after his death. His sister, Grimanesa, became a patroness of it; one of his nieces, her elder daughter, entered there.

The origin of the foundation is worth noting. A successful merchant, Francisco de Saldaña, came one day to the archbishop's office with a proposition so selfless that it left him momentarily stunned. This good man, who had amassed a small fortune by honest industry, wished to donate it all to the archbishop for the foundation of a refuge for women whose husbands had deserted them and for young girls without family or means. Living there honorably, they could be saved from destitution and possible moral ruin. Efforts were to be made to find worthy husbands for those who wished to marry but had been unable to do so because they had no dowry to offer.

The plan was too generous to be dismissed. After prolonged discussions, the home was founded and the first group of women and girls was housed there. The sum provided by the donor was more than this institution needed, so Toribio began to think of possible uses for his windfall. His archdiocese had so many wants that he could not decide which one to satisfy; then he thought of bringing the Poor Clares to Lima. He discussed it with Saldaña, who was delighted with the idea. Not only did he willingly give the extra money for this foundation, but also himself. Asking only the necessaries of life from the community, he offered his full-time services to them free of charge as long as he should live. Some additional funds were needed to finance the house, so several others joined him in his benefaction, among them Grimanesa.

It had come to Oliva's ears that Martin was to be professed as a lay brother of Santo Domingo and she immediately thought of Rose's great affection for him.

"Would you like to visit Brother Martin on his profession day?" Oliva asked Rose. "He has been too helpful to you for you to neglect giving him this mark of appreciation."

"Oh, Mama, I should be so happy if you would take me!" Rose exclaimed, flushing with pleasure.

After Martin's profession on June 2, 1603, he had more occasions to speak to Rose and she was able to share with him her grief at the long, fruitless dispute over Indian personal service. Although his compassion naturally went first to the Negro slaves, he was also agonized at the selfishness of the Spanish mine officials and *encomenderos*. With all his heart he desired justice for the Indians, whom he loved and pitied.

Both Martin and Rose began to hope anew when in the middle of 1603 they learned that the viceroy was transferred. Wishing to flee his compromising dilemma, he had asked for a recall, and the king gave in. He named him Governor of Mexico, in which capacity he had already acted once with credit. His move was an agile piece of dodging, and it showed perhaps more than any other of his acts, his innate weakness.

The new viceroy was Gaspar de Zuñiga y Acervedo, Count of Monterrey. The document appointing him was signed May 19, 1603, but it reached Lima much later. But even then, there was no sign of the viceroy. Poor health was the reason given.

Hoping that he would arrive soon, the citizens prepared to welcome him. They constructed five arches, decorated with scenes depicting the new viceroy's feats. This painting was a rush job, so the two or three artists then living in Lima prob-

ably shared the work. One of these, a Neapolitan named Angelino Medoro, had come to Lima only a short time before
with his tempestuous wife, María de Mesta. Both would one
day be close friends of Rose and of the family of Gonzalo de
la Maza, recently arrived from Spain.

Gonzalo de la Maza was Rose's signal benefactor. He it was
who introduced her to the artist, Angelino, and it was under
his roof that the artist painted the only authentic portrait of
St. Rose.

But all this was still in the mists of the future, and if Rose
thought of these decorated arches at all, it was to plead with
her parents that she be spared the outing which the family
was planning, to see them. The arches were costing the citizens of Lima a notable sum, so everyone wished to examine
the work and pronounce on its splendor.

Every day the people of Callao expected news of the viceroy's arrival. As the weeks dragged on, they thought of sending someone to Paita to welcome him. Pedro Sores de Ulloa
was chosen for this gracious role. July, August, September,
October and November went by. Still the viceroy did not
come. Finally, on December 8, at two in the afternoon, the
Count of Monterrey came. The people had waited for him so
long that they no longer felt much enthusiasm.

As Rose, Martin and Archbishop Toribio had hoped, the
new viceroy took some action in favor of the Indians. The
king's *cedula* abolishing their personal service had only made
their state worse. Not only were the men still forced into
mines and factories and fields by the *encomenderos*, but
women and children were now herded with them into service.
Reports reached Lima that in the provinces of Tucamán and
Paraguay even the old were forced into the *mita*.

An official visitor was sent; he found the facts worse than
this. The Indians were not even allowed to marry. They had
no free time to attend catechism classes or go to Mass on

Sundays and feast days. Nothing but work was their lot. As they worked from dawn to dark, they could not even raise a few garden vegetables and herbs for themselves. The prices of the food sold to them were fantastic.

When the visitor submitted his findings to the viceroy, they were soon public knowledge. Rose increased her time of prayer and multiplied her acts of penance. At night she found that she could not stay awake as late as she wished, so she tied her long, shining hair to a spike in the wall of her room. Then, kneeling at some distance from the wall, she prayed facing a large wooden cross which hung opposite. If she dozed for a moment and swayed forward, the tug on her hair wakened her.

As a result of the visitation ordered by the Count of Monterrey, the worst abuses against the Indians were rectified. Many *encomenderos*, fearing the loss of their holdings, acted more humanely. The governors, uneasy as to their own posts, were more conscientious in enforcing the laws.

At this time Lima was stirred by strong emotions of piety: a localized eruption of fervor caught the popular fancy. Public confessions of sin, processions of penitents scourging themselves energetically in the streets, and an abrupt closing of gambling houses were some of its features. Others less conspicuous were no less sincere and more lasting, such as an increase in Lima's devotion to Our Lady of the Rosary. What caused this phenomenon, in which Rose and her family were caught up with their townsfolk? The cause was twofold.

In November, 1605, a strange procession made its way from the city gate to the *Calle de Santo Domingo*, passing the Flores home and entering the Church of St. Dominic. It was led by a tall man with a well nourished look. He was clad in rough animal skins; his beard was long and his hair streamed behind him as he walked. He carried a cross formed of two timber beams, coarse and unplaned. Behind him walked his ten followers dressed in the same way, their skin blackened by exposure to the sun. Unlike their leader, they were emaciated and showed signs of great fatigue. They had come on foot from Callao to thank Our Lady of the Rosary for their deliverance from a deserted island.

Who were these Robinson Crusoes and how did they find themselves stranded? They were passengers from a ship which had hit calm weather and, with provisions almost depleted, had beeen carried to an island. The eleven men had offered to go ashore to search for food and water. Armed with a few weapons, they had braved the wild, only to find that the island contained nothing but jungle. There were a few berries and fruit trees, but no other food.

The adventurers cut their way back to the shore to report their findings, only to see the ship disappearing in the distance. The wind had shifted as soon as they went ashore and the captain had put out from the island. They were abandoned.

For two years they eked out a painful existence on this island, living in constant danger of death. Besides the savage beasts, they had hunger and storm and sun as their tormentors. They were devoured by insects, maddened by monotony and inaction. Only one among them never lost hope. This was the corpulent man with the streaming locks who now led their procession. He was Martin Barravenido, a native of Fuente del Maestre in Extremadura. A man of firm faith and practical wisdom, he had refused to give up his hold on life. He was devoted to Mary and her rosary; in this he put his trust. If he continued to pray for deliverance, she would not fail him.

Little by little, he had restored the spirits of most of his companions. On that deserted island they knelt each day and prayed before a crude wooden cross which Barravenido had made. At last, one joyful day as they peered at the horizon they saw the sails of a ship. It sighted their signals and approached them rapidly. In delirious jubilation they shouted and waved. But one of them was on his knees, weeping his thanks to our Lady. It was the feast of the Most Holy Rosary, 1605.

At Barravenido's urging the men had made a vow. If our Lady delivered them, they would make a pilgrimage of thanksgiving to her chapel of the Rosary in St. Dominic's Church, Lima. It was this vow that they now fulfilled as they plodded to Lima from Callao. Exhausted as they were by two years of frightful malnutrition, they had wished to make this gesture of gratitude to Mary.

That their pilgrimage would draw all eyes upon them had been farthest from their minds. But even at the seaport they saw that such was the case. People had flocked from Lima to welcome them. As they passed, people knelt and recited the rosary with tears of devotion. It was as good as a mission. All Lima and Callao seemed to press after them into St. Dominic's; what had been meant as a private visit by eleven men had become a *fiesta*. Thousands of rosaries were recited that day before the miraculous statue. Our Lady and the Infant Jesus showered graces on their clients; the confessionals were full and long lines of penitents waited to be absolved.

Rose, who had prepared the altar of our Lady that morning with special love, felt an inexpressible joy as she joined the throng in prayer in the chapel which was her charge. Like the rest of Lima, Oliva and the boys had followed the pilgrims and wished to make their thanksgiving with them. Even Isabel, who had been confined to bed for some weeks, forced herself to walk the short distance to St. Dominic's.

On the following day Rose met Martin Barravenido when he came again to our Lady's chapel of the Rosary. She was just finishing her sacristy work when Brother Martin de Porres brought him in to meet her. With accents rich in emotion, the grateful man retold his story. Rose listened with tears of joy in her eyes.

"And now, what do you think I should do to repay my debts of thanks for this favor?" he asked Rose.

"I do not know," she answered softly. Then her eyes flashed. "A whole lifetime would not be enough!" she added with feeling.

"That is what I have been thinking," he said. "And Brother Martin is of the same opinion. May I ask your prayers for my intention?"

Rose agreed gladly and her new acquaintance thanked her earnestly. As he turned away, Rose looked at Brother Martin questioningly and made a gesture as though smoothing his habit. Martin laughed and nodded, his teeth flashing in the shadows of the doorway.

"A little patience, *señorita Rosa*. A little patience, and many prayers."

Rose said the promised prayers and practiced patience, but she did not have to wait long to learn their issue. Only three weeks later the middle-aged Barravenido had taken his place among the lay brother novices at Holy Rosary. It was a courageous act, one worthy of so generous a soul. Through the years of his postulancy and novitiate Rose saw him seldom, but as soon as he was professed he was made porter of the convent with Brother Martin. It was a strange coincidence that threw them together in their work, for both were *"fray Martín."* He and Martin de Porres became fast friends. His humble, simple piety won the admiration of Martin de Porres, who often related to Rose conversations which he had had with Barravenido.

Little more than a month after this event, when Barravenido's vocation to the Dominican Order was still the latest news, the people of Lima again experienced a mass conversion. But before this a quite different crisis arose in the Flores household, one which shook both Rose and her mother to the depths. It began with Mariana knocking urgently on Oliva's bedroom door one morning while she was fitting a new dress on little Juana.

"Enter!" she exclaimed, "and do not beat the door down! I can hear you quite well!"

"My Lady, it is the archbishop's servant!" Mariana gasped. "He gave me this note for you from Archbishop Toribio!"

Oliva blanched and took the heavy wax-sealed parchment from the maid with an angular gesture. All her vitality left her in an instant; she shook with terror and it seemed to her that her spine would crumple.

"What is the matter, Mama?" asked Juana, pressing against her knees to peer at the archiepiscopal seal. "Why has Archbishop Toribio written you a letter?"

"I do not know, child," answered Oliva in choked syllables.

Oliva took up her scissors and broke the seal free from one end of the parchment. Her lips moved in agitated prayer. She had no doubt as to the contents of Toribio's message. Fatherly and beloved though he was, as Archbishop of Lima he was nominal head of the Inquisition in the New World. In his compassion for Rose he was doubtless warning her that her case would soon come under consideration if she did not put an end to her extraordinary ways.

Now she had the parchment opened out; it was as Oliva feared. If it were convenient, the archbishop would call to see her on the following afternoon at four o'clock. Although it would give him pleasure to see all the family and impart his blessing to them, he especially wished to speak to Rose.

CHAPTER EIGHT

The Marriage of the Lamb

How Oliva, Gaspar and Isabel lived through the next few hours they never quite knew. As for Rose and the other children, they were told nothing of Archbishop Toribio's coming visit. With the help of Gaspar and her mother, Oliva managed to insure that they would be away at the time, all except Rose.

"I am to have a distinguished caller this afternoon who has particularly asked for you," she said. "So you must be at home."

There was nothing unusual in this remark; it was one that Rose had heard a hundred times before. She did not ask who the caller was to be; it made little difference to her. The routine was always the same. At first, Oliva received the visitor; then, on her request, Rose was sent for. There were saccharine greetings and preposterous compliments. As soon as she could, Rose withdrew.

Despite her fears, Oliva achieved a composed appearance for the archbishop's visit. She made Rose wear her finest and most striking costume. She ordered Mariana and Rose to decorate the front gate, the doorways and windows of the house with garlands. Above the door leading into the living room, which was the only room Oliva had in which she could entertain guests, they had hung a cross of red and yellow roses, surrounded by sprays of fern and orange blossoms. Oliva knew that the archbishop would be pleased by this gesture in his honor, no matter what his errand. Such decorations were often used by her wealthy friends, for they frequently entertained the great.

From the moment of Toribio's arrival, Oliva was stunned. He had not come alone or with his secretary, as she imagined he would. Instead, he brought with him his young niece, María de Quiñones. Oliva had met her only once and then only for a few moments at a reception, so she was bewildered at this visit. If Grimanesa had come with her brother, Oliva would have been less astonished; in fact, she would have been pleased and flattered. But for Archbishop Toribio to come with his niece and ask for Rose at once, this sent her imagination scurrying. What could it mean?

She had not long to wonder. After a few remarks about Gaspar, Isabel and herself, the archbishop came to the discussion of the children. So! Matthias and young Gaspar had enlisted with the Chilean troops! And they had remained in the army! And her other daughters? Ah, yes. She had lost a daughter at Quive. The archbishop's face saddened. These deaths of the young are so hard to bear, so difficult to understand. But we must rely on the wisdom of God who does all things well and orders all for our good. Her daughter Bernardina had married? Indeed! He would pray for her future happiness and that of her favored husband. Ramón, Andrés and Fernando were employed? Good.

By now there was no one left to ask about except the three youngest children and Rose. Oliva was alarmed. Her intuition clamored that Toribio was about to introduce the subject that she dreaded; yet, what could he say in the presence of his niece?

"Has Rose decided what is her vocation?" the prelate asked with a broad smile. "She is not promised in marriage?"

Oliva blanched and shook her head. His words left her in little doubt as to what would follow—words as painful to the mother, in their way, as those which she had feared. He had come, not to warn Rose, but to lure her into a convent!

"No, Your Lordship," she replied. "Rose is young; one cannot say how her mind will turn."

"She is very pious," said the archbishop gently. "And so given to prayer. Has she never thought of the religious life?"

"The cloister is so delightful for those suited to it!" exclaimed María enthusiastically. "My sister, Béatriz, is in heaven with her Poor Clare vocation!"

Oliva grew still paler. The vocation of Béatriz was the archbishop's joy. She had flouted the *hidalgos* of Lima by resolving to take the veil in his cherished Poor Clare foundation. Not only that, but she was the first to do so. As Oliva thought of the opportunities that the archbishop's niece had given up, her heart hardened. Her lips drew back into a thin, firm line. No one, archbishop or not, would dictate to her as to Rose's future.

But she reckoned without Rose herself. So far, the archbishop had addressed his questions to Oliva. Now he turned to Rose.

"And you, my daughter, what do you say? Does the religious life attract you? Ah, if I could but count you among my Poor Ladies of St. Clare! They are my consolation and a source of hidden strength to the archdiocese."

Rose, overwhelmed with joy, opened her lips to answer him, but Oliva cut her short.

"Your Lordship, my daughter is not meant for the cloister. She has her vocation here at home, caring for our own family and the many sick poor who come to her. Why, so far this week alone, she has helped more than three hundred persons! Later, she will marry. Already some very noble *caballeros* have offered her their hands."

"I am sure that they have," Toribio answered, "but if you will pardon me for saying so, her work for the sick poor can scarcely be termed a vocation. It seems to me that perhaps she is attracted to the religious life."

Turning again to Rose, he looked at her as though to read her soul.

"My Lord is right," Rose answered with a simple nod. "It is true that I have often longed for the retirement and consecration of the religious state. Still, as my mother says, I have much to do here at home caring for the poor who come for medical help, as well as for the members of our family."

As she spoke of the poor, her eyes shone and her cheeks flushed.

"I would miss this work exceedingly; but if I am called to the cloister, God's will is all. I would willingly forfeit everything for this treasure."

She might have said more, but Oliva had heard enough. She was convinced that Rose would agree to enter the Poor Clares in another moment if she did not intervene. Don Toribio was about to speak again; doubtless, he would tell Rose that the cloister was God's will for her.

"We cannot thank Your Lordship enough for taking such an interest in Rose," she began rapidly. "But as you see, our circumstances are humble and we are reduced to the scantiest resources. It is this poverty that keeps Rose in suspense as to her vocation, more than anything else. We can provide no suitable dowry."

"Well, that is no obstacle if Rose wishes to enter the Poor Clares," said the archbishop with a genial smile and a deprecatory wave of the hands. "We can easily dispense with it."

Oliva suppressed a gasp. Dispense with Rose's dowry! Was there anything that Toribio would not do?

"That is most generous, but I fear that the question of our poverty still remains. Rose's embroidery and sewing provide much of our income. Then too, several members of our household are often infirm, and Rose takes care of them."

Don Toribio parried. "You have another growing daughter, my lady, and sons who are employed. Surely Rose's earnings are not essential to the household. And one so adept as yourself in the arts of homemaking will not have failed to learn the care of the sick."

This was too much for Oliva. If anyone but the archbishop had been the speaker, she would have gone into a tantrum. Now, as she answered him, her voice shook.

"I am sorry; it is impossible. Her grandmother is too attached to her; she would never let anyone else attend her. No, my daughter will not enter the Poor Clares nor any convent, although we are grateful to Your Lordship for taking such a paternal interest in her future. In my opinion, she will find her vocation in the married state."

"Ah then, I have been mistaken," said Toribio sadly. "I cannot hide from you that it is a great disappointment.

Standing, he took Rose's hand while she knelt to receive his blessing. "The fairest rose in my garden," he thought.

Aloud, he said: "Sometimes the divine Gardener must be patient. He may have to wait a long time for his choicest blossom, but while waiting, his pleasure in it only grows. So it will be with this Rose."

Rose flushed and lowered her eyes. Her heart was ready to burst. To think that Archbishop Toribio wanted *her* for his foundation of Poor Clares, and she could not go! And he would even have dispensed her from bringing a dowry! What words could convey her gratitude?

"My humble thanks and prayers go with you, my Lord," she said, scarcely trusting her voice. "I have always prayed much and offered sacrifices for Your Lordship's intentions, but now and for the rest of my life I shall never be able to do enough."

"Thank you, my daughter," answered Toribio. "The rest of your life. . . . " He looked down at the fresh young face, radiant with the bloom of the first years of womanhood. His smile was tinged with weariness.

"Ah, that is said so quickly," he continued, glancing ruefully at Oliva and his niece. "As for myself, I am near the end of my course. I count on the prayers of all this pious Christian family and especially yours, *señorita Rosa*, as we say in the *Ave Maria*, now and at the hour of my death."

Tears gathered and glistened in Rose's thick lashes. She nodded and curtsied slightly but could not speak.

Don Toribio looked around the room. "Have we forgotten anything?"

"There was just your breviary," his niece said.

They left with little ceremony. At the gate, Archbishop Toribio stopped and looked back. It was the last time that he was to see the Flores home in his life. His next gaze would be from heaven; and then, it would be to find Rose kneeling before his picture, her eyes pleading and full of sorrow.

"Good Father of my soul, you who in your lifetime wished to give me the joy of consecrating myself to Jesus Christ, pray for me now and obtain for me the permission I need."

On the night of Archbishop Toribio's visit, after having shed some tears on her own account (a rare occurrence, for her tenderness was mostly for others), Rose made a resolution. She would ask her director and all the priests to whom she had gone to confession whether, in their opinion, God was calling her to the cloister. If their answer was "yes," she would go to the Poor Clares in spite of her mother's opposition. Surely, if all the priests who knew her soul were agreed that she should enter, Oliva would come around.

Taking Fernando into her confidence, she obtained his services as escort for her visits. She began by calling at the Jesuit college. Her director, on learning of Archbishop Toribio's visit and offer, was emphatic that she should go to the Poor Clares.

Consoled by this approval, she walked back with Fernando to the convent of the Holy Rosary. There she spoke with the priests to whom she had made her confessions almost daily over the years. One by one they gave their opinions; all were in favor of her entering. However, it seemed to some of them that it would be more prudent to go to a long established community rather than a new foundation. The greater order and peace in the older community would make the atmosphere more congenial to prayer.

Rose was overwhelmed with joy, as she had been when first she heard Toribio's invitation. Now, she wished to consult her director at once on this new suggestion; would Fernando take her back to the college? He made no difficulty; on the contrary, he wanted to have the matter settled as soon as possible and so complied with her wish.

"Let us finish our journeys this afternoon," he said. "Who knows when we shall have another chance? There should be no delay in deciding a vocation; if there is, it is often lost. And anyway, even if you did not lose it, you would always be about the house like a ghost. Deliver us from that!" he added with an affectionate grin.

Actually, he felt a bit uneasy. What would his sister's director say of this return trip? Had he not given his opinion already? Perhaps he had even gone to the chancery office to see Archbishop Toribio! And, should Rose have asked her confessors after her director? It seemed to him that, if she wished to consult them, she should have asked his permission, too.

As it happened, the youth was right. To Rose's dismay, her director was piqued at her for having consulted others, for both the reasons that had occurred to Fernando.

"When you have heard your spiritual father, there is no need to seek out more advice," he told her sternly. "Such an act shows a great lack of faith and obedience!"

Shocked and distressed at his misunderstanding of her motives, Rose explained that she had consulted them only to satisfy her mother. She knew that Oliva would never change her opinion for her director alone, if she had not heeded even the archbishop. Rose's only chance of success was to marshall all the support that she could for her cause, she claimed.

"But you are not going to tell your mother first!" protested the priest sharply. "You know from experience that she will not give you up! Enter first and explain later; it is the only way. Tell your grandmother; she will approve. If anyone can win your mother's consent to the accomplished fact, she can."

Rose nodded, but with misgivings. She was reluctant to hurt her mother.

"What of my father?" she asked. "I suppose that if I cannot tell my mother beforehand, I should do the same in his case."

"It is hard, I know," her director said more gently. "But it would be more prudent not to confide in him. Has he not been pressing you to marry?"

"Very well, Father; but what do you think of this opinion of my confessors? Should I still go to the Poor Clares?"

"On second thought, no. I agree with the other suggestion. I know the prioress of the Augustinian nuns well; if I ask her to do so, she will arrange to accept you without a dowry."

Rose began to thank the priest; then he interrupted her.

"But I must warn you, Rose, I can no longer direct you once you have entered. You must have a director who follows the spirituality of your order."

Rose was astonished and pained, for she was fond of her spiritual father and he had understood her soul. Still, she saw the logic behind his words.

"Be of good cheer," he told her as she left the college. "I shall go this very day to see Mother Prioress. She will arrange about the dowry and fix the day of your entrance. You can send your brother to the convent to find out what she has decided, since you will scarcely have a chance to go there yourself without being noticed."

"But Father, are you certain that Mother Prioress will receive me?" asked Rose.

"If Archbishop Toribio wishes you for his Poor Clares and I myself vouch for you, that is recommendation enough. Do not worry; I have already told her about you."

Three days later, Fernando called on Mother Prioress and learned that Rose was accepted. The details had already been arranged; she was to enter that Sunday morning after the eight o'clock Mass. She need not think of the dowry; the council, chapter and archbishop had dispensed her from bringing one.

On hearing Toribio's name, Rose's elation was pricked. She would have preferred to go to his convent of Poor Clares, since he had wished it so. She knew that he must have felt pangs of disappointment when told that her choice was not the Poor Clares. But she brushed this thought aside, telling herself that when she had entered she would write him a letter of thanks, explaining that her choice had been made under obedience.

Glancing keenly at her, Fernando sensed her moment of sorrow. His countenance softened.

"Do not forget to pray for me when you are there in peace and quiet," he said. "I could wish for some, myself; and I think that soon I may take steps to find it," he added. "I am going to join the army as soon as our parents give me their permission."

"To find peace?" asked Rose with a smile.

"I am sure that I shall have more of it there than here," laughed the youth grimly.

Early that Sunday morning, Rose and Fernando aroused

themselves and dressed elegantly as though to attend Mass at Santo Domingo's. In the half-light, they met in the *patio*.

"Here; let me carry your luggage," said Fernando.

With a smile, Rose's brother took the small box containing her effects and hid it in the folds of his cloak.

"Now, let us go. Are you ready?"

Rose nodded. Just then, she had no voice. For a minute or two they walked in silence, but as they were about to pass Santo Domingo's, Rose laid her hand on Fernando's wrist.

"Brother, please let me pay one last visit to Our Lady of the Rosary."

"Very well, Rose, but make it brief. We have not much time to spare."

Rose went into the chapel and knelt before the beloved statue. Fernando stationed himself at the church door, from which he could see the front gate of their house. As the minutes dragged on, he grew impatient. Three times he went to call Rose; she seemed not to notice him. At last he strode angrily up to her.

"You will have plenty of time to pray in the convent," he snapped. 'Come; you are making us late."

Rose looked up at him, troubled and anxious.

"I should certainly like to leave, Fernando, but I cannot move."

"Nonsense!" said her brother. "Here, let me help you."

Taking her by the elbow, he tried to raise her. She did not budge. He tried again, exerting all his strength. It was useless.

"If God is doing this, find out why," he ordered savagely.

Rose turned to the miraculous statue. She already guessed the cause of her predicament.

"Good Mother, if you deliver me, I promise you to go back to my mother and live at home with my parents as long as you order me to do so, instead of in the convent."

Instantly, the young girl's limbs grew flexible. At once she rose to her feet and followed Fernando from the church. Outside the door he stopped, looking down at her in wordless wrath.

"I am sorry to have caused you so much trouble," she said, "but evidently it is not the will of God and our Lady that I should enter the cloister. I must stay at home, at least for the time being."

"You and your miracles!" he exclaimed, still seething. When he had gained some control of his voice, he made a gesture towards the church. "Well, if you are not going to the convent, at least you are still Catholic. It is Sunday, and we have not been to Mass."

When Rose and her brother reached home, they found that Isabel had not yet told Oliva of her intended flight. There was, accordingly, no real reason for her to hear of it. But Rose was too candid by nature to hide the facts from her mother; so, as soon as she was astir, she told her everything. Oliva was hurt, but the fact that our Lady herself had intervened a second time in favor of her opinion acted as a soothing agent. She thought that the prohibition against entering the convent implied marriage; and knowing that Rose wished only to do the will of God, she felt confident that she would now give up her stubborn refusal to accept any suitor. When Rose spoke of going to the college to explain the new decision to her director, however, Oliva grew annoyed.

"There is no use in that. Write him a letter instead. If he reads it to the end, he will perhaps be convinced. But there can never be a question of his directing you again. You have compromised him before the archbishop and the prioress. No priest could overlook that; his dignity would not permit it."

Rose was about to protest that her director was humble, but she sensed that her mother perhaps had another reason for insisting on the point. The plan of having Rose enter without telling her had been his. Oliva would not soon forget this. She would always feel uneasy while Rose was directed by him.

Accordingly, Rose fell in with her mother's desires. She gave up the idea of seeing the priest. She had already hurt her mother by going so far without her knowledge and against her will. To compensate for this hurt was her duty in justice and charity, as it was also her pleasure and consolation.

But she now had to look for another director. After a delay she found one in the Jesuit, Father Villalabos. To go to him for advice grew increasingly hard, however, for her grandmother was no longer able to make the trip on foot and Oliva did not wish to do so. Rose had to depend on one of her brothers to escort her. Fernando was the only possibility, but Oliva no longer trusted him since he had shared in Rose's attempt to enter the convent.

Scarcely had Oliva's wounded heart begun to heal than a religious revival shook Lima. It came at a perfect time, from Rose's point of view, although she would not have thought of that. Like the rest of her family, she took part in it without noticing that it helped restore peace between herself and her mother. When it was over, they resumed their daily life as though the incident of Rose's attempted flight from home to the cloister had not occurred. The soothing interval lasted until the first time that a party was planned. Then Oliva learned that Rose's return home had no bearing on her social life or lack of it. It implied no plan to marry.

The cause of the revival which gripped Lima was a Franciscan friar named Francis de Solano, a missionary in the purest sense of the word. He had a mission from God to preach the Gospel to the poor, and he lived that mission. Like St. Toribio, he tramped the South American forests and mountains, seeking the Indians, who were his children by preference. Nevertheless, on occasion he poured forth the fire of charity on others, and his charismatic gifts lent force to his words. When there was need, God supported his words with divine power to bring holy fear and penance into hard hearts.

His reputation for sanctity soared when, in 1600, he preached repentance to Arequipa's people, threatening them with scourges if they remained in their sins. His threat and pleadings were ignored. God's reply followed. In mid-February the volcano Omate erupted. Then another more distant volcano began its rumbling on February 18. They grew so uproarious that no one in the district could sleep. Brought by force to their knees, the tardy penitents prayed for mercy. The earth shook convulsively; the sky was covered with fog; a white ash, formed by small particles blown from the craters, fell on the city. A third of the Spaniards fled; with them went most of the Indians of the *mita*.

All this was still in the minds of the people of Lima when, a scant month after Martin Barravenido's pilgrimage to the chapel of Our Lady of the Rosary, St. Francis Solano emerged from his convent cell with a frown on his face. It was time for Lima to repent of her reckless ways. If she did not, she would perish from the earth.

"What is sin," asked the Franciscan of his audience, "and what is its punishment? The fires of hell! Hell was created to be a place of torment for sinners, created by a God whose wisdom and power are endless! You have read of the tortures borne by the martyrs; you have heard of the cruelty of pirates; you have seen your loved ones prostrate on beds of sickness, their bodies burning with fever, their tongues parched! You yourselves have been ill; you have suffered. You know what suffering is.

"Yet, suffering in this world, violent though it may be, is temporary. It ends. The pain of hell never ends. Never!

"You believe in hell," the Franciscan went on. "At least, you say you do. Come to your senses now, for the earth is opening before you. Hell is coming up for you! Lima and Callao have filled the cup of agony to the brim and poured it down the choking throat of Christ. Your crimes are like a sewer; the fumes of them rise to the heights of heaven!

"Repent! Since you have sinned like Ninevah, imitate her penance and save yourselves! She had forty days in which to do penance; not so, you. In the name of God, I tell you this: unless you repent at once, your city will vanish. Not a stone of her will remain!

"To your knees, sinners of Lima, lest you perish forever and your children with you!"

Meanwhile, Rose had been praying the rosary with her family. Oliva caught Rose just as she was opening the outside door of her room.

"Rose, where are you going? It is past eleven o'clock."

"Only out to the garden, Mama."

"Well, I do not want you to go out there alone. If we are going to die, at least let us be together. The earthquake may come at any time."

"But Mama! I must pray and do penance. That is all that can save us; Fray Francisco said so! Please, let me go!"

"Very well; but come to me at once if the earth starts to shake. Since Father Solano has said it, pray as long as you can and do all the penance you wish."

For Rose, who had no director as yet to replace the one she had lost, this permission sufficed. Only at dawn did she pull herself to her feet. She was covered with slashed and swelling welts, for she had scourged herself without mercy until she could lift her arm no more; then she had fallen to her knees. Did she first enlist Mariana's strong arm to scourge her still more? We do not know; but perhaps she did. The Indian woman was a party to more than one of her penances.

Now, as she stood before her bedroom window gasping for breath in the fog-laden air, her heart sang. She gazed at the peaceful garden and the quiet buildings around it rising like a vision from the gray air. God had heard her prayers and those of her fellow townsmen; he had accepted her penances and theirs. The city stood.

Early that morning, Fray Francisco received an urgent message from the viceroy and the archbishop. For once in Peruvian colonial history, Church and State agreed. Let him stay in his convent today. He had preached enough. The people were in a panic and must be allowed to regain their balance. They were converted; his work was done.

In his cell, the guardian of the convent of Our Lady of the Angels knelt before his crucifix and read the message. He had preached too well! As his eyes turned towards the window through which he could see Lima's majestic buildings in their usual calm, he must have thought of the prophet Jonas, who had preached penance to the people of Ninevah at the command of God, threatening destruction to the city if his message were scorned. His sermons sent the pagan populace into vehement penance. God saw their change of heart and withdrew his hand. Therefore, the prophecy of Jonas failed because his preaching succeeded!

The health of the new viceroy, the Count of Monterrey, grew increasingly bad. The summer heat of the year 1606 brought its stint of fever which would not leave him. In an effort to find relief, he went to Limatambo as the guest of the Dominican friars, taking with him some members of his court and a few of his private guard. The farm provided meat and vegetables to feed the friars in the city. It was worked by a large number of negro slaves who lived in barracks behind the convent of the Holy Rosary. The farm residence was used by the community as a place of vacation.

Frequently Martin de Porres was sent to Limatambo to do

some special task or to bring back a load of produce to the convent in Lima. It was there, one sunny morning, that he planted an orchard of olive trees, praying as he worked. God made them as fruitful as the humble Brother; they bore in miraculous profusion. Some of them still remain. The farm, however, is no longer open to pilgrims. The friars sold it in 1902.

Despite the care of Lima's best physicians, the viceroy's fever persisted. It seemed clear that he was about to die. Then began a none too delicate strife for his body. Although he had gratefully accepted the Dominicans' hospitality, the count wished to be buried in the Jesuit church and asked the provincial of the Company of Jesus if he might be assured of this. The Jesuit could not refuse, although he doubtless anticipated what would and did happen. Some priests of another Order, craving the honor of possessing the viceroy's body in their church, told the dying man that in the church of the Jesuits there would not be room for his coffin on the Gospel side of the altar. The viceroy summoned his faltering strength to say that any place in so holy a temple would be roomy enough. Despite all protests, he held to his choice.

He died on February 10, at about 4 o'clock in the afternoon, leaving to Peru outstanding signs of virtue. He had given all his substance in alms to works of charity. He died lacking money to pay for his funeral. On February 12 his body was brought to the church of the Jesuits where, on the following day, the funeral Mass was held.

Rose, of course, must have attended with the members of her family. Gaspar stood resplendently at attention near the coffin. All the nobility of Lima were present and a great sea of tonsured heads lowered in prayer lent luster to the scene.

When all had passed the coffin and paid last respects to the viceroy's body, it was entombed on the Epistle side of the altar, to the scandal of those who thought this beneath the great man's dignity. A little more than a year later the body was removed and taken to Spain with elaborate precautions for secrecy. Only when the *armada* had sailed away was the tomb dismantled. Such machinations may seem ludicrous to us, but they were necessary. The people of Lima looked on their viceroy as a saint and were tenacious of their claim on him. If they had suspected that his body was being moved from their midst, they might well have stopped its translation by violence.

The same problem arose at the death of St. Rose. She had to be buried in secret because the throng would have kept her coffin from being moved from the nave of the church although the prescribed time had passed since her death. And even on her death bed she had been asked to sign a document stipulating where she was to be buried, for fear of disputes over the possession of her body.

On the death of the saintly viceroy, the reins of government passed to the *audiencia*. The oldest of the judges had nominal power, but he did not live long to wield it. On May 26 he breathed his last, to be succeeded by Juan Fernández de Boan. The *audiencia*, so vigilant in guarding its rights, soon had fresh cause for mourning. The courts subordinate to Lima, notably those of La Plata and Quito, were unruly. They would not admit that they owed obedience to Lima, even though the king intervened to tell them that they did.

Rose, with other good people, began to feel that Fray Francisco's prophecy was after all coming to pass. Lima was being flattened figuratively, if not materially. This feeling grew acute when, less than a month after the death of the viceroy, Archbishop Toribio died.

He had begun his third pastoral visitation early in 1605. March brought the cruel summer heat which took the viceroy to his tomb. For Toribio, too, it was lethal. It caught him while he was in the valley of Pacasmayo. He ignored it and pressed on to visit the towns of Cherrepe and Reque. From there he drove himself without mercy as far as Saña, where he had planned to be during Holy Week. He was to celebrate Mass for the inhabitants and consecrate the holy oils. But this was too much for his failing body; instead, he needed them himself. Indomitable though he was, he took to his bed on reaching the town. He could no longer stand.

Afire with fever, almost from the first he was given no hope of recovery. When told that he would die, he raised his eyes heavenward, exclaiming: "They have given me new gladness; for we shall go into the house of the Lord!"

With profound peace he arranged his affairs; then he made an astonishing request! "Let me be borne to the church on a pallet, that I may receive Holy Viaticum there!"

It was done. To the edification of all, he received the Sacred Host. This was on Wednesday of Holy Week; on Thursday he was anointed. He kept his lucidity to the end, answering the prayers of those grouped about the bed. They were not numerous: his confessor and companion on the visitation, the parish priest of the town, the prior of the local Augustinian convent, his servants and a few other persons.

During his last hours, Archbishop Toribio often paraphrased St. Paul's words, repeating with holy ardor: "I desire to see myself freed and to be with Christ!" It was love, not his sickness, which drew this cry from him. His desire was not to be released from pain but to join the King of apostles to whom he had vowed his heart and his life.

Father Ramírez, the Augustinian prior, was an expert harpist. He had played for the prelate during his illness. Now, in the prelate's last moments, the prior renewed the favor. What did he play? Gregorian chant tones; the music which made St. Augustine weep with love when he heard its liquid sweetness. As the Augustinian prior played, he chanted in Latin the words of the dying saint's most-loved psalms. So St.

Toribio, who had found poetry in life, in death found song. In the midst of his agony, the prior's playing flung him skyward on towering surges of joy.

Scarcely had the people of Peru lost their archbishop-saint when God took from them two more exemplary prelates who were doing much for the Church. The first to go was the bishop of Quito, who died in Lima on July 5 in a bare conventual cell. The second was the bishop of Cuzco. Rose was in the springtide of pain. Almost at a single stroke, the New World had lost its viceroy, its archbishop, the senior judge of the *audiencia,* and the two saintliest and most energetic of the bishops after St. Toribio. At the same time she saw her vision of freedom for the Indians vanish like smoke. Yet, she forced herself to acts of faith and hope in God's loving providence, and she continued to bear more than her share of her nation's burden. In her first grief at St. Toribio's death, the thought occurred to her that Peru had lost its deepest well of prayer and penance. So she added to her own penances what it seemed probable to her that the saint had been doing, until she reached the limits of her strength.

After Archbishop Toribio's funeral, which Rose attended with all the members of her family, she made a sorrowful pilgrimage to the monastery of St. Clare. What were her emotions on seeing this house of God and gate of heaven which St. Toribio had wished to open for her? But God's plans for Rose were different from those that she had formed. Scarcely three months after the archbishop's death, Rose had what she really wanted: knowledge of God's will for her. Four months after his death that will was her possession.

How did this happen? Doubtless, not without many secret sighs and petitions; but the final answer came in the form of a miracle worked by God on her behalf. It occurred one day while she was seated at her embroidery in the garden. Oliva was present, as was Juana.

"Look at that black and white butterfly!" Oliva exclaimed. "Be still, Rose; I believe that it is going to light on you!"

Obedient to her mother, Rose sat perfectly still; a moment later, the butterfly lighted on her heart.

"See how it behaves!" whispered Oliva. "It is not moving, but its wings keep fluttering back and forth!"

"Look, Mama!" Juana exclaimed as the butterfly detached itself from Rose's breast and flew away. "It has gone, but has left its mark on Rose's gown!"

Rose looked down and saw the black and white markings over her heart.

"It means that God wishes me to be a Dominican Tertiary," she said gently. "I was just praying that he would make his divine will known to me, when the butterfly came. As it rested on me, I had an interior light explaining what it meant."

"Let me see that mark myself!" cried Oliva. "I do not like this; it is too strange!"

She shivered. "It is some kind of magic," said Oliva. "You have prayed for a sign, and the devil has given you one to deceive you. Go into the house and change your gown. Perhaps those stains will wash out. As for your precious sign, you will not join the Dominican Tertiaries or any religious order!"

In those few moments Rose realized that God was calling her to the Third Order of St. Dominic and she conceived an ardent desire to enter it. This alternative had but newly presented itself to her mind, despite her admiration for the Order of Friars Preachers and her love of St. Catherine of Siena. She had longed for the cloister, but the Dominican Tertiaries lived at home.

Still, it is evident that the grace of this apparition did no more than crown a long series of preparatory graces which Rose had been receiving. It is such with most of God's works of grace, in spite of an apparently sudden change of disposition. In silence and hiddenness the divine influence has touched these souls many times but its effects have not been manifested exteriorly. Then, like the eagle, the Spirit of God swoops upon them, adding but one grace more; and all their thoughts are changed. The world marvels at the sudden conversions, the abrupt changes of heart that it thinks it sees. It was so with Rose. From her childhood, the Holy Spirit had been forming her for the Third Order of St. Dominic. Like many a soul before and after her, she found, on entering the Order which attracted her, that her spirit had been tailored to fit the rule which she then embraced.

Rose's first act, on learning God's will for herself, was to take a Dominican as her director. From his guidance she hoped to learn the Dominican point of view on the inner life. She found it wholly satisfying. Fortified by the prayers and advice of her new spiritual father, Rose pleaded anew with her mother for permission to enter the Third Order. She redoubled her pleadings to St. Catherine of Siena and Our Lady of the Rosary. Archbishop Toribio did not fail to receive his share of petitions. Finally, after a few weeks' resistance, Oliva gave in. But it was in a petulant mood that she went with Rose to her investiture, which took place on the feast of Our Lady of Ransom in the chapel of Our Lady of the Rosary. The festal decorations of the chapel, the presence of the Tertiaries and many of their friends and, finally, Rose's director, Father Alphonsus Velázquez, drew from her no more than a frigid stare. She consoled herself with the thought that Rose's entrance into the Third Order would be no impediment to her marriage.

As a necessary preparation for taking the habit, Rose had received a majority vote of the female Tertiaries of Lima. She had been recommended to them as a person of virtuous life and good reputation, and in no way suspected of heresy.

The ceremony of Rose's investiture was almost the same as

that held when Brother Martin entered the Order as a *donado*, according to the established form. It was, therefore, with deep emotion that he knelt, with other friars of the community, in the chapel of the Rosary on Rose's day of oblation. How happy he had been when he dedicated himself to God, and how sure that this was God's will for him! Yet now, here he was a full-fledged friar, and just as sure that this was also God's will! Knowing that Rose had desired to enter some convent, he must have wondered whether for her, too, the Tertiaries would not be but a step on the ladder to some higher form of the religious life in which she could pronounce the vows of poverty, chastity, obedience and enclosure. As there were no active religious orders for women then, this fourth vow was an obligation, and one which few called in question. Apart from the cloister, there was no alternative for Rose in the religious life but some Third Order.

Martin, of course, was delighted that Rose had decided on the Order of St. Dominic, his own religious family. It was a choice that drew the bonds of friendship even closer between himself and Rose, so that they did not hesitate to speak frankly to one another of their inner lives. From that day on, his practice was to pass as often as possible through the sacristy when he knew that she would be there. They became a familiar sight to other members of the convent of the Holy Rosary, standing apart in a corner of the room happily immersed in spiritual talk. All took their friendship as a matter of course.

At her clothing ceremony Rose received the full Tertiary habit: a long white tunic and scapular, a leather belt, a coif and white veil. Over her tunic she wore, when outside, a black mantle which extended to the bottom of the white tunic. Although still living at home, she looked like a religious novice.

The wearing of the complete habit was customary then in

Spanish domains but elsewhere variations existed. In some places private Tertiaries wore a black and white secular garb and a small scapular inside the clothing. In many European countries the Tertiaries wore the white tunic and a black leather belt, but not the large scapular (for example, St. Catherine of Siena). The public use of the scapular for conventual Tertiaries was not authorized until 1667. There seems to have been no authorization for Tertiaries living at home to wear the large scapular, but seventeenth-century paintings of Rose show her wearing it. Probably the custom of its use in Peru was established before the 1667 authorization for conventual Tertiaries. In Rose's case and in the case of most of the Tertiaries in Lima, there was an implicit desire to live as conventual Tertiaries, a desire which was eventually fulfilled for them.

Although most of her pictures show her with the black veil, there is no reference to it in the formula of profession; nor is there any mention of it in documents on Rose's profession ceremony. In the "Glorification of St. Rose," which hangs in the church of St. Dominic, she is shown with a black outer veil and white inner veil. In the room where she died, now a shrine in the convent of St. Rose, a small painting set above her cross and other relics shows her black-veiled. The same can be said of the more modern Francisco Lao painting in the Lima City Hall and works of different schools and periods found in private collections. Perhaps, like the Tertiaries in St. Catherine's time, Rose wore a black *manteleta*, made of thin material and attached to the top of the head, covering the white veil and flowing down to the bottom of the white tunic. This *manteleta* also served as a cloak for street wear. It is still worn by some Dominican Sisters in Spain to this day.

"What do you ask?" said Father Velázquez as Rose knelt at the rail before the altar.

"The mercy of God and yours," answered Rose in clear tones.

She was too happy to feel nervous; in this moment of her self-giving to God, here in the presence of the much-loved statue of Our Lady of the Rosary, she felt no anxiety. Confidence in the help of God and those whom he had set over her lifted her far above fear.

After the opening question, Father Velázquez spoke a few earnest words on the duties which Rose was assuming by her entrance into the Tertiaries. He mentioned the original name of the Third Order of St. Dominic, the "Militia of Jesus Christ," and told those assembled in the chapel that the soldier's obedience and valor, his devotedness and loyalty must characterize the Tertiary. Then he spoke of the actual name of the Third Order, "Brothers and Sisters of Penance of St. Dominic." This name indicated its spirit. The members of the Third Order were to be brothers and sisters to one another in charity, but brothers and sisters dedicated to a life of penance, supernatural restraint. Whether married or single, they were to carry this thought with them in all their daily duties.

Now, Father Velázquez turned to Rose and spoke to her of the obligations of the Tertiary. She would be obligated to certain morning and night prayers of the Rule, to the keeping of certain fast and abstinence days, to the recitation of the Little Office of Our Lady and the Office of the Dead at prescribed times. Moreover, she would be bound to practice the virtue of charity with special zeal, visiting the sick and devoting herself to works of mercy. She was to study her Rule and attend to the formative counsels of her director.

Finally, Rose was to be punctual and faithful in attending the monthly chapter meetings. She was to listen with attentive and docile heart to the explanations of the Rule which would be given there. She was to accept reproofs and corrections in the spirit of humility and gratitude, should they be given her. In short, she was to model her life in all things on the examples of Jesus Christ and his Virgin Mother, on the life of her spiritual mother, St. Catherine of Siena and her Father, St. Dominic.

Oliva listened with supreme boredom to this sermon, so far from her interests and designs. It was with relief that she began to follow the prayers of the blessing of Rose's habit, which began at once. During the blessing, Rose and all the Tertiaries present held lighted candles, symbolic of faith, love and self-dedication.

After the hymn *Veni Creator,* chanted verse by verse alternately by the Sisters in two choirs, came the Our Father, an invocation to the Holy Ghost and St. Dominic, and a versicle which expressed all the fullness of Rose's joy.

"Be glad in the Lord and rejoice, ye just."

"And glory, all ye right of heart," was the response.

"Save thy servant."

"Hoping in thee, O my God."

Then followed a prayer to the Holy Ghost and others imploring that Rose be delivered from the weight of her sins on being clothed with the garment of penance, and that she might be helped and stirred to a better life in the example of the saints of the Order, all those who had practiced sacred penance.

After this, Father Velázquez blessed Rose's scapular.

"Receive, Sister, the holy scapular of our Order, the most distinguished part of our Dominican habit, the mother's pledge from heaven of the love of the most Blessed Virgin Mary towards us, under whose wings and mantle thou shalt find a shade from the heat, and a bulwark and defense in death from all dangers both of body and soul.

Then Rose kissed Father Velázquez' scapular and passed

from one Tertiary to another to receive the kiss of peace, as they all sang the *Te Deum*. Meanwhile, Oliva was overcome by a strange drowsiness. After the ceremony, Oliva had to go with Rose to the sacristy to receive the congratulations of all, but she still felt dazed. She forced a smile to her face, which felt as though it had been carved of wood. It was with unspeakable relief that she leaned on her daughter's arm as they walked the few paces from the church to their home.

As soon as they were indoors, Oliva sent Rose to show her habit to her grandmother. Isabel was too weak to leave her room. However, Oliva did this none too graciously; she was still far from reconciled to seeing her daughter in a Tertiary habit.

How tired she was! Before Rose left the bedroom she let her remove her shoes. Now she could feel Rose lifting her feet and placing them gently on the hassock, but she did not try to open her eyes. Then Rose took off the bedspread and turned back the top sheet.

"Come, Mama. Rest awhile," she said. But Oliva could not answer. She seemed paralyzed, but she felt no fear. Instead, her soul was flooded with peace. She felt a strange nostalgia swell within her. Suddenly, she uttered a cry. On a raised throne surrounded by cherubim in the midst of sparkling, multicolored clouds, sat the Queen of the Most Holy Rosary. She was clad in the white habit of St. Dominic. The borders of her mantle seemed sewn with constellations of stars. She held the Infant Jesus on her knee. He, too, wore a Tertiary habit, but without the mantle. He had a radiant white rose clasped in his hand.

"This rose represents your daughter, my Son's cherished flower," Mary said to Oliva with a tender smile. "I plucked her for him from your garden and he will not let her go. Only see how grateful he is to you for having tended her for him and for having given her to me!"

With these words, the Virgin of the Rosary held out her divine Son towards Oliva so that she could feel his infant hand caressing her cheek.

"Now, see the reward that my Son has prepared for those who love him," Mary went on. "This reward will be yours if you are faithful in his service."

As Mary pronounced these words, the figure of a young Dominican Tertiary appeared kneeling before herself and the Child. Her habit and mantle also blazed with glory, and as she bent to press her lips to the hand of the little Jesus, Oliva recognized Rose. The mother's cry of joy was instantaneous, but it could not be heard. It was lost in the cadences of a heavenly chant.

"Come, spouse of Christ, accept the crown
The Lord has prepared for thee from eternity."

Now the rose in the hand of the Infant Jesus multiplied itself to form a crown of roses blazing with heavenly dew. While Oliva watched in a trance, her daughter inclined her head to receive it.

"I am thy reward exceeding great," sang a seraph in muted tones.

At these words, Rose received the Infant into her arms, pressing him to her heart while he fondled her face.

About an hour later, Rose opened the door softly and tiptoed into their room. Her mother was as she had left her, in the armchair. She had not been to bed. When Oliva heard her come in, she stirred, opened her eyes and smiled.

"You are not the only one who has visions, Rose," she said. "I have just had one myself; and I must say that it was consoling."

CHAPTER NINE

Agony in the Garden

❧ ❧

IT WAS some comfort to Oliva to see how Rose's social life began to thrive in the circle of Tertiaries. The eager young novice found in them the congenial company that she had lacked until then. Coming from every rank of society, from the highest nobility to the servant class, they shared with her the same ideals, the same interests, the same family spirit. She soon won their hearts by her gentle, whimsical, unassuming ways. Her soul, already prepared by grace for the Dominican Rule, opened spontaneously to the advice of her elders in the chapter. So pliant was she to their guidance, so ready to learn, that soon they came to look on her as their model. Without in the least seeking it, she became their unofficial leader.

Now Oliva had the joy of welcoming to her home a growing circle of Rose's friends. She noted gratefully that some were wealthy and influential. A few of these had unmarried brothers. Oliva's hospitality to them was as warm as she could make it. As she watched Rose, she saw for the first time her talent for leadership. All her gifts of nature and grace fused to fit her for it. Even her impetuosity lent force to her powers. Her enthusiasm, her quick dexterity and competence made even the older Tertiaries follow her initiatives and give place to her as organizer.

Pleased though Oliva was at Rose's unexpected friendships, from time to time they brought annoyance. For example, she found that sometimes her best veil or one of her other garments was missing. On inquiring of Rose if she had borrowed it, she would learn that it had been given to some needy Tertiary or a member of her family. Oliva would not have minded, had she herself not been poor, but at the moment peso-pinching was her prime occupation. As Isabel grew more feeble, and finally a permanent invalid, Oliva lost a skilled fellow-worker whose nimble fingers had earned perhaps a third of the family income. True to her Franciscan standard, the valiant old lady worked almost to the end, propped up in bed with pillows.

It was, therefore, with scant appreciation of Rose's charity that Oliva learned one day of her latest benefaction. On looking for one of the two cloaks which she possessed, she found it missing. On being questioned, Rose admitted that she had given it to a poor Tertiary. However, she seemed so confident that divine providence would repair the loss, that Oliva soon let her anger subside. She began to wait for the next event; she only hoped that it would happen soon, and that there would be nothing supernatural in it. Rose's miracles made her uneasy.

Oliva had not long to wait. As years before a complete stranger had given Rose the exact sum needed by Gaspar to meet his debt, so now Oliva found herself being handed a package of money. She was to use it to buy a new cloak, the donor said. When Oliva told her daughter what had happened, Rose was casual in her reaction.

"You should not have worried, Mama," she said. "I knew that you would be given money to buy a new one."

Apart from her obligations of the Rule, Rose found life full of fresh challenges. More perplexing medical cases were presenting themselves at the Flores home. In her doubts, she consulted Brother Martin. When all human remedies failed, she had recourse to the Child Jesus. One of her wealthy friends had given her a little statue of the Child Jesus—a sweet-faced, appealing image, its robe adorned with flowers in Spanish style and its head gold-haloed. Rose called him her "little Doctor." Inexplicable cures at her hands were all referred to his power and love. She was only his instrument, she said.

The selflessness of Rose deceived none of the humble people who gathered each morning to be healed by her. That the Child Jesus worked the miracles they had no doubt; but the prayers that moved him to do so were Rose's. When, on occasion, she was faced by a diffident person, her exhortation was firm.

"Where is your faith?"

When faith was forthcoming, cures abounded.

As Rose absorbed the Dominican spirit, she began to change her outlook on many things. First among these was truth. She had always loved the truth, but now, as the Dominican motto, truth became her delight and trust. To defend it, to spread it, to foster it by every means was her intent in all her words and acts.

If formerly she had shared the opinion of those who think it more charitable to let an error pass unremarked rather than risk hurting the one who has made it, she now felt it her duty as a Tertiary to point out the slightest failure and to report facts in stark realism.

"Excuse me," she would say on hearing some verbal vagary, "but it seems to me that things did not happen quite as you say. As I recall them, the facts are these."

The habit was prompted by zeal for the observance of her Rule and intense love of truth, but it was sometimes annoying to others, especially her own family. Her brother Andrés called her "the voice of conscience"; Fernando told her bluntly that she was a nuisance. Oliva rebuked her for correcting Juana's childish exaggerations.

"Let her alone!" she exclaimed. "If you keep harping at her, she will never learn the art of conversation!"

If Rose did not hesitate to point out the mistakes of others in a spirit of zeal for truth, she did not shrink either from rebuking them for faults. One instance of this that was reported in her Process shows at once her fearlessness and want of self control, her freedom from human respect and her still untamed vehemence. Wisdom and prudence were certainly hers, when she took time to reflect and pray about a problem; but when she acted on the spur of the moment the result could be disastrous.

It happened that one of the salient affectations of the time was to hold animated chats at the back of churches, whether or not the Mass was in progress. This was true not only of Peru but of the Spanish motherland, and the custom dated back to the thirteenth century, perhaps earlier. So, when the Rule of the Third Order of St. Dominic was set down in writing and approved by the Holy See, first for it and then, with slight changes, for the Carmelite and Servite Third Orders, talking in church was singled out as an abuse to be shunned.

"While Mass is being celebrated, or the Divine Office is sung, or the word of God preached, let all strive to keep silence in the church and attend diligently to prayer and to the Divine Office; except that on any particular necessity showing itself, they may say something in a very low tone."

This particular necessity showed itself to Rose one Sunday morning when she and Fernando entered Santo Domingo to attend Mass. At the main altar a priest was saying the Communion prayer against a cacophony of chattering. As usual, a group of persons of high rank was engaged in a very noisy conversation at the back of the church. Rose swept down upon them, her cheeks flushed with indignation.

"My Lords! My Ladies! Is it seemly for you to speak out

loud during the Holy Sacrifice? Is it not your duty to give the example of reverence and piety? How can the Lord fail to be displeased by such conduct in his house?"

Rose paused for breath. The group of chattering noblemen and ladies stopped short and stared at her, stunned. Was it possible that a soldier's daughter was saying such things to them?

"Regret your folly and offer to God the satisfaction of your prayers," Rose went on.

A nervous titter from one of the ladies started the rest laughing. Soon, a loud chorus of laughter echoed through the church. Rose stopped it with a gesture.

"You may laugh if you choose," she said energetically, "but I have spoken the truth."

"Come, Rose," said Fernando quickly, taking his sister's arm. "Well, you have really done it!" he muttered angrily. "Who do you think you are, Father Provincial?"

Undoubtedly Rose's rebuke was ill-advised. She had taken it on herself to scold some of the foremost members of the parish. If there was need of such an act, it should have come from the prior of the Dominicans, who would have couched it in carefully soft words. By her hastiness, Rose had made foes for herself; from that time on, they watched her like monitors.

Other incidents from the next few years show Rose's need for a firmer grip on herself. Due to their nearness to Holy Rosary, the Flores family were often visited by friars of the community. At first these visits were formal, pre-announced or on invitation. At length they grew spontaneous. A group of friars out for a stroll in the afternoon or evening would drop in on Rose before going home. Missionaries about to leave for the *doctrinas* would call to ask for prayers. Priests in need of vestments would be ushered in discreetly by Dominicans wishing Rose to have the orders. Finally, friars who grew discouraged in the face of contemporary wrongs so hard to right sought in the Flores living room or *patio* a sympathetic ear.

Oliva and Gaspar welcomed these friars to their home and treated them with supreme courtesy. They were, therefore, not a little troubled on seeing how Rose dealt with them. If she wished, she could be as respectful and gracious as became her; but these were her spiritual brothers—members of her own religious family. When she found herself in their midst she lost her sense of reserve; she opened her thoughts and emotions to them with sisterly frankness. When, on ocassion, the turn of their talk displeased her, she told them so. Oliva gasped. Don Gaspar apologized. Both learned to their amazement that their guests seemed to like it.

Rose, for all her outward vivacity and the comradeship she enjoyed with the other Tertiaries and the friars as a member of the Third Order of St. Dominic, soon found herself a prey to temptation. No sooner had she taken the habit than she became a center of attention for all whom she knew. Her sensitivity to compliments was as lively as ever; she writhed inwardly in the grip of constant feelings of vanity to which she still did not consent. But the trial was fierce; and when it seemed to die it was replaced by one more cruel. Now it seemed to her that she had entered the Third Order in order to draw down on herself the praise and admiration of the world.

In her mental and emotional turmoil, she could no longer tell whether or not she really desired the compliments from which she suffered. Still, in the crisis she knew where to turn for help. Her new spiritual father diagnosed her fear as a ruse of the devil, an attempt to rob her of her peace. She accepted his word and relied on his judgment; the scruple fled from her. With renewed joy she plunged into the practice of her Rule and strove to grow in its spirit.

Since she had embraced an Order of Penance, it could be expected that she would try to extend and intensify her program of self-discipline. As, moreover, she still lacked full control of her emotions, her efforts were more zealous than prudent. We find, for example, that she tried to use a discipline with chains, a practice too severe for most men. Only when admonished by her director did she give up this penance. What was his magic formula? One open to argument, yet one which Rose accepted instantly.

"Cords," he said, "are more in the spirit of the Order."

This dictum was not without its weak side. St. Dominic himself had used a scourge of chains. In the convent of the Holy Rosary there were those of his sons who did the same. As Rose probably knew, Brother Martin was one óf them.

Later, when a series of events robbed her of spiritual help for a time, she turned, it would seem, to the Jesuit who had steered her first on the voyage to sanctity. While under his direction she tried another masculine penance—the wearing of a heavy chain about her waist. When she put it on, she fastened it tightly; then, fearing that the pain which it would cause her in the future might prove too strong for her will, she padlocked it and threw the key in the well. In time, the chain hurt her unbearably and Mariana had to break one of the links with a hammer. When she took off the chain, pieces of Rose's flesh adhered to it. Yet, scarcely had the wounds begun to heal when the intrepid girl tried again. As before, the penance proved too hard for her and she had to give it up.

Another experiment was ended by Oliva. The ardent young Tertiary longed for a penitential shirt, which she could not afford, so she got her director's permission to stick pins through her hair shirt. Presumably, she filed off the points; nevertheless the shirt made her movements awkward. Oliva noticed, jumped to conclusions and asked questions. As always, Rose answered frankly, and the improvised penitential garb served to stoke the kitchen fire.

It is probably from this time that Rose began to feel the need to renew in some form the hard bed which she had used in her childhood. She knew from experience how quickly she grew accustomed to logs. If her bed was to be really penitential, she must add something to it.

One may wonder; one may even ask: "Why this desire? Does it not smack of sadism?" The answer is "No." If Rose wished never to be free of suffering, it was first of all so that she might keep Christ company. Then, it was because souls in need were always storming her heart. Finally, it would seem that it was in order to arm herself against the assaults of the flesh. Having failed in his effort to shake her Dominican vocation by means of temptations to vanity and the fear that she had entered to attract the approval of others, the devil now began to use new tactics.

The innocent virgin, whose thoughts had never strayed to creatures from her childhood and who had always mortified her senses vigilantly, now felt the sting of concupiscence. As in the case of St. Paul, doubtless part of this trial came from her own psychological and physiological make-up, but it was stirred up by foul, lascivious visions which obsessed her through the attacks of impure spirits. It was a cruel persecution which her model and mother, St. Catherine of Siena, had borne before her. Her valiant repudiation of them gained for her a great increase in purity. Many other saints have been tormented on this score, so Rose was in good company. But she could not rest on this assurance. She knew that to conquer temptation like a saint she had to use the means of the saints. So she gave herself no comfort; ceaseless mortification as well as prayer is essential as a weapon of defense.

Rose had her director's consent to experiment until she

could find a penitential bed that suited her. Oliva reluctantly gave her consent also. She stipulated, though, that Rose should cover the contraption with a sheet tucked in around the sides. For the purpose, Rose wove a thick piece of homespun which would not readily tear from contact with the sharp points and edges of crockery fragments, pieces of broken glass and other angular objects which she strewed between the logs. More of an advantage than this, in her own view, was the fact that the loose weave of the homespun allowed many of the points to penetrate the cloth.

Rose began to rest on this bed little by little until she could bear it for several hours at a time and manage to fall asleep on it. At first, the novelty saved her from dreading it, but as the months passed, she began to feel what amounted to terror at the mere thought of lying on it. Sometimes the sight of it was enough to set her shaking like one with the ague.

At about this time Rose was approached by a white-clad *caballero* as she prayed alone in the garden late one evening. Considering the loose morality of Peruvian nobles as a class, it was a wonder that some such thing had not happened years sooner. With a prayer she managed to wrench herself from his grasp; then she ran to the door of her room which was open, although the rest of the house was locked and its occupants asleep. Once safe, she flung the bar across the door and scourged herself without mercy. Keenly aware of her human weakness, it seemed to her that she might well have succumbed to the temptation. For now more than ever, when she had to fight a daily and nightly battle to keep her purity of heart, she prized it as a thing worth dying for.

Her fiery nature flung back each assailing thought and image with youth's vehemence. She prized purity in and for others as much as for herself. She fled from the least occasion of sin and fault; she knew that to be an occasion of sin or fault to others was reprehensible in God's sight if it were avoidable. Her horror at the thought that her beauty had lured one man into sinful desire knew scarcely any bounds, although thanks to the help of her guardian angel and her agility, she had escaped him.

With this torture in her heart, Rose was forced to attend one of her mother's periodic parties. This particular one was more repugnant than usual to her, for the lady in whose honor it was being held was perhaps her most extravagant admirer. Rose had never emerged from a conversation with her, except in the throes of struggle against temptations to pride in some form. Now the occasion was renewed; Rose could not avoid it, for her mother was bent on producing her for the edification of some new acquaintances who had heard much of her. Besides, Oliva insisted, what excuse could she offer the guest of honor to explain Rose's absence?

If the party had been held elsewhere, the observant Tertiary might have found a way of avoiding it, for the Rule discouraged attendance at feasts and worldly amusements. As it was, there was no solution but to comply with her mother's wish. The afternoon was to prove painful. In her dilemma, Rose lost control of herself and insulted her mother's friend, committing subsequently an act as excessive as it was heroic —one of the most vehement acts of her life and one most misunderstood.

Precisely what Oliva's guest of honor said when Rose greeted her is not known; but its general tenor is clear from the saint's reaction. The frivolous lady had taken her hand, fondled it, and declared that its beauty would be the ruin of many a man. Rose withdrew her hand quickly; her countenance blanched.

"I hope I shall never be an occasion of sin to anyone!" she cried, fleeing from the room.

Oliva followed her with a furious glance, but she could not leave her guests. "Please pay no attention to Rose's little ways," she said hastily. "She is self-conscious; compliments affect her."

"Ah, I hope that I have not distressed my little rosebud," fluted the lady. "Will she come back soon?" she asked, her eyes roving about the room. But Rose did not come back. She had run from the scene to plunge her hands in lye. Her hope was that her hands might be scarred so that no one would admire them again, and that no one might be tempted by their beauty. She reckoned without her mother. Oliva sent Juana after the fugitive and soon Rose's hands were swathed in bandages soaked in oil. A month's time saw them wholly healed.

It is clear from this incident as well as others recorded in her Process that Rose still lacked the self-mastery which makes the soul strong enough to cling to God through every incident and crisis. It is such calm of spirit that makes it possible for the soul to live in total union with God. He had destined Rose for the highest possible union with himself—spiritual marriage. To prepare her for this state and raise her to it, he had to purify her. It will be no surprise, then, to find that her inner trials now grew acute. She had been suffering from periods of dryness for about six years; now they took on a new aspect. In the designs of God, Rose was to find her sole support in him, so he permitted that the night of the soul take a form which differed outwardly from that experienced by most souls nearing the unitive way. It was, therefore, not recognized as such by her director and the other priests whom she consulted.

Ordinarily, the "dark night of the soul" is marked by a feeling of abandonment by God. The soul feels as if it is at enmity with him, and in this state the soul experiences the worst type of suffering. In Rose's case aridity had first come in this way, but soon after her clothing as a Tertiary, it assumed the form of visions.

The enemy of souls, having failed so far in his war against her, was the direct cause of these visions. But God purifies souls by means of the sufferings he permits them to endure. Only by giving Rose a special motive for clinging to him with all her strength and seeking him in the night of pure faith could he teach her the way of peace. Detachment in all things is the key to this way; it alone frees the soul from self-will so that its acts proceed primarily from the movement of grace and not from self. It is a hard road, and all must tread it who reach perfect union with God. However, all are not asked to bear it in the frightful form which Rose endured.

For years the garden had been a source of delight for her as she prayed there alone far into the evening. In this garden she had walked and talked with God and sometimes, like Elias, felt raised by his power far above the earth. Then suddenly this was changed, and the garden of delights became a garden of agony.

"Depart from me, ye cursed!"

With terror and paralysis in her soul, Rose heard the words of condemnation hurled at her by the Savior and Judge of all. Confusion and anguish overwhelmed her. Why was she being damned? She could not remember. But she had once loved God; she knew that. Why could she not love him now?

"How could I offend him who is so good?" she cried.

She found herself in the midst of condemned souls, hideous with sin. Demons, too, of many sorts, pressed upon her from every side. Loathsome snakes, slimy lizards with distorted human faces, creatures part man and part bird, but with wings and fur like bats, swooped at her, shrieking foul things.

"Forever! Forever!"

Rose saw her guardian angel with the other angels before the throne. With an effort born of desperation, she tried to fling herself towards him.

"My angel! Plead for me! You have helped me in the past!"

The angel turned to her with a fearful countenance.

"Your place is with the goats; I have charge of you no longer."

With redoubled anguish, Rose saw the faces of the blessed through clouds of stinking pitch. Her mother was there, her father, Fernando, all her other brothers and sisters. Her confessors were there too, Brother Martin and that little negro slave who was always tagging after him. How his face shone with glory! And now, they heard her cries and turned away from her with looks of reproach. A clamor, a chorus of shrieks, and she felt herself falling. Down, down through an ocean of fire that consumed her and yet did not kill.

"Forever! I am lost forever!"

And now, could it be true? She was in her own garden. Overhead, the moon appeared, flooding the sky with silver. About her the shrubs and flowers seemed washed with silver; night birds twittered and insects sang. She was alive! She was not damned! She could still love God!

And now, her whole being vibrated with joy. God was hers; she felt herself immersed in his goodness and mercy, his fatherly compassion. She was his! No longer could demons boast that she belonged to them! A wave of consolation swept through her; she felt herself transformed as though she were no longer in the flesh.

So it would be one night, then Rose would go about her next day's work in a state of nervous exhaustion. Perhaps this evening it would be different, she told herself. But then, when her free time for prayer returned. . . .

"Back from the throne! Go with the goats!"

Rose felt herself hurled from the judgment seat into the shrieking throng of souls distorted with malice and remorse. A flaming sword pierced her; she felt its blade pass through her vitals. Demons tortured her in every pore of her body.

"Ah, my God! What have I done? Why am I here? I loved thee once!" she sobbed.

"Hell! Hell! Hell forever!" shrieked the demons around her.

Rose felt herself torn to pieces by numberless fiends in forms so horrid that she found the sight of them as so many deaths. She was shackled and gagged now; her cries were muffled and went unheard by the throng of the blessed standing before the throne. She could hear their voices through the blasphemies and vile epithets that rose around her. They were singing a hymn of thanksgiving.

Suddenly Rose cried out. Very near to Christ stood Archbishop Toribio. He would plead for her. But no; the prelate who had loved her in life as his daughter now stared at her coldly, then turned to kneel before his Lord. There was no more hope for her.

"Oh, God! Oh, my God! Mine no more! I must be separated from thee forever!"

What had she done? Why was she here?

Suddenly Rose found herself kneeling before the wooden cross that she had planted in the rocks when she prayed in the garden. No demons tortured her! Again she could love God!

Suddenly, too, she saw her Savior near. He was in the form of a lovely Infant, kissing and caressing her, filling her soul with bliss. Close to his heart, he hugged a rose, the symbol of herself.

"This rose is mine," he whispered. "I shall never let it go!"

At first, Rose managed to hide her trial from Oliva. But

her face was pale and her smile forced. Her mother was not long in asking why. Rose told her candidly what was happening. Oliva was stunned.

"It is epilepsy!" she cried. "You must go to a doctor! Now is the time to treat it, before it grows worse!"

But Rose refused.

"Mama, it is not epilepsy," she said gently. "Besides, as long as it does not interfere with my daily life and work, I must not go to the expense of seeing a doctor. When we can scarcely earn enough to buy food and clothing, and Papa is so often ill, I should rather bear it a thousand times than place him in debt!"

"You are right in saying that we cannot afford to incur more doctor's bills," Oliva agreed. "But I cannot see you going through the house like a ghost. Put your work aside for a time and go to your room. Since you cannot sleep at night, try to rest a while in the afternoons."

The visions were not long confined to the evening and night hours. Soon they came upon Rose in the midst of her ordinary tasks.

"Mama!" Come quickly! Something has happened to Rose!" cried Juana one morning, running to her mother as she sat in the *patio* with her spindle.

"What is wrong?" Oliva asked in terror. "Has she hurt herself?"

"She just sits like a statue beneath the tree, with her sewing in her hands."

Oliva followed Juana hurriedly to the spot. Rose sat rigidly on her chair, her one hand poised in the act of drawing the thread through the net that she was embroidering, her other hand holding the embroidery hoop. Her face was turned upward in horror.

Oliva tried to shake her, but found her immovable.

"It is no use, Mama," said Juana. "I tried everything. I

pinched her and pushed her; I even stuck the needle into her."

"It is an epileptic fit," said her mother. "We must not leave her alone. I cannot stay with her, for I must finish this order. Go and get your mending. Stay with her and call me when she comes to her senses."

Sometimes the visions disrupted the family's social life; then Rose met with less sympathy, above all from her brothers.

"Is Rose never coming?" asked Francisco as he looked impatiently at the slim, still figure poised among the garden shrubs. "She has been standing there an hour."

"Go and see what she is doing," growled Ramón irritably. "She will make us late. She loses all sense of time when she begins to pray."

"Begins?" snorted Andrés. "Does she ever stop?"

"Well, go and see what is wrong with her," said Oliva, looking up from her task. "We have to leave for the Montoyas' in a few minutes. Tell her not to delay us; after all, it was her idea that we should go."

The young men left the room and went together to fetch their sister. Soon, however, Ramón was back, knocking on his mother's bedroom door where she was dressing Juana.

"She is in another of those fits. She keeps staring at one of her flowers as though she saw the devil himself and has her hand out, just ready to cut the flower. We tried to take the knife away from her, but she is too strong. Her grip is like a man's."

"I think it is time that Rose consulted the doctor," said Gaspar, coming to the door. "I do not care how deeply I must go into debt; I cannot bear to see her like this!"

Once more, Rose put off visiting the doctor. Indeed, she knew that her director was the one to help her. But he did not understand. Wishing to have the advice of a priest who knew her better, he sent Rose to one of his colleagues. But he too was at a loss, so her referred her to Father Pérez, to whom she had often confessed.

"Indeed, I do not like it!" exclaimed Father Pérez. "This certainty that you have of being damned and these demons you see and hear, how can that be a form of prayer? Do not be ridiculous!"

"But Father, what do you think is the cause? Is it not some kind of spiritual trial? I do not think the visions are from God, but from the devil."

"I think the visions are from here, *hermana*," said the priest, tapping his temples. "Some of the night vapors have seeped in through your skull."

Rose flushed and bit her lips, but she did not answer sharply.

"I thank you for your trouble in listening to me, Reverend Father. I am sorry to have inconvenienced you. Since you do not wish to direct me farther, may I at least please have your blessing?"

From him, Rose went elsewhere in search of advice. This time she sought out a friar who had known her soul since her childhood.

"I fail to see how this can be part of your spiritual life," he said. "No, in my opinion this trouble is not spiritual but mental. You have overstrained yourself; too much fasting and excessive penances have ruined your health."

"Then, Father, what should I do?"

"I cannot say for sure. Perhaps, you might consult someone else. Try Father Fernández."

Rose fared no better than before. As soon as she tried to explain her visions to him, she found herself in the throes of an argument. After an hour of fruitless questions, the priest gave his decision.

"I am sorry, *hermana*. I have done my best to help you.

The only cure for scrupulosity is to obey the confessor. If you will not agree to fight these fits of depression and these figments of your imagination, how can I cure you? You say that you cannot fight them and that, although you think yourself damned, you are not in a state of depression. Nonsense!"

"But, Father, I do not honestly believe that I am scrupulous. It is true that in the past I have been troubled with scruples for a time, but not permanently. It seems to me that this is a spiritual trial."

"Scrupulosity is a spiritual trial," said the priest dryly. "And there was never a scrupulous person yet who thought himself so. Take my advice, and find another in whom you have confidence."

But Rose did not know anyone to whom she could turn. It was then that she thought of Brother Martin. Until then, she had kept her trial hidden from him; when he questioned her on her health, she had answered evasively. But would he understand? Would she lose this friend, as she had lost so many who had once held her in high esteem? She agonized and prayed, then made her decision. If she could not trust him, there was no doctor in whom she could find help. If he failed her in her need, there was no friend on whom she could count. She would take that chance.

In the meantime, Brother Martin was having his own trials, but of a different nature. Not long before, the head infirmarian had called him away from his tasks to discuss ways and means of ridding the convent of mice. Not content with rummaging in the kitchen and storerooms, the mice were now invading the wardrobe room and ruining the clothing and bed linens.

"Brother Martin," he said sternly, "we are overrun by mice. I want you to buy a large quantity of poison this afternoon and spread it around."

But Martin protested humbly: "Your idea is to rid the

convent of those little animals, not necessarily to kill them. If I can make them all stay outside, would that suffice? I think that I could do it without poisoning them. If I put some scraps in the stable or garden for them, they will have enough to eat without coming in here."

"If you can save us the price of the poison and the trouble of burying those rodents, God bless you, Brother," said the infirmarian with a grim laugh, "but if I ever see one of them here after you leave the scraps for them, I shall set out the poison myself. And no more arguments."

As soon as Brother Martin left the infirmary, he went straight to the hole where most of the mice came in on the ground floor. He crouched down and drew out of the opening the trap he had set there. A small gray mouse was caught in it by the tail.

"I shall let you out, little brother," said Martin softly, "but do not run away yet. I have something to say to you. Tell your friends not to do any more mischief. Give the word to your whole tribe to leave this holy convent. They can go to the garden shed, and every day I shall leave some food there and in the stable for them."

The mouse scurried off. Martin walked away, humming a song under his breath. He had scarcely begun to mount the infirmary stairs when he heard a rattle, then a continuous scuttling sound. Other friars whom he had passed stepped aside just in time: several chesty rats and a mouse ran past them, making their way out of the building through their favorite hole. A moment later came another warning sound, followed by agitated squeaks.

"Look!" exclaimed the prior to Father Lorenzana, the provincial, "he has done it! The rodents are all running out!"

A dozen rats and even more mice streaked past them and scurried through their exit. This was, however, only a beginning. The hall was soon crowded with rodents of all sizes, each one bent on leaving the premises as though running from a fire.

Brother Martin smiled as he leaned over the edge of the staircase to watch. As the last of the intruders vanished through the hole, he made a small sign of the cross in its direction.

"Now, we shall have peace and so will you, my small friends," he remarked as he turned back to his tasks.

If Brother Martin was a friend even to rats and mice, he was also a friend to some people no less unwelcome. So it was that, later that week, as he was busy in his cell, he opened the door to two panting fugitives.

"Sanctuary," both cried hoarsely, as they dashed into the room.

Brother Martin took charge of them with calm competence.

"Stay here until I talk to the officers," he said firmly, indicating a few baskets of laundry.

With a bland smile, he faced the two angry soldiers who were soon pounding on the door.

"Yes?" he began vaguely. "Can I be of service to you?"

"We are after two thieves," said one. "Did they come this way?"

Brother Martin smiled even more broadly. He spread out his palms.

"Do you see them here? Is our convent a likely place for them to visit? We are poor friars."

"You may have hidden them, Brother. Come; give them up. They are no good."

"Oh, I am sorry to disagree with you," said Martin. "But I feel sure that there must be some good in them. Did not Christ die for them? Be more understanding; perhaps they were hungry when they stole."

"In that case, they have been hungry all their lives," said the younger officer, "for they are professional thieves."

Brother Martin frowned.

"Then they are to be pitied, are they not? I am sorry, gentlemen; I cannot help you."

The two officers exchanged glances. Then they glanced about the room and, seeing the baskets of laundry, they felt around inside the baskets. There was no sign of the thieves any place. Then they left, apologizing to Martin for the interruption.

From these two incidents drawn at random from Martin's busy life, it is clear that even if Rose had come to him as a complete stranger with her problem and asked his help, he would have gone all out to give it. But he already counted her a friend, and that since his childhood. He who had gathered into his heart the whole world of suffering, who had compassion even on thieves and rodents, would place at her disposal all his medical knowledge and spiritual wisdom. He himself was no stranger to the kind of trial that Rose was experiencing. Having a slight advantage over her in age, he had already reached the dark night of the soul, for he too had begun the practice of virtue as a child. However, in his case the purification had been seen by his spiritual father for what it was. This was due to the fact that the trial, as it came to him, assumed a more normal appearance.

Rose did not find it hard to confide in Martin, for she was used to exchanging views on the inner life with him. But she did find it hard to keep her own composure when faced by his obvious emotion. If he had begun to listen to her account of her so-called epileptic seizures with an overtone of clinical interest, he soon lost it. As Rose described her anguish and terror, her bewilderment and cruel sense of having lost God forever, tears gathered in his expressive eyes.

"Put the thought of having epilepsy out of your mind, Sister," he said with decision. "I can tell you now that you have no such thing. Epileptics do not remember what has happened during their attacks. As for what some of the Fathers have said, I do not think that you are mentally ill. Tell me, how long is it since you began to have these visions?"

"I have had visions frequently for the past five years. However, they have always been consoling and instructive until now. That is why I believe that these come from the devil."

"Can you describe what you see in more detail, Sister?" asked Martin.

Rose nodded. "Only too well."

Taking a firm grip on herself, she began to sketch for the Brother a few terse word-portraits. He stopped her before she could go on.

"I have met this gentleman myself, Sister, and I can vouch for the fact that he is as ugly as you say, no matter which face he wears. Now, tell me one thing, if you will. I know that you have suffered from aridity before; would you say that it made you love God more?"

"Yes, for I kept seeking him and striving to be better in order to please him."

"And that, my dear Sister, is why the Lord sent you that aridity. Now, why do you think he is permitting these visions of the judgment in which you feel that you are damned?"

Rose smiled in spite of herself.

"To make me love him more and seek for ways of pleasing him better, so that I may escape hell and enjoy his presence?"

Martin nodded.

"I am not at all surprised at this purification that the Lord permits you to bear. I should be more surprised if you had not begun to suffer some such trial. It is the lot of those whom God wishes to raise to the highest sanctity to pass this way. You should find in the very violence of your trial a source of encouragement, since he purifies most those for whom he has destined the most perfect union with himself."

Rose felt the courage mounting in her heart. Still, one question remained.

"Then why have the priests whom I consulted not understood, Brother?" she asked.

Martin looked at her gravely.

"God wills it; that is all," he said. "While you have support from creatures, you lean less on him. Enter into his rest in the midst of all that you suffer, although you neither see him nor feel his support. This is what I try to do myself, Sister," he added. "You see, you are not alone. It is true that my trial is not the same as yours, yet in God's plan it is perhaps meant to serve the same end. But forgive me for preaching. I am no priest," he said humbly. "I am only a poor *mulatto* on whom Jesus Christ looks with mercy."

"You have helped me, Brother Martin."

Rose returned from her talk with Martin strengthened in hope. It was well that she had gone to him. She was to find herself in the same trial almost till the end of her life. During much of that time, she would lack the sympathy and guidance of a priest. Her talks with Martin, then, meant much more to her than they had before. They were like oases in a desert.

Through the years in which Rose bore this purifying of the soul, she was not spared other sorrows almost as grim. In 1609, when her visions of the judgment were growing frequent for the first time, came the long-deferred royal decree deciding the issue of Indian personal service. The decree was a foregone conclusion to all but Rose, Martin and a few hopeful die-hards. The rapacious landlords had their way. The mine administrators and Indian *caciques* needed fear for their graft no more. The *audiencia* had triumphed.

For Rose, it was as though someone had let down a trap-door beneath her. Yet she still hoped in God. He would bring good out of this breach of justice; meanwhile, she would do all she could in the way of prayer, penance and the offering of whatever pain came to her. She soon had much to offer. The damp atmosphere of Lima during six months of the year had always caused her oppression of the chest. Her long hours of gardening and her prayer in the evenings now took their toll of her health. She found herself afflicted with asthma. This in itself was a heavy cross; but with it came another disease which, combined with it, could make her life a martyrdom and take that life from her. This was arthritis.

When she could scarcely breathe on account of her asthma, Rose had to take her hours of rest seated in a chair. She found this a frightful torment because her spine was so stiffened, especially at the waist, that she could hardly sit down. And after being seated, when she tried to stand she could not straighten up. At times, she should have been lying perfectly flat because of her arthritis, but then she would be gasping for breath and would have to be propped up in a sitting position because of her asthma. There was no escape from the dilemma, it seemed, except death. Then the fog would thin and her condition would ease for the time being.

This was enough, combined with her nightly visions of hell, to make Rose's life a constant torture. Still, she did not lose courage. She did not fall back from her self-imposed works of charity. So far as she could, she went on caring for the sick poor who came to her; when she was well enough, she walked valiantly with some Tertiary companion to visit sick members of the Order or indigent sufferers who had come to her notice. Unsatisfied by what she was already doing for the poor, she even conceived the idea of building an infirmary behind her home so that she might take on the care of bed patients. With her own hands she helped Mariana mix the mud and straw and fill the *adobe* brick molds. It was good for her, she said.

When she could kneel, she went serenely to her gardening as though nothing had happened. Oliva reproached her for this in vain; Rose was determined to ignore her own pain as much as was prudently possible. So, lifting bed patients became a part of her daily routine. When her arms were too stiff or she could not bend her back, Oliva replaced her, but unwillingly. For Rose to assume this extra work when she was ill herself seemed to her mother certain folly.

Martin shared Rose's pain in his compassionate heart, but there was little or nothing that he could do to help her. As she surely knew, her salvation lay in driving herself to exercise as much as she could. Once she stopped moving even for a minute, her back stiffened. As for her new venture, the infirmary, he approved of her motive; still, since she could not rely on her own strength to turn her patients, he thought that perhaps she should have waited. She might restrict her infirmary work to the dry months, he thought. Then her asthma and arthritis receded.

Had Martin been less unselfish, he would have been hard put to it to enter into Rose's joy over her infirmary. He himself had just received one of the hardest obediences of his life. He had been forbidden to bring sick paupers off the street into his cell or the convent infirmary. The dirt and vermin, the stench of their wounds, and their garrulous company distracted the friars—at least, those who had complained of Martin's charity to their prior. The fact that Martin bathed and deloused these abandoned wretches with tireless patience did not suffice to soothe the plaintiffs. His pleas were dismissed as a lack of charity for his brethen. He was told to desist from his ways and he did, but with breaking heart. In this great sorrow, faith alone sustained him. He saw in his prior's prohibition the will of God, and he offered the pain it caused him for the poor whom he could no longer help. For the present, the daily bread line alone was all that was left to him.

The next four years passed more or less without event in Peru. For Rose, they meant much suffering but more grace. She clung to God without seeing his hand, and she grew in calmness and self-mastery. But in 1613 came a crisis which shook the whole nation. No one with any vestige of conscience could have failed to feel alarm, frustration, righteous anger, grief and anxiety. For the religious orders of Peru, notably those which had furnished the *doctrineros*, it brought ruthless exposure of their failures. For Archbishop Toribio's successor in the see of Lima, it meant shock, disillusionment, and a desperate readjustment to a deplorable situation. For the King of Spain, who had received his title to the western colonies in virtue of his promise to christianize the Indians, it was a time of humiliation before the pope and the whole civilized world.

While the Flores family was living in Quive, Archbishop Toribio had named as parish priest of San Damián in Huarochiri a zealous diocesan priest named Francisco de Avila. Armed with a keen mind, an inquisitive eye, and his Quechua dictionary, this enterprising priest attacked the barriers posed by the Indian language, customs and hatred of Spaniards. He meant to reach the souls entrusted to him, to make himself as far as possible one of them. After the example of St. Toribio, he dealt kindly with their harshness, bore their insults with calm, and gradually won his way into their confidence. Then came the revelation. The Indians of his parish were idolaters as well as Christians. They saw no sin in their dual cult.

When he had regained his balance after this blow, Father Francisco began to explore other districts with the utmost cautions. As the months and years passed, he reached the conclusion that idolatry was almost as widespread in Peru then as it had been at the time of the Conquest. Almost as many sacrifices were made to the sun, almost as many prayers offered to *huacas*, as when Pizarro and his men first picked their way over the Incan highway to Cuzco. Christianity had been forced on them from without, yet inwardly the Indians kept their old faith. To them it represented all their lost heritage.

If we consider the elements of the Incan idolatry which were similar to the Christian religions and if we recall the superficial way in which Christian doctrine had been taught to the Indians, the discovery of almost universal idolatry among them as late as 1613 will be no surprise. When the Spaniard first raised the cross over Peru, the cross was already reverenced. It had in those times the same standing as any *huaca*. Seventy odd years later it had much the same value in the eyes of the Indians.

When the missionaries first began to preach the fundamentals of that faith through interpreters, they found to their amazement that most of those fundamentals were part of Incan faith. The Spaniards believed in an omnipotent, infinite Spirit-God, Creator of all; so did the Indians. The Spaniards preached the four last things: death, judgment, heaven and hell; the Indians nodded in agreement. The Spaniards preached the existence of purgatory, angels, and devils. They met no argument. They preached the sacrament of penance; they found a receptive audience.

What was, in fact, left to them to preach? Christ; but the Indians believed in Vira-Cocha, the bearded, human Son of God. The Trinity? Even this doctrine was preserved in a distorted form; they had but to use what they found as the apostle Paul had used the Greek pagan *data* as foundation for his Good News.

In fact, had the Christian missionaries been able to strip Incan idolatry of its superstitions, they would have been left with a sound basis for the true conversion of the Indians. But blocked by the language barrier and the quasi-military method of Spanish preaching, which antagonized the Indians, this ideal remained a dream. For all Peru and all Christendom, the awakening was rude.

How blameworthy the Indians were for the crimes committed in the course of their double religious life is debatable. How blameworthy colonial priests were is less so. But the state also shared the blame for the evident failure; it had constantly fought the bishops' efforts to crush the evils. The miseries of the Indians under the system of the *mita* fed the traditional Indian craze for fortune telling. Driven underground, the various castes of diviners who had flourished in Incan times found eager clients.

Deplorable though it was, the continuation of divining showed that, as a race, the Indians had not yet lost hope. They always looked to the morrow for some stroke of good fortune to ease their burden. Tales of past generations, told nightly in barracks and squalid huts by exhausted *mitayos*, nourished the flame.

It would be callous to dismiss the cult of Our Lady of Copacabana at the Cuzco and Lima shrines as that of just another *huaca*. If the Indian converts were confused by diabolical locutions coming from objects which seemed to them *huaca*, and hence worthy of worship, they accepted what they learned of the life of Christ as more detailed knowledge of their legendary God-Man, Vira-Cocha. Vira-Cocha is a composite figure of Christ and some apostle who preached him. Therefore, when the Indians who accepted Christianity without abandoning idolatry came to learn of Mary, they had no reason to place her on a level with their many *huacas*. To pay homage to some object or beast thought to possess a "grandfather spirit" was very different from paying homage to the

Virgin-Mother of Vira-Cocha, human Son of the omnipotent Spirit-God.

In her compassion for the Indian peoples, Mary had shown herself their mother with wondrous tenderness. In Mexico at Guadalupe, in Peru at Cuzco and Lima, she showered prodigies on her simple children. To these Indians who flocked to her shrines, she was the all-powerful, loving Mother of their God-Man, whatever their doctrinal errors in other respects.

The violence of Rose's grief on learning that the majority of Peru's Indians were still idolatrous seems understandable. She had devoted most of her prayers and penances to their welfare all her life. Now she saw them as lost almost to a man, unless. . . . It was this "unless" that sent her sense of the possible shooting sky high. Her mind was wholly taken up with the hope that she might gain for them a true conversion. Necessarily, this meant frantic efforts to revitalize the work of the clergy. This, in turn, required the conversion of many priests from tepidity or worse. It was much to hope for, yet Rose soared above all apprehensions. She never faltered in her trust in God's copious grace.

Still, she found her former peace shaken; her ordinary prayer had been changed to one unbroken act of tense petition. It was more than any soul could bear for long; yet, how could she do anything else? She wept and agonized, yet in vain. Her aridity grew. It seemed that she could no longer make a single act of adoration, of simple contemplative love of God. In the instant in which she first heard of the tragic discovery, her soul had leaped towards God in petition; now, she could not turn it to another act. Yet, she found no comfort in this petition; as she flung herself Godwards, God receded. Where he had formerly been waiting, she found nothing.

At first, Rose thought that the state would pass; but it did not. She found that she could not think of God. Her memory, her imagination, her understanding were obsessed by one thought: what was happening to her Indians. Gradually, her soul seemed to dry up for want of God. In this state, she felt as though she had offended him in some way. The sense of loss which caused her such anguish in her visions of the judgment and of hell was now diffused throughout her day.

Despite this, she had to carry on as best she could with her usual tasks. As the months passed, Rose groped for something that she could cling to until she should find peace, and with it God. At length the thought came to her that a more frequent use of ejaculations might help. She had tried saying the beads as she worked, wearing them slung over her shoulder. Interruptions came too often. She needed simplicity in her prayer; so her ejaculations, without being always the same, had to be fused in some way. But how? The answer came as an inspiration which filled her, for a time, with her first taste of joy for many months. She could not fail to share it with Martin as soon as she saw him again.

"I want to begin the practice of making an ejaculation each time that I take a stitch when I am doing needlework," she told her friend, her face aglow with enthusiasm. "And when I am engaged in other tasks not too absorbing, I shall use them, too. That way, it will be easy to keep the thought of God in mind."

Martin gazed down at Rose, his heart pierced with shafts of sympathy. The nature of this idea and the evident joy that it gave her told him better than anything else how dark her night was.

"That sounds splendid, Sister! What ejaculations will you use?"

"The names of God," Rose answered vivaciously. "All that are in the Bible."

"Do you know them all?" Martin asked in astonishment. Rose shook her head.

"I know some of them, of course, but not nearly all, I am sure. That is just the trouble. To find what I want myself, I should have to read the whole Bible; and of course I cannot do that."

Martin smiled. Throughout the Catholic world at that time, the only bibles available were huge Latin, Gothic-printed volumes.

"We have a number of bibles in the convent," mused Martin. "Perhaps you could ask one of the Fathers to make out a list."

"That is what I thought of doing," Rose answered. "Indeed, that seems to be the only solution. But which Father shall I ask?"

"Why not ask Father Provincial?" said Father Juan de Lorenzana, coming up behind them. He had just caught the last of Rose's words. "What can I do for you, Sister?" he inquired pleasantly.

He was glad of this opportunity to make the acquaintance of the young Tertiary whose miracles were the talk of the parish. Of course, the continual presence of out-of-season flowers on the altar of the chapel of the Rosary was a fact that faced him daily. Then, too, he had had occasion to see Rose at prayer in church and note her rapt expression. Sometimes, especially when she received Holy Communion, her face was transformed in a way that made him wonder if the glory of the blessed would differ from it. Her ardor when she received was so great that it affected her body, and a burning heat came from her lips.

Recently, the provincial had heard a story that made him wonder even more what was passing in this Tertiary's soul. She had been seen saying the Office of our Lady in the gar-

den, and when she bowed at the *Gloria Patri*, the shrubs and
flowers bowed with her. How he would like to know the interior of her soul! He had heard that she could not find a director. How tragic it would be if, lacking direction, she should
go astray! Now he turned to her affably, his ascetic face
softening as he smiled.

"I should like to obtain a list of all the names of God that
are in the Bible, so that I may use them as ejaculations while
I work," she said.

"That is easily done," the provincial answered. "But I may
need a little time to get you the complete list. If you promise
to be patient, I shall have it for you as soon as I possibly
can."

Rose's cheeks flushed with embarrassment and gratitude.

"I am so grateful, Father. I should never have dreamed of
putting you to such trouble."

Father Lorenzana waved his hands in a deprecatory gesture.

"That is nothing, Sister; I shall be happy to help you."

Several months passed before Father Lorenzana was able to
give Rose the list. For the sorely tried Tertiary, they were
months of painful aridity. She tried to hide her feelings and
succeeded for the most part; but once or twice she lost her
patience. Unfortunately, in one instance when she did so,
it was in front of friars from Holy Rosary; and her ire was
directed at them.

Then as now, there were fascinating dogmatic questions
still open to dispute, and the Dominicans were as fond of ex-
ploring them as any other priests of the time. One of the disputed doctrines was that which held that our Lady had been
conceived without original sin. Champions of the Blessed
Virgin as valiant as St. Bernard held that she must have been
conceived in original sin and sanctified later. As it was still
not clear how the privilege could have come to our Lady prior

to the Redemption, the whole question was quite obscure.

For the Dominicans, brothers of St. Thomas Aquinas and heirs of his doctrinal teaching, the question was especially difficult. Not only were there Thomistic documents to prove that the saint opposed the doctrine, but others to show that he favored it both as a young theologian and in his final years. However, the authenticity of one document—the final one—was hotly challenged by some of the friars.

Rose found herself present at one such debate. At first, she listened with concealed annoyance; but soon she could bear no more. Turning on her spiritual brothers with flaming cheeks, she vented her ire on them.

"This is not how the sons of St. Dominic should conduct themselves, wasting their time in useless disputes while souls are perishing!"

After her death, the reprimand was cited as a sign of her zeal, which in part it was. But at the time it did her reputation no good. To Rose it must have been a source of humiliation.

One day about four months after Father Lorenzana had made his promise, he stopped Rose on her way out of the church.

"Here is your list, Sister," he said. "I am sorry to have been so slow in giving it to you, but I do not have much free time and the Bible has many books."

Rose gasped. "Surely Your Paternity did not read the whole Bible to satisfy my wish!"

"Never mind, Sister," said the Provincial. "I could not obtain the full list any other way. But how many names of God do you think are in the Bible?"

Rose guessed, but her guess fell far below the total. It was one hundred and forty-nine. With effusive thanks, the young Tertiary took the list and hurried home. In the privacy of her room she read it with mounting delight. The names were so

beautiful! They filled her soul with light. For the first time
in many months, she tasted briefly her former union with
God.

What were these ejaculations which came to form so vital
a part of St. Rose's prayer? This is not the place to cite the
whole list, but it will be well to mention some of them. She
divided them into fifteen verses of ten ejaculations each, ending with a *Gloria Patri*. After this she made five petitions
found at the end of other litanies, adding a prayer in honor
of the triune God, praying for freedom from adversity and
peril. In view of her struggles at that time, it is of interest to
note which of the names Rose chose to repeat in her litany.
It was: *"Dios manso"* or *"gentle God."* Gentleness, the twin
sister of patience, was already characteristic of her in times of
calm. And although an upsurge of enthusiasm or a wave of
anger could still sweep her off balance, the time was to come
when her peace would be permanent and unruffled.

So, as she worked at the gossamer veils and opulent gowns
ordered by her mother's friends, the cupid's bow of her lips
shot arrows of love in rapid fire at the heart of God.

"Dios Espíritu!" (God, Spirit)

She finished one stitch.

"Dios simple!" (God, simple)

She took another.

"Dios inmortal!" (God immortal)

She poised her needle.

"Dios perfecto!" (God, perfect)

She plunged it through the stuff.

"Dios infinito!" (God, infinite)

She snipped a thread. So it went all day. In the mornings,
when she tended the sick who came to her for treatment, she
recited other snatches of her litany.

"Pacific God! God of longanimity! Loving God! Affable

God! Generous God! Patient God! Clement God! Sweet God! Meek God! Glory be to the Father and to the Son and to the Holy Spirit!"

When she went to the infirmary to nurse her bed patients, her mind turned to Christ the healer.

"Immaculate Lamb! Son of the Virgin! Good Shepherd! True Life! Seed of the Lord! Gate of heaven! Life of heaven! God, our life!"

As she went briskly and cheerfully from patient to patient, her heart expanded. She forgot her own sorrows, immersed in the love of God and his sufferers. All kinds of miseries found their way to this *adobe* room, but she had a remedy for each.

"Prayer is the great pharmacy where we can find the medicine for all our ills," she told her sick. They voiced their agreement and followed her movements with grateful eyes. But if she noticed these glances she gestured at her statue of the Infant Jesus which she had set in the window. "There is your little Doctor," she said. "He it is who will cure you; I am only doing his work and his will."

No disease was too loathsome for her to treat, although her stomach might turn. Sometimes she would leave the sick for a few minutes, retch painfully, then come back smiling. She set fragrant rosemary in wide-mouthed jars here and there through the room to help clear the air; nevertheless, often she was forced to turn hastily and gasp in the doorway. From day to day she fought her repugnance; but she never lost it till her death.

Once, while tending a negro slave at the home of her owner, her stomach quailed at the stench of the woman's ulcerated wounds. Rose fled from the room with a pan of bloody pus which she had drained off, and in a nearby alcove gave vent to her feelings. In her emotion she spoke aloud to herself, unaware that she was heard. With a scornful word of self-reproach for shrinking from her suffering sister in Christ, she drank the contents of the pan as a penance. That time, her stomach did not turn.

Here it must be mentioned that this summons by an eminent lady to tend one of her slaves is of utmost importance. It demonstrates the revolutionary impact of Rose's infirmary on Lima's society. In the humble room built behind her father's house, the young Tertiary upset the most cherished prejudices of her time and class. Until she began her work of mercy, race pride and an exalted sense of their dignity had kept Spanish ladies from tending the sick of subject peoples. Charitable though they were, they confined their care to the sick poor of their own race. Only through a money donation did they help Negroes, Indians. or *mestizos*.

The fact that Rose was asked to visit this slave woman shows that her mother's friend gauged her charity aright, but not all would have approved of it. But Rose's heart knew no barriers of race, color or class. Her interracial infirmary was a revolution in love.

If some of Oliva's friends were scandalized at Rose, Oliva feared worse than scandal. It seemed inevitable to her that Rose would catch a disease from those she tended. She looked on each patient as another threat to her daughter's life. Then, too, time taken to tend the sick was lost work time. We gather that from the time Rose built her infirmary, tension in the household tautened quickly. Doubtless other factors helped increase it, but the presence of the sick poor did not sweeten relations between Rose and her family. The quasi-miraculous nature of many cures worked by Rose on her patients alarmed them and some of her practices of devotion annoyed them. The utter disregard of convention which characterized her was too much for her family.

As life with her family grew more and more of a trial to herself as well as them, Rose began to look for some way of easing the tension. What she needed most was a place where she could be alone, working or praying as the case might be. Now that Juana was old enough to sit at needlework with her mother, Oliva did not need Rose's help so much. Indeed, there were days when the mere sight of the Tertiary habit set Oliva nagging. Why would Rose not marry? Being a Tertiary she was free to do so. Why run the risk of catching those diseases? When would she find a director to her taste?

This last was a matter that occupied Rose as well as her mother, but for different reasons. Oliva hoped that Rose would take as her new guide some priest who could curb her ardor and bend her will. Above all, she looked for the day when Rose would be forced to give up her penitential bed, although Oliva had to admit that her daughter's powers of endurance were clearly superhuman. During one Lent, when the new archbishop was trying to call a Council to deal with the Indian scandal, Rose simply stopped eating. Nothing but Holy Communion passed her lips, except for five pomegranate pips a day, which she chewed slowly in order to keep their bitter taste in her mouth as long as she could. During this time she began to say the Stations of the Cross in a way that suited her spirit but made her mother shake her head. First, she would scourge herself without mercy and then, taking a heavy wooden cross, make the rounds of the garden meditating on the various stations as she went. To her, this was no more than a sincere showing of her will to share Christ's sorrows. To her mother, it seemed a spiritual excess. However, she did not think of the practice as we would think of it today. In that time and place, devotion was shown in ways which seem to us extravagant.

Needless to say, Rose's wish to find a director was based on different motives. She loved obedience and looked on it as a guarantee of safety. In her fears and desolations, she needed a guide prudent and well versed in the ways of God with souls.

Where could she find him? For many months more she went on wondering. Then one day she came home, her face radiant with joy.

"I have found a new director, Mama!" she announced gaily. "And he is one of the most able priests in the city. Is God not spoiling me?"

Oliva drew her lips into a thin, firm line. God was not spoiling Rose, and she knew it. But she said nothing of her own anguish. Instead, she asked her daughter the all-important question: "Who is he?"

Rose laughed. It was the first time that she had done so since her visions of hell began.

"You would never guess, Mama, if I gave you till doomsday! He is our neighbor."

Oliva frowned.

"I suppose that he is one of the friars at Holy Rosary. How could I possibly guess his name? There are so many!"

"Well, I shall tell you; then you will see how blessed I am. He is the Provincial, Father Juan de Lorenzana!"

Oliva screamed and jumped to her feet, dropping her fragile handwork on the floor. Tears began to flow from her eyes; as she began to speak, her voice rose to a shriek.

"Oh my God! What will become of us! You have taken the inquisitor as your director! You are going to open your soul to him! Daughter, you are mad!"

CHAPTER TEN

Vigil in July

WITH THE HELP of her new director's calm counsels, Rose regained her spiritual balance. The use of the names of God which he had looked up for her still proved a balm to her soul, as did the writings of the Venerable Louis of Granada, which came into her hands at this time. Soon she saw that they contained the nourishment that she needed in her life of prayer. From that time on, they were her constant companions. His *Book on Prayer and Meditation* has been called her *vademecum*, and his reflections on the Passion filled her with love, pity, compunction, and zeal for Christ's honor.

Written in a simple yet forceful style, these books helped her find Christ when she felt arid. No matter what her anxieties, a few moments of reading from these meditations brought her peace. She lost herself in the mysteries of God's love with a child's delight. Never could Louis of Granada find a more diligent reader of his treatises. If anyone should ask why Rose never looked for another writer to fire her piety once she came upon the works of Louis of Granada, he need only read them to learn why.*

More intensely now, Rose felt the need for privacy and silence; she needed a place of retreat. As the leafy hermitage had been her refuge in childhood and young girlhood, it was normal that her thoughts should turn to ways of building

---

* Cf. *Summa of the Christian Life,* 3 vols., translated by Jordan Aumann, O.P., and published by Herder of St. Louis.

some such hut again. Then, the living boughs had shielded her; now, however, she needed more light than a leaf-hermitage could admit. She had her sewing to do; she had her Office to say; she had her meditation book to read. To build an *adobe* hermitage for herself became her ambition, one which she lost no time in confiding to Father Lorenzana.

The friar looked kindly on Rose's project and gave his consent to her campaign to gain her mother's permission. The Queen of heaven and the Infant Jesus added their all-vital support. Rose went to the statue of Our Lady of the Rosary, placing her dilemma in the Virgin's hands. As a sacrifice, she gave up her sole possession of worth, a coral rosary which had perhaps been the gift of one of her rich admirers. Brother Fernando, the sacristan on duty at the time, took it and hung it around our Lady's neck. To reach the statue, he had to use a ladder. When Rose came back later to pray before the statue, her beads were in the Infant's hand. The Brother was confounded; he had not moved them and no one else had access to the ladder.

"It is surely a miracle, but what can it mean?" he asked.

Rose knew. She was to keep after her mother until she had her consent for the building. In the meantime, she began on another project still dearer to herself and all the Tertiaries: the establishment of a Tertiary convent in Lima. This annoyed Oliva even more than the plea for a hermitage, as it meant soliciting the names of prominent persons for a petition to the king. Also, she was still obstinately set on Rose staying in the world. Just lately they had met the very *caballero* for her. He was a newcomer to Lima who had moved, with his brother, into a neighboring house. He was pleasant, handsome, well off financially, and quite fascinated by Rose. His name was Vincent de Montesino.

But if Oliva would not yield to her daughter's pleading, divine providence soon gave Rose the ally she needed. Don

Gonzalo de la Maza, a noble and eminent court official, had heard of her holiness and he determined to make her acquaintance. Gaspar seems to have retired before this from his post in the viceregal guard, so the royal accountant had to have recourse to a casual meeting. Enlisting his wife in the cause, he sent her to Santo Domingo with the purpose of speaking to Rose. When she did so, her own gracious ways and genuine piety charmed the young Tertiary. She soon asked the Mazas to her home to meet her parents. The Mazas found Oliva and Gaspar congenial hosts; soon they invited them to their home. The more they saw of Rose the more they loved her. It was not long before she ranked, in their hearts, with their own two daughters.

Don Gonzalo's fatherly love for Rose made him partial to her every wish, so he could see no flaw in her plan for the hermitage. Sensing his need of a second for the verbal duel with Oliva, he called on Father Lorenzana. The provincial affably sided in with the great man's plan, and together they went to the Flores home to ask for the hermitage.

Had the friar come alone, Oliva would have held out, inquisitor or no. But she esteemed Gonzalo too highly and set too great a store by his friendship to say no to him. It was, therefore, not long before Rose had her hermitage. Fernando helped her mix the mud and straw for the bricks. It was his last friendly act before leaving for the army and Chile.

Rose did not have her hermitage long before she grew gravely ill. Oliva blamed the dampness, but words were no remedy. One night she and Gaspar sat up with their daughter in vigil, fearing lest she would die; then, as soon as morning came, they called for a priest to give her the last anointing.

"Let us pray for Sister Rosa de Santa María, who is being anointed," said the prior of the convent of the Holy Rosary as the community knelt in thanksgiving after the conventual Mass. A shocked gasp came from the community as he began

the prayer. *"Ave Maria, gratia plena, dominus tecum, bene-
dicta tu in mulieribus et benedictus fructus ventris tui Jesus.*
. . ."

What were Brother Martin's thoughts as he prayed for the
friend whom he thought was dying? We can well imagine; we
can picture, too, the purity of his prayer for her. He wanted
her to live, humanly speaking; yet if God wished to take her
now, what could he say but: "Thy will be done"? As soon as
he could spare a moment from his work, he went to the
chapel to pray for her; it was there that Father Lorenzana
found him.

"Brother! Brother! Come to yourself! You have missed your
luncheon!"

The holy mulatto roused himself and looked up at his superior, his eyes full of tears.

"Pardon me, Father Provincial. I forgot about the time.
How is Sister Rose?"

"She is much better, Brother. Go in peace and eat your
bread. She is eating hers."

While Rose was still convalescing, her mother paid a visit
to Father Lorenzana. He was no stranger to her purpose. She
had already asked him twice for leave to destroy her daughter's
bed. Now she was coming to ask him again. This time, he
agreed. Perhaps she was right; perhaps the penance had undermined Rose's health. Oliva left the convent in triumph.
After so many threats, tears and remonstrations she had her
way.

At home, Oliva stood staring at Rose's bed, that object
which had been the cause of such grief to her and which she
was now free to destroy. How to begin? The pent-up frustrations of her past life were hurling themselves at the breakwater of her will. Swaying a little under the force of the
waves that surged against her, the breakwater suddenly
crashed. With a sob of grief, she flung herself at the accumu-

lation of broken glass and pottery which she hated as though it had been living. She would sweep this detestable litter into the Rímac.

Snatching up a sack which Rose had filled with dried bitter herbs and hidden under the bed, Oliva emptied the contents onto the floor. Then, standing ankle-deep in the herbs, she began to drop the pieces of broken glass and pottery one by one into the sack. There was nothing real in the world but these vile fragments of old glass jugs, cups, vases, pipes, nails, and her hands—her hands which kept snatching them up one by one. At last it was over. She let herself out the door and ran along the path beside the dining room towards the *patio*. But it was not this that was her destination. The kitchen and infirmary lay beyond, and behind them the fringe of wilderness along the Rímac.

At last Oliva reached the river. Half laughing, half sobbing, she summoned her strength. First she wrenched the heavy sack behind her, then forward. She let it go; it struck the water. The violence of the wrench threw her to the ground. For a long time she lay there, panting and gasping. Then she began to sob. Her sobs were hard and racking; they shook her whole body. She sobbed without knowing why, for had she not just done what for two years she had yearned to do?

When Rose resumed her ordinary life, she found Father Lorenzana firmer in his discipline. Previously he had gently urged her to curtail her penances; now he commanded her to do so.

"I do not want you to scourge yourself so much, Sister," he said. "Heretofore I have allowed you a hundred strokes at a time. Now, take no more than a hundred a week. You must be prudent. If at any time you feel unwell, leave off the penance until you are able to take it without undue strain."

Rose nodded meekly, although it cost her something. It was a great sacrifice; but God asked it of her through her director. The thought of arguing or disobeying did not occur to her.

"And another thing," the priest added. "You have been taking all the strokes on one part of your body. That is too severe for you now. I want you to dispose them over your whole body so that no one part will suffer much."

"Yes, Father. And now, may I beg your blessing?"

"Surely, Sister, if you will take it standing. I do not wish you to kneel in your present state of health." As Rose opened her mouth to answer, he added brusquely: "No arguments, if you please. Obey and win merit."

As it happened, Rose's fever came back that week and she was too ill to take the discipline, but by the following Thursday she was well enough to go to Mass and Holy Communion and do her daily work. On Friday she recalled Father Lorenzana's permission; if she divided the hundred strokes into several acts of penance he would approve. So, at an opportune time she went to her hermitage and began to scourge herself. Since she had not done so for some days, she made up for lost time by using all her strength for every blow. If she had known that she had an audience, she would have stopped at the end of one *Miserere,* but her visitor had come unseen and silently to her hermitage door. It was her friend, Isabel de Mejía.

Isabel had already gone to Father Lorenzana, begging him to force Rose to have mercy on herself. He had assured her that she already had her wish. She therefore assumed that Rose had disobeyed. As she listened to the seemingly endless whine of the lash and the sound of Rose's voice reciting the penitential psalms more than once, her anger knew no bounds. She had thought Rose a saint; now the reverse seemed true. She was a fraud, this *beata* whom half the nobility of Lima sought as an oracle!

Inside, Rose went on with her discipline. For priests and

missionaries, for the conversion of sinners, for the Indians, for the poor black slaves.

Isabel went straight to Father Lorenzana. She found him in a bad mood. He had just received a complaint about his penitent, Rose de Flores: she practiced witchcraft; she healed by magic arts; a light was seen shining around her grotto when she was there at night. Now he listened to Isabel with mounting impatience. So Rose was disobedient! She was dishonest with him! He had been deceived!

When Rose came to the convent as usual for direction and sent the sacristan to ask for him, Father Lorenzana came briskly towards her, his face impersonal, as though he were looking through her.

"You wished to speak to me about something, Sister?" he asked blandly.

Rose looked up at him in bewilderment.

"Why, Father, I have come to review my permissions as I always do on Saturday. Did you not ask me to?"

The friar looked at her in feigned astonishment.

"There must be some mistake, Sister. I am not your director. I am not the one whom you obey."

Rose turned pale.

"Why, Reverend Father, what have I done to offend you?"

"You have no idea, of course," said Father Lorenzana. "Well, if you wish to know, ask your friend, Isabel de Mejía. It is from her that I have learned how perfect is your virtue! What sincerity! What obedience! What religious simplicity!"

"Then, Your Paternity no longer wishes to direct me?" asked Rose with pain. "Really, I cannot understand in what way I have disobeyed you. Nor have I had any quarrel with Isabel. It is all a surprise to me."

"It was to me also," answered the friar. "I had formed

quite other impressions of you. And now, Sister, if you will excuse me, I have important work to do!"

Father Lorenzana was indeed exceptionally busy, which may account for his hastiness in judging Rose. It may have some bearing, too, on the fact that he had failed to ask Isabel de Mejía for more specific evidence before condemning Rose in his mind. When one is in the midst of a serious problem, he is apt to deal briefly with new problems that present themselves.

The provincial was in the throes of such a problem. It was a question of the loss of the convent and church entrusted to him as well as the University of San Marcos. So heavily was the Province of St. John the Baptist in debt that disaster loomed before him. He had spent sleepless nights in prayer and penance, asking for light that he might find some way out of bankruptcy. Still no help came.

Moreover, his work as inquisitor kept him engaged much of late. Don Francisco de Avila, the parish priest of San Damián in Huarochiri, who had first learned of the idolatry practiced by the Indians, had sent for two Jesuits well versed in Quechua. With them he had gone on with his investigation, visiting first the five towns of his *doctrina*. In the following October they had gone to Lima to see the archbishop, bringing with them a collection of small idols, *huacas*, and *conopas* or mummies.

On Sunday, December 20, a sort of *auto de fé* was to be held in the main *plaza*, solely for Indians. All Indians living within four leagues of Lima were to come at four in the afternoon. A procession was being planned; its members were to meet at the house of the *corregidor* of the Indians, called the *corregidor minor*, in the University *plaza*. From there they would march to the *plaza mayor*. An idolatrous Indian priest (baptized) named Hernando Pauccar, was cited. He was to hear the charges and sentence from a pulpit erected there for the purpose. Together with his colleagues, Father Lorenzana had set the punishment at two hundred strokes of the scourge in public. In addition, Pauccar was to have his head shaved and be moved to Chile. There he was to live in the college of the Jesuits.

A bonfire would then be lit in which 3,000 idols, some mummies and bodies of Indians which had been receiving worship would be burned. It was to serve as an example to the Indians who would see the fire, and it was to be reinforced by a sermon in Quechua, the text of which Father Lorenzana had already checked. Plans were being made to name an investigator of idolatry who, with priests capable of the work, would go on with the visitation until every corner of the land under Spanish rule had been covered.

Other tasks of major import would soon tax his prudence. Research was in progress on the Chilean apostolate. Father Valdivia, who had been in charge of it, had died a martyr on December 14, 1612. He had to be replaced; and the joint consultations of Lima's most eminent priests would offer some help to the archbishop who had to name the successor. It was not a pleasant task, for whoever might go would probably follow Valdivia, who had met his death at the hands of the Araucanians after spending himself without stint for their good.

With all these grave problems in sight, Father Lorenzana soon put his displeasure with Rose out of his thoughts. He would learn by experience; never again would he take on the work of directing a soul as long as he had the office of provincial and inquisitor. Now that he had learned that Rose was disobedient, he would be forced to review all that he knew of her supernatural acts and the charismata which she seemed to possess. There was the accusation he had received against her, charging her with witchcraft. Dared he dismiss it as the work of some malignant hand?

But he must not act hastily. It would suffice for the present to keep her in sight, to mark any behavior out of keeping with the sanctity that she seemed to have. Then later, if some specific evidence should show itself against her, he would be forced to proceed.

Viceroy García had died on August 5, 1610. He was succeeded by the Count of Montesclaros, no model of morality. As his affairs became known, Gaspar thanked providence that he was no longer at court. The viceroy had come to Peru wifeless, but spent no lonely hours. Soon he had sired a son and daughter by different ladies, one his kinswoman.

Later, the viceroy seems to have married or been joined by his wife from Spain. At any rate, he acquired a consort. Rose soon found herself the object of this lady's attentions. Well aware of Rose's power with God, she wished to assure herself of her friendship. In her domestic trials she needed the encouragement this would give her. If Rose's prayers could not smooth her path, nothing could.

How did the lady hear of Rose? From Gonzalo de la Maza. The radiant description that he gave of his young friend's charms and sanctity intrigued her, and at her request he and his wife, María de Uzateguí took her to visit Rose in her hermitage. Gaspar and Oliva were supremely honored; such an attention left them in a state of shock. It was a shock that they were to feel more than once. Often, too, they were to see the viceroy's carriage drive up and be handed a gift which the lady had sent to their daughter. Rose could not understand why the countess was interested in her and wished heartily that she could escape notice. Still, she knew how to return the great lady's kindnesses graciously, for instance, by sending her a cross of flowering rosemary which she had trained to grow in that shape.

These marks of affection on the part of Peru's First Lady filled Oliva and Gaspar with fresh hope as to Rose's future.

The climax came when she was invited to the palace. She went with her parents and the Mazas. All passed during the visit as Oliva wished; Rose's etiquette was flawless, her manner frank yet dignified. If only she would use her opportunities, she could take a foremost place in society and her family with her.

It was at this juncture that Vincent de Montesino, the Flores' new neighbor who had aroused Oliva's hopes, called specifically for the first time on Rose. When at other times he had met her socially, they had been chaperoned. Now, perhaps, since he wished to speak to her only for a moment about an order for collars, they would be left alone.

Unfortunately for his plan, Rose was working that day with her mother and Juana, not alone in the hermitage. Oliva brought Vincent in with a gracious smile. She was not deceived; if Vincent wished to have collars made, he had no need to come in the daytime. He was frequently an evening guest at the house.

Rose, too, was not deceived. She greeted her caller coolly and looked with downcast eyes at the collar pattern which he had brought with him. It was for a plain, turnover collar; some of the more daring gentlemen favored them now rather than the cancillated ruff. Raising her glance to the crucifix which hung on the wall across from her, she treated him to a sermon.

"Ah, good Jesus," she exclaimed, "how admirable is thy patience! And you," she added, turning to Vincent, "know that there are no secrets from God. You are here for quite another thing than this affair of the collars, and I would say it aloud if I did not fear to make you blush."

Her admirer stood, open-mouthed and silent, listening to her homily. His handsome face flushed and he was about to answer angrily when Rose went on, this time kindly.

"What does not lead to God is a lie; what flatters the flesh endangers salvation. Do you not know the danger you risk in letting your eyes enjoy what they wish? Is it not written: 'He who loves danger shall perish in it'?"

Evidently, Vincent grasped one fact during this speech, and that was the ardent love of truth that made Rose turn on him. If he had been sincere in his wish for new collars, she would have served him pleasantly. Instead, it had been a mere ruse; and now he was in her bad books. However, he could congratulate himself on this: before, her manner had always been distant though polite; now, it was informal though fiery. Now too—and this consoled him in his mortification—she seemed to care about him. If her interest was in his soul, so be it; he would use this means to win her. She had read his heart and knew that he loved her; she knew, too, that he had not thought overmuch of his soul. Very well; he would think of it now to please her; perhaps by this means he would conquer.

It was with these sentiments that the young man answered Rose in tones of gentle humility. She was already ashamed of her outburst, for she knew that it had hurt him deeply. He had, after all, done nothing to deserve it, save to use a mental reservation in stating his reasons for asking to see her. As she listened to his answer her heart expanded maternally and took him into her friendship. If she could strengthen this soul and lead him to God, she would spare no words to do so.

So it was that, early next morning, worshippers at weekday Mass in Santo Domingo's saw Vincent kneeling gravely among them. They were not a little amazed, for in the short time that he had lived in Lima he had made a name for himself as a carefree gallant. What was their edification when, at Communion time, they saw him receive devoutly! After Mass, he made a long thanksgiving; however, he did not walk

home with Rose. Rose had her sacristy work in the chapel of
Our Lady of the Rosary.

Later that day, Vincent called again on his neighbors. This
time there was no talk of collars. He had come to see Sister
Rose, he told Gaspar and Oliva. Hearts brimming with joy,
smiles wreathing their faces, the two parents announced him
to Rose. To their astonishment, she greeted him cordially,
gesturing to him to sit near her while she went on with her
needlework. For more than an hour he sat with her, Oliva
going discreetly to the opposite side of the room to teach
Juana an embroidery stitch. But her joy at Rose's evident
pleasure in receiving Vincent would soon be punctured. Indeed, Oliva would feel a wound that went straight through
her, piercing her dearest dreams mortally.

Rose had kept her vow of virginity secret till now, knowing
the pain it would give her parents. When the time came for
her to make her profession as a Tertiary, she had not
pronounced the vow of chastity which Tertiaries wearing the
full habit of the Order were free to make if they chose. She
had her private vow of virginity, and that sufficed for the moment. If later she should find it possible to take the vows of
religion in a Tertiary convent, she would do so. Now, however,
there was need of reaching a true understanding between herself and her new friend. Rose was not the one to let him
cherish delusions. If she agreed to let him call daily, as he
now asked leave to do, it was strictly on a friendly basis with
no tinge of courtship about it. For this reason, she told him
what she had so far confided to few, that she had vowed her
love to Christ.

Vincent took the blow manfully and came back for more.
He loved Rose enough to take what she gave him, so long as
it was affection of some kind. And that she was fond of him
he had no doubt. So it was that from this time on Rose re-

ceived Vincent daily and spoke to him of all that interested
her. She strove to arouse in his soul a life of piety. He followed her guidance as simply as a child.

Soon she had him making mental prayer like Fernando;
and he began on his own to practice gentle penances. Not the
smallest of these was to rise every morning in time to go to
early Mass, where Rose would see him. And every morning,
too, he received Holy Communion.

In an age when frequent Communion was rare, the fact
that Vincent had begun to receive daily could not escape
notice. When, at Rose's suggestion, he went to one of the
friars at Santo Domingo's for daily confession and direction,
the furor grew. It loudened when his daily visits to Rose became known, and his frank praise of her came to the ears of
her former confessors. There were in the convent at least a
dozen friars who knew that Rose had a vow of virginity, not
counting Martin, in whom she had probably confided. They
were not at all pleased by her familiarity with this gentleman.
Father Lorenzana was pained when he heard of it. But worse
was to come.

When some weeks had passed and Vincent still came to
see Rose daily without proposing, her parents grew anxious. If
Rose spent all her time with him though he did not intend to
marry her, other young men would not court her and she
would be left. One evening, therefore, at the close of the
visit, Gaspar drew Vincent aside and asked him adroitly as to
his plans. Great was his dismay when the *caballero*, with tears
in his eyes and voice, answered that he had none. How could
he, when Rose was pledged to Christ!

"But, what do you mean, Vincent?" asked Gaspar. "She is
not a nun. As a Tertiary, she is free to marry."

"I mean her vow of virginity, my Lord," said the young
man openly. "If she were free to marry me, and would do so,
I should be the happiest man in Peru. But she is God's. May

his will be done! At least I have her friendship and, I believe, her esteem. I count myself blessed to have that much. She has shown me the beauty of virtue and the charms of a life of prayer. I would never try to deflect her from her vow."

Gaspar had rigid control over his facial muscles and voice, when he chose to use it. Such control had been needful in his life at court. Now he laid a paternal hand on Vincent's shoulder and replied as though he were not in a fury.

"Well, then, continue your visits to our daughter. So far as we are concerned, you are always welcome. And I shall tell you frankly that we could have wished for another course for Rose than the one she has chosen. Still, as you say, God's will be done!"

Vincent left, consoled. He did not guess that he had unleashed on the head of Rose an unparalleled storm. The instant that he left, Gaspar charged into the room where Rose sat sewing with her mother and Juana. In raging words he assailed her for taking her vow against their will. Obedience to one's parents was the law of God. How could she think to please him by disobeying?

So went the first sally. What followed? Hysteria. First Rose's mother, when she grasped what Rose had done, gave vent to her frenzy. Then Juana, worked up by her screams and tears, added her own. Then her brothers came in, drawn by the din, and their rage surpassed all that had gone before.

Rose listened in silence to all that was shouted at her. But at last, with a cry of anguish, she rushed from the room. No one pursued her; their rage had exhausted them. Besides, by now they realized that they must calm their passions and compose themselves; the Mazas were due to come for supper.

That evening Gonzalo came again to Rose's rescue. On being told that she had made a vow of virginity against her parents' will and that she had refused an eligible suitor, he offered to give her a dowry to enter the Poor Clares. At first, Oliva and Gaspar argued, but Gonzalo turned to Rose. Would she be able to find the life she desired in the Poor Clares? Rose hesitated; and while she sought for words in which to couch her answer, Oliva gave in. If Rose wished to be a Poor Clare, she would consent to her entry. Then Gaspar, seeing his wife's change of heart, gave his consent.

But Rose was a Dominican Tertiary; she had no wish to leave her order, even though it meant being able to enter the cloister and take the vows of religion. She esteemed the Poor Clares, she said, but to enter it was not for her. What she needed was a convent of her own order in Lima. When that was established she would gladly accept Gonzalo's generous gift of a dowry.

This refusal to fall in with their friend's suggestion enraged Rose's parents more than ever. Next morning when she appeared at her mother's door to call her for Mass, she found Oliva in no mood to go. What was more, she informed Rose that in the future Sunday Mass and Communion would suffice. As for visits to the Blessed Sacrament, their home was surrounded by chapels. Let her make her visits from her hermitage.

Rose took this outburst calmly. During the past night she had been through so much that she was emotionally drained. It was only later, as she knelt in her hermitage and began to follow the Ordinary of the Mass in spirit, that the fullness of grief came over her; but God caught her up into himself and she was consoled. It is to the zeal of a fellow Tertiary that we owe our knowledge of the nature of this consolation. When, for many days, Rose had failed to attend daily Mass, receive Communion, or make her visit to the Blessed Sacrament and our Lady, this Tertiary came to rebuke her.

"Sister, I feel it my duty to tell you what I think and what all are saying. You carry this affair of being a hermitess too far. You have not been at daily Mass or Holy Communion for three weeks. Is this the spirit of the daughters of St. Catherine? I cannot understand you; you were so fervent. Can you not see that, leaving the ordinary path of virtue, you endanger your soul?"

"Pardon me, Sister," Rose answered. "I do not stay at home of my own accord. But how generous God is! Every morning for this past three weeks I have been able to go to three or four Masses in spirit, at Santo Domingo's, the chapel of the Holy Ghost, at St. Sebastian's or St. Marcel's."

From this revelation, it is clear that Rose now enjoyed the gift of being present in some mysterious way in several distant places. This same charism was also enjoyed by St. Martin de Porres, who was reported as being seen in Morocco, in China and in Mexico, without having left Lima.

The charism of apparent bilocation assumes different forms in the lives of the saints. In some cases the soul seems to leave the body for a time and go to another place where it takes on visible form. Sometimes, on the other hand, the individual is engaged in some activity or other, while in another place the likeness of the person is seen, perhaps through angelic intervention. Finally, the individual is sometimes transported only in spirit to some place other than where the person actually is, but is in no way visible in the distant place. Rose was not seen by anyone when she visited various places in spirit.

The Tertiary who thought Rose deluded because she stopped going to daily Mass and Communion was guilty of rash judgment; yet she was frank enough to face her friend with the charge. Others who had noticed her absence from church drew the same conclusions but acted less openly. So it was that one day, just after Vincent had left her and Oliva was entertaining the wife of Gonzalo de la Maza in the patio,

Rose had callers. Father Lorenzana and his fellow inquisitors had come to examine her spirit.

The inquisitors were five in number; four were priests. Rose knew them all: Fathers Martínez, Velázquez, Luís de Bilbao, and Pérez. The fifth was a layman remarkably versed in theology: Doctor Juan de Castillo. As a medical man, he could judge when a suspect was a mental, not a spiritual case. It was a strange choice of personnel that drew together three persons whom the Church was later to single out as models of Christian holiness. Rose, of course, is canonized; Doctor Castillo is beatified; and Father Martínez is Venerable.

Since the hermitage was too small to accommodate them, the inquisitors led Rose to the house. Oliva and the wife of Gonzalo de Maza were allowed to attend the examination. Their presence was both a source of strength and anguish to Rose. She felt secure because she had never acted save with an upright will. If she should prove to be in error, she would be the first to change her opinion. But her mother feared that she was deluded or worse. She expected an adverse verdict, and María de Uzateguí also feared the worst. Therefore, although Rose was grateful for their concern for her, to see them suffer on her account was an added trial.

To Rose's surprise, Father Lorenzana did not question her, nor did any of the other priests. It was Doctor Juan de Castillo who took charge of her inquisition, the one examiner whom she did not know. He began with a general question as to how long she had practiced prayer. She answered that she had done so since her earliest years. She spoke of her sense of the presence of God within her; the happiness she felt in it kept her from finding consolation elsewhere.

Had she ever read books on mystical theology? Rose shook her head. She had never had such books at her disposal.

"Experience alone has taught me the little I am saying; that is why I have such trouble in making understood what takes place within me. I do not even know if my kind of prayer has a proper name."

Doctor Castillo then explained Rose's prayer to her in words that leave no doubt as to what degree she had already reached. She had been in the dark night of the soul long enough to be purified of most impediments to divine union. She had already entered the third stage of the spiritual life, the unitive way. Human faculties do not reach this kind of prayer by their own effort, he told her. God himself raises the soul to it. It is not an acquired science; it is a kind of infusion that comes from the Holy Ghost.

María de Uzateguí smiled and nodded at Oliva. She, however, did not return the smile. She was in a state of shock; nothing that passed around her registered, although she heard it. The doctor's manner would have bewildered her, had she fully grasped its import. She had steeled herself for threats, denunciations, accusations of false mysticism or a declaration of insanity. At the very least, she had looked for a medical diagnosis of Rose's visions as epileptic. Instead of this, the doctor was speaking to Rose paternally.

"In this state," he continued, "the spirit is first wholly stripped of earthly things, then filled by the Lord by a wholly heavenly light and inflamed with a very pure love which, to the creature, is a kind of foretaste of eternal joys."

Rose breathed a prayer of relief and thanksgiving. She had not been deluded after all! With lightening heart she listened as the doctor went on to explain her prayer in more detail. Then he asked how long and how she had fought the evil inclinations of nature, the demands of self-love, the vices, the passions. She explained that from infancy she had been drawn to practice virtue; if some involuntary movement arose in her against good, she had only to recall God's presence to repress it.

The doctor smiled. Inwardly, he himself prayed for light.

This was usually the most vital moment in an inquisition, the moment when false virtue tore off its mask, when delusion showed itself, when malice and pride revealed their vain disguises. He phrased his next question with care, yet easily. He had often asked it.

"The soul does not rise to the degree where you are without passing through trials. Tell us if you have suffered contradictions or persecutions on the part of men."

A frown passed over Father Lorenzana's already grave countenance. What would Rose say? He himself was present as her judge, and he had cast her off as his spiritual child. Then her mother, too, was present, and as Rose's former director, he knew something of the intimate family trials that centered on her. In these trials Oliva had often been foremost, acting as aggressor. How could Rose tell the truth without wounding charity? But he silenced his thoughts, Rose was speaking. He watched the movement of her lips for the slightest grimace that might show insincerity.

"The singularity of my life has sometimes merited vexations and insults." She drew a deep breath. Her examiners waited tensely for her next words; would she inveigh against those who had troubled her? If she did, it was a danger signal. True charity alone meant true sanctity. This formed the key to her soul which would soon lead them to knowledge of her true dispositions. "But I had to bear troubles more terrible than those which come from men; those are interior desolations."

It was all that Father Lorenzana could do to keep from clapping.

"Bravo, Sister Rose," he murmured to himself.

Rose had turned the accusation against herself rather than others by drawing attention to her way of life and calling it singularity; then, she had done what he knew was more heroic for her than a thousand disciplines to blood: she had herself introduced the question of her inner trials, the very trials which had brought on charges that she was deluded or unbalanced mentally.

"Can you describe these desolations for us, Sister?" asked the doctor.

Rose began to speak of her visions of hell and the judgment. Oliva was still in a daze, but she caught the gist of what her daughter was saying and her heart sank despondently. Now the paternal manner would change; now she would hear Rose's life stripped of its deceptions and delusions. What would happen to those miracles, those incredible fasts and penances? Would they not be called the work of the devil?

Now the doctor asked Rose how long she had experienced her visions of the judgment and of demons. Rose told him.

"What advice have your directors given you on these experiences?" he asked.

"I have sought help from them without success," she answered in a gentle voice, sad yet full of resignation. "Some have not understood the explanations I have tried to make of the source of my torments; yet I am not surprised, for I cannot explain myself well."

Father Lorenzana's facial muscles relaxed. His tension was lifting. Again, Rose had denounced herself and spared those who had caused her suffering. If this soul were deluded, he could wish all souls to be so deluded.

Doctor Castillo asked Rose to describe what she felt.

"The torment of fire would seem little beside these interior pains," she said slowly. "The visions that appear to me and the terrors I feel are so ghastly that they would suffice to tear my life away a thousand times if God did not save it by the miracle."

The young Tertiary paused; she drew in her breath sharply. The sound was audible in the grave silence.

"I can say, like the prophet-king," she concluded, "the sorrows of hell have surrounded me, and I am in the toils of death."

The doctor leaned forward and grasped the arms of his chair. He seemed to have forgotten that there were others in the room besides Rose and himself.

"When you were in these thick shadows," he said in a voice full of pity, "conceiving the hope of seeing them end, you suffered the desolation of souls held fast in purgatory. When, on the other hand, the hope of escaping was taken from you, you felt something of the pains of hell."

Rose nodded.

"Now, why does God send you such torments? Because they teach your soul to know yourself and him. In passing thus from light to dark, from dark to light, she sees on the one hand her own nothingness, on the other what she has from God; on the one hand, what she is in herself, on the other what God does in her. Several saints canonized today have passed through the furnace in which you yourself have been thrown; they asked God to spare them this trial, offering to bear every other trial save that, which proves what it is in violence."

Oliva's face wore a look of incredulity. What was she to think? Was this the doctor's method of questioning, to gain the confidence of the person being examined and so bare the truth? María de Uzateguí began to smile; the worst was over. Rose's case was being heard sympathetically.

"Now, will you tell us what happens to you on leaving this hellish night?" the doctor asked.

Rose remained silent, trembling and blushing. The priests frowned in disapproval; Oliva sat stunned.

"I asked you, Sister, to tell us what happens to you when you are freed from this night," Doctor Castillo repeated.

Rose still sat with lowered head, her cheeks burning. Oliva

roused herself and gave her daughter a nudge. Still, the Tertiary did not speak.

"Sister," said the doctor, his voice now razor-edged, "I have
asked you twice to describe your experiences on leaving this
hellish night. You do not answer; I remind you that you
must. To fail again would be a sign of ill will."

María de Uzateguí's lips moved in prayer; she fingered her
beads. Rose began to speak. She told her examiners of her joy
on escaping from these visions, of her sense of union with
God, refreshment and transformation in him.

"In these happy moments," she added with hesitation, "I
feel convinced that my union with God is consummated forever; and I feel sure of never losing his friendship again.
There is in me a gift that I cannot explain, but which tells
me that I shall never sin more, and I can say with St. Paul:
'Nothing will divide me from the love of Jesus Christ, not
death, nor life, nor hunger, nor thirst, nor anything that is in
this world.'"

Then she revealed the reason for her hesitation. She had
feared that what she was about to say would seem false doctrine, for as she told them: "I know, indeed, that the elect
alone are confirmed in grace; and still, since I am ordered in
the name of obedience to say what I feel, I cannot hide the
fact that, in these moments, this conviction is in me."

Rose did not know it, but mystical theologians think it
likely that souls reaching the state of spiritual marriage are
confirmed in grace. As St. John of the Cross puts it, "the
faithfulness of God is confirmed in the soul." Now, Rose had
not yet experienced this in a way that could tell her she had
reached this state; this was to come later as the spiritual climax of her life. But baring the conviction that she had in this
regard, she was simply giving more proof of her unitive state
and firm rectitude.

"After the martyrdom I bear in hours of darkness," she

added, "I often see our Lord in the form of an infant or a young man full of majesty. At other times, it is the Blessed Virgin Mary who appears to me with a sweet and lovable face, a thousand times fairer than I could say."

Half an hour later, after many questionings on her visions, the illuminative way, the mystery of the Holy Trinity, the hypostatic union, the real presence in the Eucharist, the glory of the blessed, predestination and grace, Father Lorenzana rose to his feet. His countenance wreathed in smiles, he turned his eyes to heaven and spread out his hands in a gesture of gratitude.

"I give thanks to thee, Father, because hiding these things from the wise and prudent, thou hast shown them to the small and humble!"

The inquisition was over. It remained for the other priests to give their opinions.

"The Holy Ghost speaks through the mouth of this child," said Father Louis de Bilbao. "He alone could have given her a knowledge like that which shines in her."

The other priests nodded; Doctor Castillo smiled.

"And now," said Father Lorenzana, "how shall we word our conclusions?"

Methodically, the doctor went over the ground he had covered; the priests discussed each point with him. At last they had their verdict in writing. The inquisitor read it with relish.

"First, that Sister Rose of St. Mary, has reached the prayer of union by the most direct way and almost without passing through the purgative way, the Lord having drawn her heart to himself from her tenderest years. Second, that she has borne with heroic courage the most crushing trial that can be imagined; and that she has kept, in this state of abandonment and desolation, a perfect submission to God's will."

As the examiners were bidding goodbye to Oliva and María Uzateguí, Father Lorenzana drew Rose aside.

"Sister," he said earnestly, "there is one thing that I wish you to tell me for the love of God. In so doing you will not be defending yourself. I beg you to tell me, did you exceed the permissions I gave you?"

Rose shook her head.

"No, Father."

The priest pressed her hand paternally and with a voice full of sadness, he said: "I have been hasty in my judgment. Forgive me, please."

Rose flashed her smile upon him.

"It was nothing. Would you be kind enough to direct me again?"

"After what I have done to you? Surely you cannot wish that, Sister."

But, as he saw Rose about to protest, he added quickly: "If you wish it, I shall do so with pleasure. If it suits you, I shall see you on Saturday as before."

Rose had her director back, but she still could not go to daily Mass and Communion. There was no one at home to take her. Mariana would have done so gladly, for it grieved her to see Rose confined to her home and deprived of what she held dearest. But her mother kept them busy from early morning till evening. And although Rose had been found blameless by the inquisition, she blamed Rose endlessly. In her mood of the moment, she would have died rather than do her child a favor.

Gaspar, too, was bridling with humiliation. The case against Rose had collapsed, it was true, but just this time, he said. She must change her life; unless she did, she would be charged again and shut up in prison.

"How would you like to lie on the rack?" he kept asking. "Do you not see that you will end in the fire?"

Some of her brothers had other ideas.

"No; they will not burn her. They will keep her in a dungeon the rest of her life, doing penance for her sins," said one of them.

"I do not care what the rest of you do, but I am leaving home," said a third. "I do not wish to stay here, exposed to her influence. If she has a pact with the devil, she may be able to throw a spell on us."

"As for me," Juana chimed in, "it is a scandal and a heartbreak! Who will marry me now? Everyone will say: That is the sister of Sister Rose, who was examined by the inquisition."

Indeed it was the scandal that Oliva felt most, for it was great. Rose was so well known throughout Lima on account of her beauty, her care of the poor and her charismata, that her examination was a seven days' wonder. Father Lorenzano and most of the five inquisitors had directed her at one time or other. Her enemies saw to it that the news reached as many persons as they could.

Some of Rose's friends were faithful to her through the weeks that followed. Vincent kept calling daily as usual, and his friendship was a joy to Rose. He continued his daily Mass and Communion and took every possible means to refute the rumors about her. Still, every time he visited her, his visit was followed by renewed scenes with Oliva, Gaspar and the whole family. She was threatened, mistreated, humiliated; all with the aim of making her ask for a dispensation from her vow of virginity. She had only to ask the confessor, and she could have been free to marry.

In the Flores household there was only one person besides the enfeebled Isabel who took no part in the persecution. This was Mariana. Only God knows what she suffered at Rose's distress; yet she could do nothing to stop the outrages heaped on her.

Other friends called at the hermitage to ask for prayers as though nothing had happened. First among these, of course, were the Mazas. Friends of theirs who had made Rose's acquaintance through their good offices came faithfully, too. One couple must be specially mentioned: Angelino Medoro and his wife, María de Mesta, who had moved to Lima at about the turn of the century. Angelino was an artist, one of the few in the colonial city. The fame of Rose's beauty had reached his ears, and to this Gonzalo and his wife had added tales of her sanctity. It had taken little urging on Angelino's part to bring about a meeting.

Of course, as soon as he knew her well enough he had asked Rose to sit for him. She had refused.

"I am sure that you can find better models than myself," she had said. "I cannot see why you are so anxious to paint my portrait."

That had been that. But Angelino had not given up. Some day, he felt sure, Rose would relent and he would paint her. Both the Neapolitan artist and his wife felt convinced that she was a saint; her portrait would be a cherished treasure for the world.

They had private evidence of her power with God. When they first met her, their married life had been made wretched by María de Mesta's violent temper. Outbursts of fury, followed by equally vehement tears of contrition had brought the household near despair. Then she thought of confiding her case to Rose's prayers. Rose had listened intently to all that the lady told her of her inner turmoil and had given her sound advice. What this advice was we do not know for certain; probably it was to make a particular examen on the virtue of meekness. Rose herself had learned the practice from her Jesuit directors; she knew its worth as a source of good. Soon, thanks to her prayers and help plus María de Mesta's good will, the Medoros were living in peace. Her transformation was lasting, and she remained a marvel of edification to all who knew her.

Probably before this, when life with María de Mesta was more thorns than roses, two slaves belonging to the couple had run away, taking with them the key to the house. The Medoros had been distracted; the act had hurt them because they were fond of the women, who as runaway slaves would be liable to death if caught. In addition, the malice implied in the theft of the key seemed to point to future robbery, perhaps with violence.

In their distress, Angelino and his wife had run to Rose for prayers. After a moment, she had reassured them.

"Go home in peace, my friends, and do not worry," she had told them. "The women will come back of their own accord and bring the key."

It turned out as she said. Scarcely had they reached their home when they were met at the door by one of the runaway slaves, contrite and begging pardon. The other followed this good example, and peace reigned again in the artist's home, at least for the time being.

Other eminent women friends of Rose continued to call despite the scandal. One of these was Lucía de la Guerra. She was sincerely devout; her conversation interested Rose and vice versa. Married and a mother, Lucía was seemingly far removed from Rose's ideal for herself, yet Rose predicted that she would be the superior of the convent of St. Catherine when it should be founded. This angered Oliva, who thought Rose wished to swindle her friend out of her fortune to found a convent which would never succeed. Rose merely smiled. Then she made another prediction: Oliva would also enter there, and be one of the first to take the black veil.

During their visits with the Flores family, Gonzalo de la Maza and his wife saw that Rose's presence made life painful for all. They were attached to the whole family, so they felt some sympathy with them as well as with Rose, but she was their darling. They loved her as a daughter. So the idea came to them of asking her to live with them. Perhaps if she moved, her family might be less hostile to her and she would enjoy greater peace. They would count themselves happy to bear the small expense of supporting her, for they thought her a saint.

At first, Oliva and Gaspar refused to part with Rose, saying that they needed her earnings. But when they understood that she would still be able to help Oliva with her sewing they agreed to the change. Rose was to move in with the Mazas as soon as she could.

She had no say in this. She was stricken by her family's attitude; what she dared say was spoken faintly in a breaking voice. Of course, she felt grateful to the friends who were coming to her rescue with such love, but her anguish was cruel. Once Oliva and Gaspar had agreed to let her leave, her move was taken for granted. She had no choice but to go.

In leaving home, Rose was leaving more than a roof, a family and a hermitage. She was leaving herself. Her transfer to the Maza home marked the outset of the final stripping of her soul of all save God. During the time of her severe trials, when the visions of hell and the judgment grew frequent and she was unable to find a director, and again in the misunderstanding with Father Lorenzana, she had received signal mystical graces. Towards the close of her life she summed them up as "the mercies of the soul." Her detailed account of the way in which she received them and the exact dates has been lost. Still, we know the facts in general.

The first mercy was the piercing of her heart by a lance which left her inflamed with love. From the account given by St. Teresa of her own experience and from the physical condition of her heart when it was examined after her death as well as the accounts of many other mystics who have shared this grace, we can say for certain that the piercing caused Rose extreme pain.

The second mercy received by Rose was the burning of her heart by the Infant Jesus. Rose left charming illustrations of all her mercies; her illustration of this shows an empty heart with part of an artery attached. In this stub of artery a hefty black cross is planted. In the middle of the heart, slightly above center, sits the Infant Jesus, unembarrassed by swaddling bands but wearing a plain white halo. Around the bottom of the heart Rose has written: "*Aquí descansó Jesús, abrasándome el corazón.*" The extraordinary thing about the Infant is that he seems to have no hands. Both his hands are plunged into the heart.

When exactly did Rose receive this mercy, which was a great infusion of grace and charity received suddenly? We have her word for it: it came just before her great tribulations. Before they came, too, she received a third mercy: a flight to God, which Father Getino, O.P., with others, interprets as the spiritual espousals. This tallies with what we know of the findings of the inquisitors as to the unitive state of her prayer, for the spiritual espousals are the end to which the passive purification of the soul is ordered. They mark the beginning of the purely unitive life which, in turn, if it reaches fruition here, is climaxed by the highest state known as spiritual marriage. As we have learned from Rose's lips, before her examination by the inquisitors she felt that she had been confirmed in grace. This in itself was a sign that she was approaching the state of spiritual marriage.

Other mercies received by Rose before she left home show the signal work of the Holy Spirit in her. Wounds of love were received in different forms with different effects. At one time the wound was inflicted by a ray of light; at another time by an arrow. Then the crucifix was implanted in her heart, followed by the wound of the nail, the wound of fire, the wound of fever, the wound by a harpoon, the wound by a dart. At this point, when her trials grew most acute, she received what she called a wound by lightning. She has drawn a cross reaching full length from the top of the artery to a distance far beyond the tip of the heart. Then, as she is about to leave home, she depicts her heart sending forth flames and winged with love, but the immense cross is still there, plunged deep into her body. At the bottom of this cross she has written: "*La vida es cruz.*"

Life was indeed a cross for Rose when she took her flight from home and family. In moving to the home of her patrons she lost many things that were dear to her. First among these was her privacy. Although their home was exceedingly large, they did not give her a room to herself. They loved her as a daughter and treated her as one. Their two young daughters shared a room, so Rose shared theirs.

Why did Gonzalo and Maria make this arrangement? It is a secret of their souls, but we can guess. They loved Rose with a supernatural love. They wished to have her in their home not only because of her need but because of theirs. They were both Christians in the thorough sense of the word, and if they were attached to Rose it was that they might profit by her example. If they did not give her a room to herself, it was that their daughters might have the privilege of living with her. They were to watch her every movement, imitate her virtues as well as they could, and report all supernatural happenings to their parents.

Since her childhood, Rose had spent herself in the care of the poor. This was a second sacrifice. At the Mazas there was no infirmary, there was no daily line-up for medicine. Without doubt, bread was given to the poor by this family, but Rose's nursing skill had lost its outlet. There was nothing left to her but prayer.

Moreover, in moving out of her own home, Rose moved

far from Santo Domingo, far from its friars who were her spiritual brothers, far from the chapel of Our Lady of the Rosary. She could no longer make her daily visit to that precious shrine; she could not tend the altar as she had done for years. Neither could she call on Father Lorenzana for help when a problem arose; she had to wait until his weekly visit. She could not confide in Brother Martin or share his joys and trials. She rarely saw him again.

In leaving home, Rose also left Mariana. The Indian maid had been her firm and loyal friend since her infancy; they were united in the closest bonds of love. For both of them, Rose's departure was a kind of death. Their conversations from this time on were rare and for the most part not in private. Such conversations were more painful than none at all.

At this time, too, Gaspar grew very feeble. The emotional strain of Rose's examination had drained him of his strength. Then had come the humiliations of the months that followed it. As a target for the capital's gossip, he suffered keenly. But this was nothing compared with his grief when he learned of Rose's vow of virginity. Vincent had seemed the ideal husband for his daughter; the poor soldier's dreams for himself had vanished, but not those for Rose. He had hoped and prayed that she might be secure, that she might be happy, that she might enjoy all that he and Oliva had missed. She refused it; she spurned it. It seemed to her father that she spurned him with it. Therefore, while Rose was receiving wounds of love from God, he felt a bitter one that struck him low. The domestic storms in which he took part prior to Rose's move made him so weak that he could not leave his chair. Soon, like Rose's dear grandmother, he was a confirmed invalid.

His visits to the Mazas were cut short abruptly. Oliva and Juana often went to see Rose, taking with them work to be done by her and calling for work that she had finished. Their manner with her was friendly but not cordial, let alone loving. And if they found themselves alone with her they scarcely spoke. When their host and hostess came into the room again, however, their smiles returned. To the Mazas their relations with Rose must have seemed almost normal. They had no idea how much bitterness still lurked behind those smiles.

Rose had always been close to her father and grandmother and now she missed them sorely. Their illnesses grieved her and she longed to care for them. What if her father scolded her? What if he frowned? He was hers; she was his. She loved him intensely.

Such were the crosses Rose bore in the home of her patrons. Yet, to most of her friends her life there seemed easy. She had moved to one of Lima's most distinguished homes; she had left a feuding family for one where all was harmony. She was reverenced by its members, idolized by their friends. They thought her a saint; but this did not please her. She had been happy in her garden, among her roses, passion flowers, her sweet and bitter herbs. She had lost that garden too.

One of her old friends who called faithfully at her new home was Vincent. Every day he knocked on the door of the imposing mansion and asked for Rose. He was a charming *caballero* and he found a ready welcome in the circle of the Mazas. Soon they counted him as one of their favorites. His way was gentle but genial. In Rose's presence he seemed like one in church. When he spoke to her, he almost prayed. She, on the other hand, talked readily to him of all that crossed her mind. He had become as much a part of her life as Fernando or Mariana or Brother Martin. Her daily schedule had to take his visit into account; the Mazas arranged theirs to suit him. He was one of their adopted daughter's few contacts from her former life; they felt that they owed her that consideration.

The first months of Rose's stay with the Mazas were anxious ones for this family as for all Peru. In the peril that threatened them, they were happy to have a living saint in their home. On August 8, 1614, a Dutch-hired pirate, George Spilbergen, had set sail from a port in Holland with six armed ships. He skimmed past the islands of Cape Verde, coasted along Brazil and St. Vincent, pausing to make savage sorties in search of loot. By March 7, 1615, he neared the Strait of Magellan. News of his hovering reached Peru some months later. Meanwhile, he had ravaged the coasts of Chile. Mocha and the island of St. Mary were invaded. The people of Valparaiso fled to the hill and set fire to the ruined naval barracks.

On June 12th, Spilbergen left Valparaiso. The viceroy of Peru, warned of his approach, ordered the fleet manned and armed and he readied the bastions of Callao that shielded Lima. All this was done in 24 hours; there was not an instant's respite.

If three hundred of Spilbergen's pirates had landed, wrote one observer, the port would have fallen and with it the capital. Was this estimate true? It came from a brave man, the provincial of the Jesuits. He was not likely to exaggerate the sorry state of the land defense.

News came that Spilbergen was in the Bay of Cañete; the viceroy ordered the fleet to meet him. Three ships were all that could be sent to the spot. The battle was bloody and indecisive. On July 17 the first canon discharge was fired. A day's heavy fighting followed. At night Spilbergen tried to flee; the Peruvians lost a sloop and some prisoners were taken by the Dutch. The pirates offered to spare the admiral, Rodrigo de Mendoza. He chose death by drowning. In the battle another Peruvian ship was lost and the pirates went triumphantly to the island of St. Lawrence to calk their ships. They had suffered small damage, and by July 21 they were again bound for Callao.

That evening saw Lima in a state of turmoil that could not be described. Rose, like her townsfolk, thought of nothing but the horrors to come. The sack would rival that of Rome; churches would be pillaged, priests and nuns martyred with revolting savagery. No one would be spared: the old, the sick, infants—all would fall at the sweep of the cutlass.

When the news came, Rose was sick. With heroic courage she forced herself to her feet and dressed. Gonzalo had her taken to Santo Domingo where she met the other Tertiaries. In all the churches the Blessed Sacrament was exposed. Women and children kept vigil before the Eucharist while their menfolk swarmed to Callao, armed with anything they could find. Through the night hours the watch went on.

Rose knelt with her Sisters while candles spluttered and sent an eerie light which reflected on the wrought gold monstrance. In the halflight of the altar, she could see the pale disc of the Sacred Host gleaming as Christ watched with his panicked children. Much of the night she spent in ecstasy, pleading for her Spouse's mercy on his own. Still, she received no answer.

Dawn came relentlessly. As the first streaks of light touched the windows of Santo Domingo, a horseman galloped to the main door. He reined his mount in and left the horse in the hands of a stranger while he rushed into the church.

"Courier! Make way for the courier!"

The weary throng of women and little ones pressed back on each side to make room for the newsbearer. As he pushed through the opening and raised his trumpet to his lips, a tense silence gripped the nave. In one of the front rows with her fellow Tertiaries, Rose waited for his words, but she did not take her eyes from the Blessed Sacrament.

"The foe has landed!" he cried. "The battle has begun in the town! We are defending it valiantly!"

A great cry arose from the throng of women and children. Anguish, fear, supplication, welled into one sweeping wave. Amid the chaos, Rose reached quietly into her habit pocket and drew out her embroidery scissors. While her fellow-Tertiaries watched her stunned, she began to cut off her skirt just below the knees.

"What are you doing?" Francisca de Montoya shouted through cupped hands into her ear.

"I am preparing to defend the Blessed Sacrament!" she shouted back.

Then they began to pray, each in her own way: some in silence, some with impassioned cries, some kneeling, some prostrate, some working their way up and down the crowded aisles, joggling wailing babies in their arms. No one really believed that the pirates would be stopped.

But Rose had not surrendered. As she gazed at the monstrance, all at once she saw her Lord above the Sacred Host. Blood was dried in his hair and on the thorns that pierced him; blood trickled down his temples into his eyes. Blood dripped out of his heart and wrists and feet. His mouth, open from his last cry, was bruised and swollen. His eyes looked straight at her.

A prayer was wrenched from her lips.

"Ah, my Jesus, ever living in the Sacred Host, thou shalt not be crucified again today if I can save thee. I could not save thee then when thou didst hang on the cross and die for me, but perhaps I may save thee now!"

"Who will die with me for Jesus?" she cried to the throng. "Who will stand with me against his foes? He is here, protected only by our bodies. Help me! Let us die for him together! Let us tell them that they must cut their way through us to reach his sacred body!"

At the supernatural force that moved her, the souls of that multitude of women and of children were fused in an extraordinary way. In a single act of love they offered their bodies and their lives to their God as a shield for him in his sublime helplessness. No more in terror for themselves or their loved ones, they flung themselves as one soul against the sacrilege they felt would soon take place.

The courier had come somewhat ahead of the news. Until that moment, the pirates had fired on Callao just twice. The first ball struck the church of St. Francis and destroyed some nearby homes of adobe; the second had been aimed too high. It passed over the buildings, doing no harm.

As Rose and the throng of women and children in Santo Domingo offered themselves in defense of the sacramental Christ, Spilbergen stood on the deck of his ship. All this cutthroat army depended on him; his was the brain that had conceived the attack. His was the cunning that had planned the details of the street fighting and the push to the capital. Now, with a smile curling his lips, he strode to his cabin.

On his table a map was spread, showing Callao and Lima. All the streets were on it, the principal buildings marked and identified. Churches were marked ominously with a black cross. He looked up and laughed, with the laugh of a man who has long ago throttled his conscience.

Now the pirate went to the corner of his desk where a heavy metal cylinder lay in its velvet lined case. It was one of the first telescopes. He took it up, squinted through it, polished the lens with his handkerchief, and began to leave his cabin. He never did. With a cry, he suddenly crumpled to the floor, grasping the legs of a chair for support. It was apoplexy. Within fifteen minutes of his stroke, the pirate fleet had put out to sea. Without their captain, they could not fight.

One legend has them land, take Callao, and surge through

Lima on a stream of blood. According to this tale, they entered Santo Domingo's church and rushed to the main altar where Rose confronted them. Let them cut her in small pieces, let them take as long as they could to kill her! The slower her death, the longer would the Sacred Host be spared! Then, it is said, the pirates saw her transfigured, blazing with light. They staggered back and fled from the church without touching anything. How strange that, in his account to the king of that year's events, the viceroy gave one small paragraph to these pirates! And in that paragraph, not a word of any land fighting! Strange, too, that we have no historical data to show that they landed.

On the contrary, facts reported by witnesses then in Callao show what did happen. While Rose and the women and children offered themselves, Spilbergen fell. The cutthroats fled in confusion; Lima was spared, and with her the Sacrament of Love.

Still, Rose is called rightly the "savior of her city." Had she not rallied all those who had run to Santo Domingo, perhaps Spilbergen would have lived on awhile. But she did, and such was God's answer to prayer.

There is a more probable sequel to this incident than what legend says, namely, what happened later to Rose. She had cut off the skirt of her habit just at the knees. She could not walk through the streets in that condition. She had to pray on until Gonzalo could send his carriage to drive her to his home.

As for Oliva, she was mortified more than words can tell when she heard what Rose was saying and saw that she had cut off her habit. What she told her daughter has not come down to us, but surely it was no eulogy. As for Rose, when she learned that the pirates had fled without landing, she could only sigh: "What a chance it was to die for Jesus!"

CHAPTER ELEVEN

Vigil in August

WHILE ROSE sighed in regret, Lima sighed in relief. Life took up its normal course. In the Maza mansion, Rose went on with her work and prayer. From time to time her host and hostess had to run to their diaries and jot down some charismatic act of their adopted daughter's.

One day, for instance, she astonished her foster mother by asking for pen and writing paper. Now, Rose was no writer of *belles lettres,* so María de Uzateguí asked her to whom she wished to write. The frank young Tertiary laughed.

"To Fernando," she answered. "I am going to give him a piece of my mind. He has married without telling us."

María de Uzateguí exclaimed in astonishment; then Rose went on.

"And do you know, Mother, what the good God will do for them? He will give them a daughter who will be very holy. And when she is born she will have the mark of a rose on her forehead."

Not only was this prediction fulfilled, but Fernando's daughter entered the convent which Rose was just then trying to found. She lived and died there like Oliva herself; and the rose on her forehead was a constant sign of her aunt's protection from heaven.

Another time, a miracle took place when María de Uzateguí went with Rose and her daughters to the family oratory to say their thanksgiving after supper. Gonzalo was not at home;

he was to dine later. When they had finished their grace, as always they stayed kneeling a few minutes before the *Ecce Homo* which hung above the altar. It was a perfect work by Angelino Medoro.

As often happened, Rose was carried out of herself when she knelt before this picture.

"Lord, when then will men love thee as thou dost deserve to be loved?" she exclaimed. "How long wilt thou let sinners offend and outrage thee? Who will make known to all how good, how lovable thou art for thine own sake, not for rewards? Bend thy bow, Lord; let fly arrows of love on every side, that they may pierce hearts! May all men adore thee, O thou the supreme Good! May all their love focus on thee, who dost love them so tenderly!"

Rose had scarcely stopped speaking when one of the Maza girls cried: "Look, Mother! The face of our Lord is covered with sweat!"

María de Uzateguí hastened towards the altar. The face of Christ in the painting indeed trickled with sweat. Rose, coming to herself, also saw it and cried out in shock.

"What can this mean?" her adopted mother asked. "We must call the priests from San Pablo's."

Hastily she summoned one of the servants and bade him bring at least two priests. Before they came, Gonzalo reached home. When he saw the sweat on the Holy Face, he paled with alarm.

"I fear some crime has been committed in my house!"

Hastily as his wife had done, he sent a servant for Angelino. If there were a natural cause for this phenomenon, he could trace it.

Angelino arrived and so did the priests.

"Let me dip my finger in the liquid to see if it is oily," he said. "It might be from the paints or the oil I used in mixing them." He drew his forefinger across the canvas. "No, it is not oily," he told them. "And none of the paint comes off when I press my finger on the canvas. It is perfectly hard. Let me see whether or not the back is dry."

With Gonzalo's help, the artist took the picture from its hook. All present looked at the back; it was completely dry.

"Not a trace of moisture," murmured Father de Peñaloza.

"There is nothing natural there!" cried Angelino. "It is a miracle!"

"Let us see whether, when this liquid is wiped off, more will appear," suggested a priest.

He took a towel, then a piece of paper and sponged the liquid from the Holy Face. The first sweat was replaced by another.

"The liquid is colorless," said Angelino.

"What is your opinion of this prodigy?" asked Father de Peñaloza's companion, turning to Rose.

"I do not think it a sign of the divine anger," answered the Tertiary. "The Savior simply wished to recall to men the ardent love he bears them, to excite them to return it."

"Why, that is what you were saying just when the miracle began!" her foster mother exclaimed. "You asked him to let fly arrows of love on every side so that they might pierce hearts; this is what he has done, for who can look at this *Ecce Homo* bathed in sweat without feeling a greater love for him?"

Not long after this miracle, Rose lost the use of one arm, which she broke in a fall. We do not know the cause of the fall, but the doctor could not restore life to the paralyzed arm. Then María de Uzateguí had an idea. Taking a piece of cloth which had been soaked in the miraculous sweat, she bound it on the dead member. Life came back to it at once.

For Rose, the trial had been brief, but she was not deceived. Death was knocking at her door. Still, she went calmly on with her daily tasks. Perhaps she thought with longing of her hermitage. At any rate, we find her spending whole days in unbroken prayer in the Maza chapel. Sometimes she stayed there two and a half days at a time, lost in God. When she was there she kept the door locked. Once María grew alarmed at the long silence and tried to enter; but Rose did not let her in. She heard the rap of her foster mother's knuckles outside, but she could not move. When her prayer was over, though, she seemed like anyone else, only more charming.

Among those who had long been frequent guests at the Maza home were several Jesuits of San Pablo church, in addition to Father de Peñaloza. They came to rely on Rose for prayers in times of necessity. One appeal that they made was recorded after her death due to her unique response. A Jesuit was dying; he had lived a good religious life but now faced eternity in frightful scruples. It seemed to him that he had no merits to show for his long years of labor for Christ. Rose understood his anguish, for she had suffered temporarily from scruples. When her visitors told her that the dying priest had confidence in her, she made a bargain.

"Tell him," she said, "that I exchange half of my merits for half of his. I am sure that I shall not lose by it."

The exchange was made, to the Father's great joy. He died relieved of his scruples, filled with childlike confidence in God. As for Father de Loaiza, when he heard Rose's words, he smiled gratefully. He had once directed her, and he knew that she had only half her merits to offer, as she had already given half to a diffident missionary.

Without flagging in her interest in priests, Rose began at this time to center her thoughts also on seminarians. Her heart went out to young men who wished to be priests but could not pay the seminary tuition fees. She confided her plan to Martin on one of her rare calls at Santo Domingo's.

"Brother, will you laugh at me if I tell you my latest project?" she asked.

"Never, Sister," said the saintly mulatto.

"I have always longed for a blood brother who would be ordained, but none of my brothers wished to be priests. Now I want to adopt one. I shall look for a young man who has no resources, yet longs for the priesthood; I shall work to earn his tuition fees as long as I am able."

"Wonderful!" cried Martin, clasping his fingers together and smiling with delight. "You will have no trouble in finding one; Lima has many."

"I know that you often help such youths through your wealthy friends," said Rose. "Could you recommend one to me who is worthy of help?"

"Not at the moment, Sister, but I shall bear it in mind," he said. "By the time next year's term begins, I shall have one for certain. I shall let you know."

Martin himself had a project afoot, for which he asked prayers. Lima was overrun by bands of homeless youngsters who lived by their wits and their fists. The civic authorities had given them up as hopeless; there were too many and their number seemed growing. What could they do? Martin had a plan; he went to his prior for permission to try it and was given a hearty "God bless you."

He had his superior's confidence after the painful withdrawal of permission to bring in the sick poor. One day, a poor derelict had been left knifed in the street near the convent. In spite of the prohibition, he had carried him in. When questioned on his reason for disobeying, he had said that he thought charity higher than obedience. So pleased was the prior that from then on Martin had complete freedom in helping the homeless. Therefore, his plea to start begging for an orphan asylum met friendly approval.

This project was no dream. Large sums passed weekly through Martin's hands: donations from wealthy persons who entrusted their alms to him for distribution. They had full trust in his virtue and discretion. It would not be hard for him to find men to donate funds towards the new institution he had in mind.

Rose, in the meanwhile, promised to pray for his begging tour of Lima's great homes and business establishments. Martin knew what a wealth of grace she would gain for his works, and he left the sacristy wafted on wings of joy.

Rose wanted to see Father Lorenzana, so the Brother sought him for her. He found him, for once, in his office.

"Little Rose is in the sacristy waiting to see you." Father Lorenzana looked up from his work. He smiled at Brother Martin.

"This Rose whom you call little the whole world will one day call great," he remarked.

The Brother nodded. More and more when he saw her, he revered God's work of grace in her soul.

That work was now near completion. A few months more would elapse, and before Martin could find the seminarian she wished to adopt, she would be dead—hailed by the Church of Peru and her people as "Mother of the Poor."

Lent came, and Rose asked for a room to herself. The one she chose was a small room, downstairs in the servants' quarters. The reason for her asking? She had Father Lorenzana's permission to sleep on a hard bed again.

What her interior trials were just then we do not know, but we do know that she was still grappling with demons. Once, in the cellar, she met one in horrible guise; then a wonderful thing happened. Rose was not afraid. She ordered him off and he went. Perhaps at this time she was still suffering from impure temptations, but whatever the reason her director allowed her the penance that had cost her most. She did not wish the two Maza children to know; they gave her the room at once. Unlike Oliva, they felt sure of the spirit by which Rose was led.

That Lent brought her powers to fresh heights of beauty and maturity. Even her natural talents, for singing for instance, were still more perfected. Her adopted family noticed this; their wonderment grew. She still lived on her *gazpacho*, or bread soup. Her very life was a quasi-miracle.

Each day at sunset a bird came and sang with her a song that she had composed. Then it flew off, at her bidding. First the children, then María herself heard that song with enchantment. Unnoticed by Rose, they came to her door and there listened to the strangest duet ever sung.

"Ah! It is sunset, and here is my little friend," exclaimed Rose, laying down her embroidery. As she spoke, a small bird presented himself on her windowsill. "Well, are we ready?" she asked, reaching out a finger to caress him. He blinked his gratitude. Then she began singing:

> Tiny singer, flirt your wings;
> Bow before the King of kings.
> Let your lovely concert rise
> To him who gave you songs and skies.
> Let your throat, full of carols sweet,
> Pour them before the Eternal's feet
> That we his praise may magnify
> Whom birds and angels glorify.
>
> I shall sing to him who saved me:
> You will sing to him who made ye.
> Both together, we shall bless
> The God of love and happiness.
> Sing, sing with bursting throat and heart!
> In turn our voices will take part
> To sing together, you and I,
> A canticle of holy joy.

For an hour, then, Rose would sing alternately with her bright-eyed, feathered caller. Then at her signal it was time for him to leave. As his small, plump body flickered off into the dusk, Rose was left to sing the last verse alone.

> The little bird abandons me:
> My playmate's wings ascend.
> Blessed be my God, who faithfully
> Stays with me to the end.

Little Andrea turned to María with a troubled look after one of these concerts.

"Mother, listen! Isn't Sister Rose crying?"

That Palm Sunday Gonzalo had her taken to Santo Domingo's for Mass. It was a favorite feast of the Tertiaries. According to a cherished custom, each Tertiary was given a palm and all marched in procession through the church, behind the community of friars. Rose had looked forward to this ceremony; it seemed to her that she was more fervently prepared for it than she had ever been. Her trip to the church was made joyful, too, by the fact that Fernando called for her. He was home on leave with his bride.

"Jesus of my soul, how happy I am to carry this palm in thy honor!" Rose whispered as the friar distributing the palms approached the kneeling Tertiaries. "This palm will be the symbol of my soul, which with the help of grace will always praise thee and move in harmony with the slightest breeze of the divine Spirit. Its greenness points to the hope I have that, by this time next year, I may crown thee King of my heart by pronouncing the vows of religion that will wed us to one another forever."

Fearing that she might die before the convent of St. Catherine was established, Rose had asked a friar who was going to Rome to obtain an indult allowing her to make the three vows, although not in a convent.

Now the sacristan approached with the palms. First came Luisa de Santa María, then Catalina, Francisca and Felipa de Montoya, Bártola López and Ana de los Reyes, daughters of Andrés López, one of the Maza servants. Then came the turns of María de Jesús, Leonora de Vitoria, and María Antonia, widow of Juan Carrillo. It was Rose's turn. She put out her hand.

As though he had not seen her, the friar turned away and began giving palms to the people behind them. Rose alone had no palm!

Grief seized her heart. Was she displeasing to God? Was this a sign that she would not make her vows? There was no time for tears. The procession was moving. She took her place at the end of her chapter with empty hands and soul torn by fear. No one noticed that she had no palm.

At last, after what seemed an eon, the procession was done. Rose left the Tertiaries and slipped alone into the chapel of the Rosary. There, kneeling before the blessed image, she poured out her woe to the Consoler of the Afflicted. Little by little, calm came back to her. Her usual sense of humor rescued her; with a rueful smile, she looked up at Mary.

"Please God, O my Mother," she said, "may I no more regret a palm given by mortal hands! Art thou not the great palm tree that enriches the desert of Cades? Thou wilt give me one of thy branches, and that will not wither!" ("Palm tree of Cades" was one of the more fanciful titles given our Lady, taken from reference to a palm which grows abundantly in Peru.)

The compassionate Mother smiled and looked joyfully at the Infant Jesus whom she held in her arms. He gazed on Rose with tenderness, and her soul was filled with the sense of God's presence. Was she in this world?

Suddenly, the lips of the Infant Jesus seemed to move. His words were distinct.

"Rose of my heart, be thou my spouse."

It was the mystical marriage, the highest state in the soul's life of union with God. What went on in her then? St. John of the Cross sums it up when he describes the graces that come with this state as "complete transformation into the Beloved." Rose yielded herself entirely to Christ; he gave himself wholly to her. Her soul, though still human, was divinized. She knew no evil, having lost all evil habits such as she had ever had; she was innocent. She might henceforth see evil and hear evil, but she would not be able to understand it, having no evil habits to judge by.

Love alone absorbed her; she had lost particular notions and forms of things, acts of the imagination and apprehensions having form or figure. God's purity, God's simplicity were hers. She was cleansed and empty of all but him. At that point, says the Mystical Doctor, the soul can quote David: "My heart hath been inflamed and my reins changed; I am brought to nothing and I knew not." Centered on love, it lives by love, its sole exercise is to love.

Rose's reply to the Infant is worthy of note. It reveals how devotion to Mary had molded her heart. When she could speak, what she said was a paraphrase of the words that brought us Christ: "Behold the handmaid of the Lord," the Virgin had said. "Be it done to me according to thy word."

"I am your servant, Lord," said Rose. "I am the docile slave of your ageless Majesty. Yes, if you wish what I should not dare, I shall be yours and ever be true to you."

Moved at these words so like her own, our Lady inclined towards the kneeling Rose and spoke.

"See, daughter, the rare honor Jesus deigns to pay you in taking you as spouse in so wondrous a way. Can he better prove the greatness of his love?"

What words can express the plenitude of grace that Rose received then? None known to human language. She could only have said that her soul was wedded to Christ's, and that, she believed, forever.

Yet, unlike many mystics, she had no wedding ring. What could she do to fill the lack? Fernando had given her money for a birthday present, and she told him she would like to have a ring with a religious emblem. Her brother thought a moment, then took a sheet of paper. On the instant, he drew the design of the ring she had longed for. It had no stone; the collet bore the inscription: "I.H.S."

Fernando looked up for approval.

"And a little inscription inside?" Rose asked.

Taking up the pen, without knowing a thing of what had passed in the chapel, he printed the words: *"Rosa de mi corazón, sé mi esposa"*: "Rose of my heart, be thou my spouse."

Fernando had the ring made; Rose took it to the sacristan at Santo Domingo.

"May God be with you, Brother, and may Jesus be our love," she said. "Would you do me a kindness?"

"Anything within the Rule," the Brother grinned down at her.

"I should be so pleased if you would put this ring inside the altar of repose."

"Until we take the altar down on Good Friday?" he asked.

"Yes. Father Provincial will know about it. You can give it to him."

And now, Rose planned a solemn ceremony. She invited her mother, María de Uzateguí and Gonzalo, and, of course, Fernando and his wife. Father Lorenzana agreed to officiate at the ceremony. Rose had told him of the graces received on Palm Sunday, and he well knew their worth. He was going to bless Rose's wedding ring and place it on her finger when she received our Lord at the Easter Mass.

But God intervened with his own plan.

The alcolyte's bell announced the priest's Communion. Rose bent her head and lowered her eyes. There, on her finger, was her wedding ring. How had it been put on? By no human hand, but by Christ's power.

Now it was time for the faithful to receive. Hastily, Rose slipped the ring off and hid it in the palm of her hand. She would pass it quickly to Father Lorenzana. He would place it on her finger as agreed. No one would know of the miracle.

What graces were given to Rose that Easter? We know from her own sketch of her heart what this "mercy" was: the consummation of her spiritual marriage on Palm Sunday. The sketch of the fifteenth "mercy" shows a six-winged heart. No flames escape from it; in it there is no cross. The cross, a large one, stands beneath it. "Once one has made up one's mind to suffer," said St. Teresa of Avila, "the suffering exists no more." Above the heart, Rose wrote her brief note on this state: "*unión con Dios estrechísima*": "most intimate union with God."

Her sketch of the sixteenth "mercy" shows her heart with no cross, in the midst of the Blessed Trinity as a fourth person. Two angels complete the group—one beside our Lord, the other near God the Father. This is the perfection of Christianity: to live the life of the blessed here below, with this difference, as the Saint of Avila said, that here we suffer and there they rejoice.

As a rule, the soul does not stay long on earth once it has attained this highest union. So it happened with Rose. Her first intimation of death came during prayer in Gonzalo's chapel. She saw herself in a radiant light that flowed from the God-head present everywhere, a light that seemed to extend without limit. In the midst of the light stood a brilliant rainbow, incredibly varied and lovely. Under it stood a second rainbow, equally radiant, bearing in its center a cross bedewed with blood. Over it were inscribed the words: "*Jesus Naza-renus Rex Judaeorum*": "Jesus of Nazareth, King of the Jews." Nail-holes could be seen in the cross.

In the space within this double rainbow stood Jesus. Never had she seen him clothed with such glory. Never before had she seen him at full length. Usually she had seen only the upper part of his body, and that at some distance.

What was it to find herself so near Jesus? How could she fear the pains of death which would bring her at last to this beloved goal! The flames that gushed forth from his heart penetrated her soul; she seemed freed from the flesh and carried to heaven.

Yet, what was this now? Near Christ stood a set of scales: a balance and weights. Numberless angels came and bowed low before him. Souls too, like herself, bowed and returned. Then some angels approached, took the balance, placed weights on one of the plates and loaded the other with trials until the weights were equal.

As though he would trust no count but his own, he now raised the balance. The weighting was perfect. Next, he gave the afflictions to all the souls present; Rose's share was out-standing. The one plate was empty; now Christ piled graces on it until in their weight they equalled the first load. He passed out these graces proportionately to the weight of afflic-tions held by each soul. Rose's share was as great as before.

Now, Jesus spoke! "Affliction is always accompanied by grace; grace is proportionate to suffering. The measure of my gifts is increased with the measure of trials. The cross is the true and only road that leads souls to heaven."

Rose had no sooner grasped what he said than she felt her-self seized with so burning a zeal that she wished to run through the streets and squares crying out like the Baptist: "Christians, listen to me! Delude yourselves no more about pain! Trial is the road to perfection! It is by this that we reach beauty of soul, the fullness of grace, the glory of God's children! Believe me; I have learned it even from the mouth of Jesus Christ!"

While Rose felt this impetuous ardor, God gave her his cross. She knew when she was to die, and what pains she would suffer. She knew that those pains would exceed all those of nature, especially an excruciating thirst. Jesus himself had asked for a drink when he was dying; could she not do the same? And something else would be needed when all was over: hands to prepare her body for burial. No curious person must see her body, scarred all over by scourges. They would think her holy; and she knew herself to be the vilest sinner on earth.

These are the thoughts of the saints, their estimates of self so far from those we form of ourselves. Seeing their imperfections in the light of God's spotless purity, they seem to them lethal. Seeing their evil propensities, they look on what they are of themselves, what they would do of themselves, and they shudder.

"Mother, I am going to die in four months. The pains of my last illness will be atrocious, and I shall claim two services of your friendship."

María looked at Rose, her countenance plunged in sorrow.

"Ah then, dear daughter, you are going to leave us? We have had you with us for so short a time! What do you wish of me? I shall do it with all my heart!"

"When devoured by a burning fever, I shall beg for a glass of cold water to refresh my throat and my scorched interior. I beg you in the name of Jesus Christ, do not refuse me. The second grace I beg of you is that, after my death, my body may not be given to strange women for the preparations for burial, but that you and my own mother may do me the needful services alone."

Strange words! Grim presage of the future! Surely Rose knew, even then, that when she should ask for a drink she would be refused.

Soon after the vision in which she learned that she was to die in four months, Rose paid a last visit home. She did not know whether or not her illness would last long, so she wished to make sure of this farewell. She was especially tender with her parents and grandmother, spoke long and lovingly with Mariana, teased Juana gently about her fiancé, and then, escorted by Fernando, went to Santo Domingo. Her brother had business to attend to elsewhere while she prayed, so he took his leave of her, promising to call back in two hours.

"Do not let me find you kneeling like a statue in the chapel of Our Lady of the Rosary," he said with a laugh. He had not forgotten the miracle that had kept her from entering the Augustinian convent.

"You will find me in the sacristy, Fernando," answered Rose with a smile. "I am going to ask for Brother Martin after I have had my spiritual direction. Just look in the corner and you will see us talking as usual.

That afternoon, when Rose saw Father Lorenzana, she told him of her vision of the Sacred Heart. She told him that she was to die at the end of August, on the eve of the Feast of St. Bartholomew. She described the pains that she would suffer and asked him earnestly for prayers.

"Be sure that I shall pray for you, Sister," said her director gently. " But I do not wish you to fly to heaven yet, if I can prevent it. Let your vision rest a while; we shall see whether God will not change his mind!"

Rose shook her head.

"No, Father; it is certain that my course is run. Let me go, then, to receive the crown of justice prepared for those who love the Lord."

As the Provincial was saying goodbye to her, Rose asked if Martin were at home.

"It would not matter, Sister, whether he was at home or not," said the friar. "If he knew that you wanted him, he would be here on the instant if he were in Quito!"

When he saw Rose waiting for him, Martin's smile was like the moon bursting through the clouds on a dark night. Rose laughed at his expression.

"Do not look as though you were seeing a ghost, Brother; it is really I. I did not wish to leave without seeing you."

"Why, what is it that you wish to tell me, Sister?" asked Brother. "If I can help you in any way, you know well that I am ready for anything."

"I am in dire need of prayer, Brother Martin," answered Rose. "I have before me a trial such as I have never experienced and shall never experience again. To pass through it according to God's will, I must have extraordinary help. It is for you and my other friends to obtain this grace for me. Without it I shall fail."

Martin shook his head.

"No, Sister, you will not fail even should this mulatto fail to pray for you. But, wretched as I am, and the least of all, I shall promise you in God's name all the help you will need. And since so often you honor me with your confidence, may I ask what this great trial will be? You have suffered so much; surely there can be nothing you have not borne!"

It was Rose's turn to shake her head.

"There is no comparison between this trial and what I have suffered in the past," she said. "In it there will be nothing natural. All will be far beyond the strength of any mortal to bear. But, blessed be God who gives me this share in his cross! It is my death of which I speak; it will come on the vigil of St. Bartholomew."

There was a long silence in the sacristy. Then, Martin spoke, his voice charged with emotion.

"You were ready; I have known it this long time. But, I hoped. . . ." His voice broke. "See how I am the one weak in virtue, who needs your good prayers! I shall pray for you, though, since you ask me. . . . Ah, be mindful of me when you are there with the saints! When shall I have that joy?"

Rose did not answer. She touched Martin's hand, with its long, supple fingers.

"In the hour that God has laid up in his heart. There is yet work to be done, my friend, by these dexterous hands. You must bring to the poor the great healing skill God has given you. Trade till he comes; as in the parable he paid those to whom he had given his talents, so in that hour he will be your very great reward."

That was the last time that Rose saw Martin while still in the flesh. Her remaining weeks were made up of waiting. Others had to be consoled: chief among them, Vincent. Telling him was not easy, but he knew the truth long before she had murmured the tale of her vision to him. To his devoted heart she had always seemed perfect, not of this world and ready for heaven. For him, her prediction was grievous; still he hoped, like Father Lorenzana, that prayers might avert what he feared, for a time. Even oftener now, he spent hours in prayer in the church of Santo Domingo.

Other friends called to see her; she told them to pray for her. More and more, what she knew of her weakness impelled her to seek help from others. For many years now, they had come to her asking for prayers; now she gently forestalled them, pleading for theirs.

So the time passed until, late one evening, María de Uzateguí and her husband found Rose lying on the floor of her room. Her groans had attracted them, but they came too late.

Their hearts wrung with anguish, they carried her upstairs to her bed in their daughters' room. She was paralyzed on one side.

"Ah!" whispered Rose. "These pains exceed the bounds of nature!"

When she had prayed for suffering, she had imagined no torments like these. She felt as though a hot iron were being passed over her whole body, from the crown of her head to the soles of her feet. At the same time, a sword of fire pierced her heart. A ball of red-hot iron seemed to roll across her temples; her head felt crushed in an iron helmet and struck by the blows of some giant hammer. The fire that raged within her reached the marrow of her bones; pains racked each joint, as though her body were being torn apart. Each member was given up to its peculiar torture. Her bones were slowly dissolving into dust; they were being scorched and reduced to cinders. Her life was being taken little by little under the action of these torments; surely, her prediction would prove true and she would die tonight.

"May God's will be done in me without reserve," she said, raising her eyes. "My sole affliction is the pain I give to those who care for me."

But the thirst! She could bear it no more! Jesus understood; he himself had felt this fierce fire. She was alone for a time, as she had asked to be, that she might prepare for her judgment. But surely, of all her loved ones downstairs, someone would bring her a glass of water! She listened intently. Was that not a footfall outside her door? Was that not the rustling of a woman's skirts? No! It was her thirst that had caused this illusion. There was no one outside; she was going mad with thirst. Oh, would her Jesus not send someone to help her?

With a stifled sob, Rose clasped more closely the crucifix she held in her arms. What a coward she was! What had

Jesus not suffered for her! Would she dare to refuse him?

"Do not spare me, then, Lord, while the illness lets me breathe. Do all thy will in me; weigh down the measure of sufferings, but increase my patience!"

A terrible cough rent her chest and throat. With her un-paralyzed hand, she kept handkerchief after handkerchief held to her mouth to stanch the blood. Still it flowed in streams, gushing forth from between her cracked lips.

A phrase from one of the psalms came to her. "Lord, do not rebuke me in thy fury nor chastise me in thy wrath; the voice of my blood cries out to thee for mercy. It is in my blood that I wash away my sins to find grace in thy sight."

If only someone would bring her a drink! Would her holy angel not send help? He had helped her so often. Would he fail her now?

There was a footstep at the door. Someone knocked gently and slipped into the room. Rose raised her eyes and saw the servant girl, Iñéz, with a tray in her hands. On the tray stood a glass. But it was not of water! It was a thick, cloying essence that they mixed with some healing extract. This was the drink, exquisite and sweet, that they brought her in place of gall and vinegar! But she could not force it down her swollen throat. Even the savor of its sweetness redoubled the fire of her thirst.

"I cannot take this drink," she told the servant. "It is impossible; my throat will not open to receive it."

"My master will not be satisfied, as it is by his order that I bring it to you," said the servant.

What could she do? As she had done all her life: in her crisis she turned to her guardian angel. He had not brought her water, but he would help her swallow this drink for love of obedience.

With a superhuman effort, Rose drained the glass, forcing the thick essence down her throat.

"Go and tell your master that I have been able, by his order, to do what was impossible to me by nature. Even at the gates of death, I forget not a whit my dependence on him."

She let her hand fall back on the bed and clasped her crucifix close. Like the furnace of Babylon, she felt the fire within her stoked to sevenfold heat. Now it was surely the end! She would never live until midnight! Yet, she had been so sure of the time!

The young Tertiary kissed her ring, that blessed memento of Jesus' love for her soul. It was the sign of her wedding with him. She had not the vows of religion, for these were denied her. The answer had not come from Rome. Death was snatching them from her, with her dream of the cloister. Yet, her Spouse was coming. Was this not enough?

"I thirst!" she murmured. He thirsted for her love, and she for its fulfillment in her.

Now María entered. She knelt beside the bed and whispered consoling words, but Rose did not hear them. She had lost consciousness. In the flickering lamplight, her face gleamed with translucent brilliance. Was this her last agony? Startled and fearful, María called her husband, Rose's parents, her brothers, and Father Lorenzana, who was reciting his breviary in the chapel. It was a chastened Flores family that grouped, with the Mazas, around the bed. Now that Rose was dying, they began to feel shame and confusion. Oliva and Gaspar, who had always loved her but whose hopes for her future had been blighted by her life of prayer and penance, felt their coming loss to the full. This was the second daughter they were to lose, and one who had long been their favorite. As for Fernando, he and Rose had been close since their childhood. His Chilean bride shared his grief. As she entered the room, Rose came to herself.

Seeing her parents weeping, she let them express their sorrow. Then she turned to her father, who was seated in a chair near her bed. He had been carried from his own bed to see her.

"I am going to leave this life you have given me; I beg you and my mother to bless me."

They blessed her.

"Have you been sleeping, daughter?" Oliva asked.

"No, Mama. I have not been sleeping. Sleep will come to my eyelids no more. Have no illusions about me; I am nearing the end. Still, I must drink the chalice prepared by my Beloved, to the dregs."

Now Father Lorenzana approached the bed. He had stayed in the house since early morning. He had helped Rose review her life; he had placed on her tongue the Living Bread, the pledge of eternal bliss. Rose had renewed her private vows and the formula of profession as a Tertiary, with her scapular spread on the bed before her. He had said the prayers for the dying with her, not once, but several times. He had watched at her bedside during her frequent ecstasies. Now, he looked gravely at his penitent. What more could he do? He had to go home to his convent; in his office, a whole day's work was waiting to be done before Matins.

"My child, I can stay no longer today. I shall come back very early in the morning," he said softly.

"But, Father," Rose protested. "I beg Your Reverence not to leave without giving me your last blessing!"

"I shall give it to you then."

"But I shall not be alive in the morning."

What could he say? Did he dare claim that she did not know the future? He blessed her and left the house. Outside, he met Angelino. Gonzalo had summoned him, bidding him bring his oils. He was to paint Rose's portrait at last, not in life as he had longed to do, but in death. But he would have to work in haste. He would have to finish her portrait that night, by the light of the wake candles. He brushed back his tears. His work must be perfect. He owed it to Rose; and he owed it to the world.

"How is she, Your Paternity?" he asked. "Is she still alive?"

"She is sinking slowly; but she will live till morning, I think. Yet, she says she will not last that long. What she suffers is terrible!"

Father Lorenzana's departure seemed to act as a signal to all the forces warring against Rose. They redoubled their fury. Sometimes, she prayed for strength.

"Ah, my good Jesus, do not let these pains and this thirst take my reason. Grant that I may have use of my reason and consciousness to the end!"

After an interval of coughing and spitting blood, she turned to María de Uzateguí.

"Good Mother, remember the promise you made me four months ago and give me a glass of water for the love of Jesus Christ."

With tears flowing down her cheeks, María shook her head.

"Child, I cannot! The doctors have forbidden it!"

"I thirst!"

Oliva began to weep inconsolably.

"Do not weep so, my dear Mother," Rose pleaded, "and above all, do not weep for me. The suffering is just for a time; the body is used up, and the soul remains."

Someone spoke of purgatory.

"It is a great joy to be saved from it," remarked Gonzalo, "but this exception is rare. God already shows himself merciful enough in calling souls to himself by this way, so purgatory is the aim of my desires."

Rose aroused herself to answer these words, not intended for her.

"As for me, I raise my hopes higher. Jesus Christ is my Spouse; and great favors, though they exceed what I deserve, do not exceed his power. The good that I expect from him, I expect to be as great and complete as possible."

Now she looked at her brothers, who were kneeling close to her.

"My brothers, keep faithful to God and devoted to our parents."

Now her gaze fell on Fernando. He was near her, turning on her a last look of understanding and love. Beside him knelt his young bride. His eyes wet with tears, Fernando moved his lips as though about to speak, but Rose turned her gaze from him to their mother, whose sobs still tore at her heart.

One thought consumed Rose. In life she had tried to live like Jesus. In death she would follow him. He had given his Mother to St. John. But to whom could she give hers? Papa would soon be with her in heaven; then Fernando and his wife would go, leaving their little daughter. On whom, then, could she count? Raising her eyes to those of her mother, she prounced the words of her last will and testament.

"Lord, I return her into thy hands. Strengthen her; uphold her; and do not permit her heart to be broken by sorrow."

Then she looked at Fernando.

"*Señor hermano,* my brother, for the love of God pick me up and put me on the floor. I wish to die, not on a comfortable bed, but as my Beloved died for me."

Fernando looked at his father. The trembling old man shook his head.

"No!" cried Oliva. "Do not lift her! She already suffers so!"

Fernando gazed with pity at the sister so dear to him. She had asked him to do her this service and he must refuse.

"*Hermana*," he said in a breaking voice, "I cannot. What you ask is impossible."

"Then at least take away the pillow," she pleaded, "for the love of God, so that, like Jesus, I may die with my head resting on wood."

This time, he did not ask their parents' permission. With gentle hands, he supported his sister's afflicted head and removed the pillow from beneath it.

Now Rose spoke again, this time with more effort because of the lowered position of her head.

"Bring me the blessed candle."

Rising from her place at his side, Fernando's wife moved back so that Oliva might carry the candle to her daughter. Signing herself with a great cross, Rose raised her eyes to heaven. She waited for freedom. Three times she pronounced the Holy Name.

"Jesus! Jesus! Jesus!"

Then after a pause, she repeated that name in accents of indescribable love.

"Jesus, be with me!"

And as she spoke, he came. It was just striking midnight.

"At midnight there was a cry made: behold, the Bridegroom cometh. Go ye forth to meet Christ the Lord" (Mass of St. Rose of Lima).

In the sickroom there was silence. Oliva withdrew from the bed and left the room. The others thought that she had gone to weep, but Oliva's anguish was turned into a joy that she could not hide.

Rose lay motionless, her eyes half closed, her mouth open slightly, her lips curving in a smile of ineffable peace. Could she be dead? They looked at one another. Fernando sought her pulse; at his request, María brought a mirror. They held it to those gentle lips that had lost their parched dryness and resumed their soft, warm lustre. There was no trace of breath on the glass. But she could not be dead! Surely, she had gone into an ecstasy!

Yes, Rose had gone into an ecstasy, the final and endless rapture prepared for all who die in Christ. Many streets away, in another quarter of the city, Luisa lay asleep. Suddenly, she was wakened by a brilliant light. She saw Rose beside her, rising to heaven in an aureole of glory, surrounded by saints and angelic choirs. Her gleaming white habit was strewn with roses. Another person in the death chamber saw her crowned. Still another lady, pious and prayerful, saw her crowned by the Virgin Mother as Oliva had, on the day of her clothing.

In his choir-stall, Father Lorenzana intoned the *Te Deum*. The community had just sung Matins.

"We praise thee, O God! We acknowledge thee to be the Lord! All the earth doth worship thee, the everlasting Father! To thee all the angels cry aloud, the heavens and all the powers therein: To thee the cherubim and seraphim continually cry: Holy! Holy! Holy!

The chant of the Dominican friars cleft the heart of the night and soared through the vault of the sky. It sundered the locks of heaven's gate. Rose was freed from her body and welcomed into the New Jerusalem.

Where was Brother Martin at this moment? In the church, as was his custom during Matins. There, in the sacred hush and darkness, he knelt in wordless adoration of that Lord whose official praises were being sung by his priest-brothers. The rest, we can only guess.

Martin rarely spoke of the graces he received; Rose had been one of the few in whom he confided. He was not asked to testify to her heroism or sanctity, although he might well have done so. Nor are we told that Rose visited him after death, as she did others whom she knew less well.

For 22 years he lived on; to his consolation, he saw her torrents of miracles, saw her raised to the honors of the altar.

Hidden yet famous even in his time, industrious, always spending himself for the poor, he went on with the work of mercy which God had placed in his hands. How often did he pray, in accents of trust, to her whom he called familiarly, "*Rosita.*"

What of the portrait by Angelino? It hangs, today, in St. Rose's Sanctuary, still lovely after almost three and a half centuries. Rose's eyes in this portrait gaze out with a brooding, maternal love on the City of Lima, and beyond this, on all the Americas. We are her children.

How is Oliva remembered in Lima? Not as the woman who harassed a saint; not as a bitter, frustrated, ambitious woman; not as an overworked, impoverished mother. She is venerated as a saintly religious who turned on herself with that holy violence dear to our Lord. Jesus, to whom Rose had willed her mother, accepted that bequest. He took Oliva, on her husband's death, as his consecrated spouse.

Arriving very early the next day at the Maza home as he had promised, Father Lorenzana knelt beside Rose's body as it lay in the coffin, clothed in her white Tertiary habit and crowned with roses from St. Catherine's statue.

"O Rose, blessed be the authors of your days! Blessed be the hour in which you came into this world! Blessed those who have known you and occupied some place in your heart! You have died as you lived, bearing to heaven your baptismal robe in all its purity. Follow, follow the Lamb wherever he goes!"

The cover picture of St. Rose of Lima is from *My Forgotten Prayers and My Forgotten Saints*. It is reproduced with the kind permission of Benziger Sisters Publications.